Learning by Heart

LEARNING
BY HEART

AIDS
and Schoolchildren
in America's
Communities

DAVID L. KIRP

with Steven Epstein, Marlene Strong Franks,

Jonathan Simon, Douglas Conaway and John Lewis

Rutgers University Press
New Brunswick and London

Kirp, David L.
    Learning by heart : AIDS and schoolchildren in America's communities /
David L. Kirp, with Steven Epstein . . . [et al.].
        p.   cm.
    Includes bibliographical references.
    ISBN 0-8135-1396-0
    1. AIDS (Disease) in children—Social aspects—United States—Case
studies.   I. Epstein, Steven.   II. Title.
RJ387.A25K57   1989
362.1'9892'97920—dc19   88-29789
                                                                CIP

British Cataloging-in-Publication information available

To

Ndebe Jackson of Ocilla

Jamie McCardle of Wilmette

Marcus Robinson of Lorraine

David Swenson of Chicago

Ryan Thomas of Atascadero

Ryan White of Kokomo

To the memory of Mark Hoyle of Swansea

And to all the other children whose lives have been touched
by AIDS

C O N T E N T S

Prologue   1

Chapter One: Telling Tales   5

    Two: "No Place to Die": Kokomo, Indiana   26

    Three: Ordinary Heroes: Swansea, Massachusetts   65

    Four: Passion Play: New York City   94

    Five: Buried Feelings: Ocilla, Georgia   133

    Six: "Clear and Present Danger": Fletchers Crossing   161

    Seven: The Bite: Atascadero, California   198

    Eight: Triptych: Chicago   228

    Nine: Our Towns   276

Notes   295

Acknowledgments   303

P R O L O G U E

Late at night on Friday, August 28, 1987, the Arcadia, Florida, house of Louise and Clifford Ray burned to the ground. By the next day, all America knew the story, even if most people did not fully sense its portent.

The Rays had fought to get their three sons, hemophiliacs infected with the AIDS virus, into the grade school of the small farming town where the family had lived for generations. They had tried unsuccessfully to convince the superintendent and school board that their boys posed no risk to classmates, and then they had gone to federal court and convinced a judge.

But Arcadians were not reconciled. They formed a Citizens Against AIDS in Schools Committee to pressure the Rays into changing their minds and, when that approach failed, they organized a boycott of the school the Ray children attended, which kept half the students home. The mayor took his own son out of the school and enrolled him in a public school in another county. A handful of Arcadians telephoned the Ray household with death threats. And one or two among them torched the Rays' home.

It was easy for the rest of us, watching these events unfold on the nightly TV news, to dismiss the people of Arcadia as ignorant bigots—easy and wrong. The people in this central Florida community, with its shopping mall and rodeos, think of themselves as decent and ordinary, no different from anyone else. Likely enough they are right, which is what makes their story so hard to shrug off. That burning house is part of our lives, even as AIDS has become part of our lives.

Imagine for a moment that your own eight-year-old came home from school and told you that a classmate had AIDS. How would you react?

By now, there is durable scientific evidence on what is called casual transmission of AIDS: it says that the risk of spreading AIDS in the classroom or the schoolyard is infinitesimally small, far smaller than risks we expose our children to daily. But infinitesimally small is not zero. And the news your child is bringing home means you are being asked to make your own risk assessment, with the risk borne by your own child.

"I'm kind of glad my grandkids won't be around them. There's enough risks in this world without taking them deliberately," one Arcadian told a reporter. It is understandable that wise and caring parents would not want to invite even the remotest possibility of death into their children's lives, that they would imagine themselves responsible for preserving childhood as a kingdom where no one dies. It is understandable too that such parents could criticize a family like the Rays, as the Arcadia school superintendent did, for "parading their children in front of TV . . . not protecting them." To the superintendent and to many people in the town, it seemed that the Rays had forgotten to care for their own children, that instead they had turned them into a cause.

Arcadia, Florida, reveals just one aspect of the drama of AIDS among the young. Days later, in another Arcadia—this one in Indiana—Ryan White, a fifteen-year-old hemophiliac with AIDS, enrolled at the local high school. Ryan's new classmates went out of their way to greet him and made sure to invite him to a dance after the first home football game of the season.

Two years before, when the Whites lived in nearby Kokomo, they had taken on the same kind of highly publicized fight as the Rays and for their pains were frozen out by their neighbors. Hoping to start over again, the Whites had moved a few miles away, not knowing how they would be received. What they found was hospitality.

There is nothing out of the ordinary about the Indiana Arcadians either, no reason to suspect that their town is the Peaceable Kingdom incarnate. Yet their school superintendent and school board, as well as the community itself, had calculated the risks very differently. They had learned the depths of significance imbedded in the cliché that life means taking risks. And they comprehended risks that their counterparts in Florida never talked about—the risk that hardening their hearts against Ryan White would be wounding not only to him but to themselves as well, and the risk that building a wall to keep Ryan out would teach the wrong lesson to their children.

Across the country, when confronted with the news that a child with AIDS was in their midst, some towns behaved like Arcadia, Florida, turning themselves into communities of exclusion. Others, like Indiana's Arcadia, became communities of openness.

The reasons that people responded as they did—first as parents, then as citizens acting together—cannot be rendered as a tale of us versus them, liberals versus conservatives, bigots versus the enlightened, rich versus poor, or big city versus small town. AIDS strikes with an awful democracy. And everywhere people have wrestled with the same powerful feelings, the same conflicting impulses for self-preservation and communion, that AIDS brings up.

This book tells a series of closely-linked tales about AIDS, communities, and children, beginning with Kokomo in 1985 and ending two years later. They are charged stories: of a mother with the AIDS virus, forced to choose between living with her child and his being allowed to attend school; of an AIDS-infected black teenager accused of having sex with his classmates; of a junior high school selecting a boy with AIDS as its "first citizen." Together, they reveal something about how we regard our children, how we deal with sex and dread and death, how we are led in times of crisis by politicians and bureaucrats and judges, and how we govern ourselves.

Many of us have tried to distance ourselves from AIDS by

thinking of it as a disease that affects someone else, some outsider. But when that psychological stratagem fails, when this
disease enters our households (as in the moment when the
eight-year-old comes home with the fateful news), AIDS offers
startling and compelling insights. It becomes something like a
mirror that we have happened upon unexpectedly. And when
we look into that mirror, comprehending the two Arcadias and
making sense of the Arcadias lodged within ourselves, the unfamiliar faces revealed there are our own.

Telling Tales

July 30, 1985, started out as a typically uneventful summer day in the boxy brick buildings of the Western School Corporation, headquarters of a crossroads school district in the Indiana heartland. Situated in the village of Russiaville, Western serves several farming hamlets as well as a slice of the nearby town of Kokomo. With students gone, summer is a quiet time for school anyplace, so teachers and administrators were scarce. Anyone who could get away had disappeared, as likely as not to go boating in Mississinewa Reservoir or to laze in a cabin in cooler country.

But the superintendent, James O. Smith, happened to be at work. Smith had taken the post just a year earlier and, though he had already been an Indiana superintendent for nearly a quarter of a century, was still very much the outsider in Western. Perhaps it was his newness on the job, or perhaps it was the newness of the issue, that led him to miss the significance of a call from an Indianapolis TV reporter. How was Western going to handle the request of Jeanne White that her thirteen-year-old son Ryan—diagnosed as having AIDS—be admitted to school, the reporter asked.

Smith didn't pause to ask how the reporter had gotten hold of the story. He himself had been over the White case, off and on, for months, and had made up his mind to take what seemed the only safe and sensible course: to keep Ryan home. But, as he told the reporter, he hadn't been able to reach Jeanne White. The reporter gave Smith the number where White was located and Smith telephoned with the official word. "She didn't sound too surprised," Smith recalls. "She seemed to expect it."

What Smith did not expect—what no one expected—was that this seemingly routine decision would make headline news, that Ryan White would become the nation's AIDS poster child, while Kokomo, a town that until then had been best known for its mentions in Bob Hope monologues, would acquire a reputation for its stance on AIDS. Ryan White's protracted fight to return to school won him no friends in Kokomo, where people still shake their heads at a boy and a family whom they regard as unduly keen on self-advertisement. But the Whites' determination, their insistence that a boy with AIDS be treated no better and no worse than anyone else, made Ryan an exemplar for other families and other towns across the country.

The conflicts over schoolchildren with AIDS that unfolded in Kokomo and elsewhere seemed to come from nowhere, like a tornado that caught the nation off guard. During the early years of the AIDS epidemic, children were not regarded as being at risk. This was a gay disease, the conventional wisdom went.

That belief was reflected in the name that the Centers for Disease Control (CDC) in Atlanta, the nation's AIDS monitor, initially gave this mysterious killer. GRID, it was called: Gay-Related Immune Deficiency.

The CDC suspected that some toxic agent linked to gay sex— tainted poppers, perhaps, or a batch of bad lubricant—might be the cause. Even when those leads proved dead ends, even when it became plain that AIDS could be passed through blood as well as sperm, by heterosexuals as well as homosexuals, the scientific community still resisted the idea that AIDS might reach children.

In 1981, Dr. Arye Rubinstein, chief of pediatrics at Albert Einstein College of Medicine in New York City, prepared a paper describing five infants, children of drug addicts, whose immune deficiencies mirrored those displayed by gay men. But the editors of the *Journal of the American Medical Association* (*JAMA*) and the *New England Journal of Medicine*, gatekeepers to scientific respectability, refused to publish Rubenstein's findings: GRID was a gay disease, they insisted, not a disease of children.[1]

While the experts were fixated on homosexuals and, later, drug abusers, hemophiliacs, and Haitians, these infants and many hundreds of others like them were being infected with AIDS *in utero*. One-third of these doomed youngsters were abandoned by their AIDS-afflicted mothers at birth, left to live out lives of undetermined length in the impersonal wards of public hospitals.

And while the scientific establishment was assuring the public, quite without justification, that the chances of contracting AIDS through blood were less than one in a million, many of the nation's 20,000 hemophiliacs under medical treatment, including 8,000 youngsters of school age, were being infected by AIDS-tainted batches of the blood-clotting product they depend on to lead normal lives. Although no one suspected it during those early days of the epidemic, the proportion of young hemophiliacs carrying the virus was far higher—estimates range between 60 and 90 percent—than of gay men living in the sexual fast lane.

In May 1983, the prestigious *JAMA* reported—erroneously, as it turned out—that routine household contact might spread AIDS, and the first signs appeared of what was to become an epidemic of panic. But despite the fact that the *JAMA* story concerned immune deficiencies detected in children living with an adult who had AIDS, the fear it aroused had nothing to do with the young. Instead, it was the apparent ease, the casualness, of transmission that seemed so ominous. Police officers and firefighters balked at touching the clothing of anyone who might conceivably have AIDS unless armored in face masks and rubber gloves. Prisoners at New York's Attica Penitentiary launched a hunger strike because the cafeteria's eating utensils had been used by an inmate who later died of AIDS. Many morticians declared their unwillingness to embalm the bodies of those felled by the disease.

When Ryan White was turned away by the Kokomo public schools in the fall of 1985, public attention finally focused on children—and furiously so. Across the entire country, the CDC asserted, no more than fifty children with AIDS were well enough to attend school, but the attention they commanded was far out of proportion to their number.

Ryan White's story developed into a staple of the nightly news, along with the theatrics of thousands of protesters in New York City, who carried a coffin bearing a sign reading "Is This Next?" through the streets of Queens to protest the enrollment in school of a child with AIDS. Two years later came the infamous burning house in Arcadia, Florida. Although these were headline-grabbing stories, they were not the only stories to be told. In dozens of cities and towns across the country—as diverse as Granby, Connecticut, and Sun Valley, Idaho; Asheville, North Carolina, and Chicago—youngsters with AIDS have been accepted in school.

These dramas of acceptance and exclusion, and the moral backdrop against which they were played out, depended on shared understandings of what AIDS meant, understandings that had taken shape before children with AIDS ever enrolled in school. While AIDS and children were not linked in people's awareness, AIDS itself evoked a wide range of deeply disturbing meanings. What happened in Kokomo and Arcadia, and everything that came between, makes sense only within the larger framework of what AIDS conjures in the popular mind.

Not in the beginning, not even as the 1980s drew to a close and the epidemic spread across America, was AIDS understood simply as a disease. At first it was ignored, indeed almost unspeakable; later it was the subject of countless headlines. But so much of what was whispered or shouted, though ostensibly about AIDS, really was about other things. People claimed to be talking about an epidemic, and no doubt believed they were doing so. But what they actually discussed often was somewhat different: their attitudes toward homosexuality, perhaps, or their doubts about science. "Nothing could be more punitive than to give a disease a meaning." writes Susan Sontag, but AIDS has been loaded down with many meanings. Most fundamentally, it has become impossible to talk about AIDS without talking about death, sexuality and deviance.

The nature of AIDS would have made it a source of panic no matter whom it struck first. As an inevitably fatal disease, it evokes a special sort of dread. Some fears draw people together—the assault of an enemy on one's country, for instance. But death too starkly and directly glimpsed can confirm individuals in their essential isolation, and so set one against another.[2] That is why most cultures take such care to ritualize death, to cover it up. AIDS offers an unwelcome reminder of the reality behind the mask of ritual.

And AIDS was—is—medically frightening. It devastates the immune system and leaves the body vulnerable to an onslaught of bizarre diseases normally held at bay, many previously unknown among Westerners, some previously unknown in humans. Plagues typically bring swift death to their victims, but the long incubation period of AIDS makes it hard to know who has been exposed and who has not—who, in the sensationalized imagery of the early news stories, were the "walking time bombs."

AIDS is an epidemic attacking ever-greater numbers, and epidemics have historically incited finger pointing. Jews were blamed for the outbreak of bubonic plague in central Europe during the fourteenth century and were slaughtered and loaded onto wine casks, which were then floated down the Rhine.[3] In turn-of-the-century California, the plague was described by doctors as an "Oriental disease, peculiar to rice-eaters."[4]

In the late twentieth century, when medical heroics have become commonplace, and when "medical science epitomizes the postwar vision of progress without conflict,"[5] epidemics have come to be regarded as a horror of the past. The day before yesterday, on the swiftly moving scientific clock, came the polio vaccine; yesterday, the eradication of smallpox; tomorrow, it is confidently supposed, will come a cure for cancer or the near-infinite prolongation of the life of the human heart.

It is easy to forget that epidemics have been historically ubiquitous and that the present thicket of interconnections among people from far-flung quarters of the globe makes diseases potentially much easier to spread. In a matter of months, years at most, viruses that emerge in the remote African bush can find

their way to New York harbor—and Kokomo, Indiana. But that
knowledge was lost to a generation of Americans who had
known no serious epidemics. If epidemics like AIDS should not
be happening, the unconscious logic proceeds, then someone
must have done something terribly wrong.

   The condition of being ill usually exempts individuals from
ordinary responsibilities without moral disapproval. But AIDS
is widely seen as a "disease of passion"—a disease of sex and
deviance—that seems to single out individuals for judgment
and guilt.[6]
Rarely is sex regarded neutrally. Whether whispered or
shouted about, it remains our great mystery, invested with
enormous power for good or evil, treated variously as the ultimate revolutionary act and the great unspeakable. For all
our supposed modernism, all our in-your-face bluntness about
once-shocking intimacies, much about sex remains taboo; and a
disease spread sexually, through "body fluids," still appears sin-
ister and suspect.[7]
Not so long ago, sexually transmitted diseases defined entire
classes of people. At the turn of the century, American blacks
were described by doctors as "an especially syphilis-soaked race,"
and a few years earlier English prostitutes had been characterized as "mere masses of rottenness and vehicles of disease."[8]
That judgmentalism seemed to have vanished during the decade or so before AIDS appeared, when America acted out
its sexual revolution. Then, we were our own most wondrous
toys, playing with each other with religious—almost childlike—
intensity.
All this freewheeling sexuality scandalized the moralists. Indeed, what prompted the emergence of the fundamentalist
Moral Majority as a political force was its ambition to tear down
the signposts of the sexual bazaar, to end abortion (with the casual and nonconsequential view of sex it seemed to connote),
pornography, and homosexuality.
These were ancient moralist themes with powerful appeal in
an America that, for all the bra burning, gay-lib parades, and

X-rated videos retailed at local 7-11s, had never entirely abandoned its Puritanism. When the herpes epidemic emerged at the outset of the 1980s, commentators quickly extrapolated its moral implications. "[Herpes] may be a prime mover in helping to bring to a close an era of mindless promiscuity," opined *Time* magazine, which emblazoned the story with a scarlet "H" on its cover. "For all the distress it has brought, the troublesome little bug may inadvertently be ushering in a period in which sex is linked more firmly to commitment and trust." The evangelist Billy Graham was more plainspoken about the meaning of herpes in God's plan. "We have the pill. We have conquered VD with penicillin. But then along comes Herpes Simplex II. Nature itself lashes back when we go against God."

To those on the religious right, herpes was the prophesy of doom. AIDS was its confirmation.

Almost immediately, the epidemic was transformed into a debate about sexual irresponsibility—especially homosexual irresponsibility. A 1983 *Newsweek* cover story sounded this note: "For Gay America, a decade of carefree sexual adventure, a headlong gambol on the far side of the human libido, has all but come to a close. The flag of sexual liberation that had flown as the symbol of the gay movement has been lowered."

AIDS meant gay in the American equation even though, from the outset, groups other than homosexuals were being devastated by the disease. In New York City, which has the largest number of AIDS cases in the nation, the majority— 53 percent—of those who died from AIDS between 1982 and 1986 were intravenous-drug users; substantially fewer—38 percent—were gay men. But that fact became known only after a retrospective study of the causes of death of several thousand drug users was conducted in 1987. Until then, statistics had pointed to gay men as the primary AIDS victims in New York.

Here again, social baggage had shaped scientific expectation, and scientists' findings shaped popular perceptions. Homosexuals had made themselves visible, in their dying as in other aspects of their lives, while drug users had often died unnoticed.

It was not, after all, affluent white cocaine imbibers who were dying off but heroin users, disproportionately black and Hispanic, and mostly poor. These drug users were as distrustful and as hard to reach as any group in America. Unlike gay men, who are often well educated and well connected, they rarely had access to decent medical care, and the meticulous documentation associated with such care was lacking. Unlike gay men, whose rich history of sexually transmitted diseases had already made them a subject of considerable medical curiosity, drug users were no more than medical John Does. And unlike gay men, drug users did not set about to make their decimation by AIDS the impetus for a cause.

To the New Right, AIDS was an act of divine retribution against the wicked sodomites. Some members of the medical establishment also adhered to this view. "[AIDS is the] fulfillment of St. Paul's pronouncement: 'the due penalty of their error,'" declared an editorial that appeared, not in a fundamentalist screed, but in the *Southern Medical Journal*. In 1983, Patrick Buchanan, who would later mold the social policy agenda at the White House, wrote a syndicated newspaper column entitled "AIDS Disease: It's Nature Striking Back." "The poor homosexuals," Buchanan said, "have declared war against nature, and now nature is exacting an awful retribution." The epidemic was also a happenstance to be exploited for political gain. A fund-raising pitch from Christian Family Renewal warned: "You may soon fall victim to an irreversible fatal disease! And it won't be your fault! But you'll have to pay the terrible price anyway because of the promiscuous homosexuals, whose lustful life-styles have created this uncontrollable incurable plague."

Yet most Americans did not see AIDS as God's punishment of homosexuals. In the decade before AIDS, many gays had "come out," announced their presence. Once people acknowledged that gay men weren't rare hothouse flowers—that there were gay doctors, gay truck drivers, and gay Republicans; indeed, gay sons, brothers, and uncles—a sea change in social attitudes became apparent.[9] The transformation was strange and incomplete, though. Gayness was, more and more, a legitimate social identity, but homosexual acts themselves were still unspeakable to many. Even as sodomy remained illegal in a number of states, big-city mayors routinely marched in gay-freedom-day parades.

This ambivalence toward homosexuals and homosexuality is reflected in Americans' varied responses to AIDS. Homosexuals were not forced back into the closet, or quarantined as enemies like Japanese-Americans during World War II, for they were no longer so far beyond the social pale. And when ultraconservatives tried explicitly to target homosexuals for punishment, their efforts went nowhere. In 1986, by a three-to-one margin, Californians defeated an initiative authorizing the quarantining of those with AIDS, which was widely regarded as inspired by homophobia. A year earlier, when Louie Welch, a former mayor of Houston trying for a political comeback, proposed dealing with AIDS by "shooting all the queers," he instantly dropped eight points in the polls—and that in Houston, not exactly the Mecca of tolerance.

But the instinct to assign blame for AIDS endures and the scapegoats are usually the homosexuals. In recent years, reported incidents of gay-bashing have dramatically increased. The assailants, who used to shout "faggot," now shout "AIDS." In the fall of 1987, North Carolina's Jesse Helms could declare on the floor of the United States Senate that "every case of AIDS can be traced back to a homosexual act"—a statement that, to many, belabored the obvious. Long after the doctors who fashioned the connection between homosexuality and AIDS had abandoned the simpleminded attribution of culpability, it survived in the public mind.

Unlike the victims of polio, who were mostly middle-class children (and who numbered among them a popular president), the AIDS high-risk groups are not generally beloved by Americans. Drug addicts used to be pitied as victims of an illness who needed help; now they are pursued as moral menaces. Haitians, a designated high-risk group during the first years of the AIDS epidemic, have in the past been branded as syphilitics who practice bizarre rites. ("We know that our Haitian patients are often involved in voodoo and spiritualism," said AIDS specialist Dr. Sheldon Landesman in 1983. "But we

don't know what in their rituals might be relevant to the transmission of AIDS.") As recently as a generation ago, before
medical advances dramatically changed their lives, hemophiliacs
were castigated as stupid and idle dopeheads who lived off
welfare.

Those with AIDS who do not belong to a high-risk group
nonetheless sense the stigma that AIDS carries. When Lester
Maddox, the rabidly racist former governor of Georgia, feared
he had contracted AIDS from a blood transfusion, he expressed
the feelings of many: "I'd rather go with straight cancer than
with AIDS. There's more dignity with cancer."

Even children with AIDS are touched by its taint, and such
manifest unfairness seems only to deepen the passion to blame
some culprit for the disease. "If I could just catch the queer
who did this to that innocent kid," said one parent in Kokomo,
and he is not alone in that sentiment. Someone—significantly, a
gay someone—deserved to suffer for the infliction of harm not
just on a child but on an *innocent* child.

The juxtaposition of AIDS and children, innocence and
blameworthiness, offers a powerful angle of vantage on how
America is coping with an event that is both a medical and a
social crisis.

Despite Freud, despite, too, the media's depiction of children
as violent and full of sexual innuendo, America still dreams of
its young as undefiled innocents, vulnerable but as yet untainted by temptation. "An immortal bud just commencing to
unfold its spotless leaves," one popular nineteenth-century man-
ual of childbearing called the child, "a beautiful flower opening
to the sunshine, ignorant of right rather than bent to wrong." [10]

From the early days of the republic, children in America
were treated as priceless objects, invested with deeply sentimental—even religious—meaning. And with advances in medical
science, the death of a young child, accepted until the nine-
teenth century as a familiar if lamentable circumstance, became the most painful and least tolerable of all deaths. [11] "What
is more sacred," asked Dr. Felix Adler, crusading against child

labor at the turn of the century, "than the life of a child?" From Benjamin Spock to Bruno Bettelheim, our contemporary authorities on childrearing dress up similar characterizations in the language of science.

This extraordinary attachment to the young, especially to one's own progeny, is one reason that national character portraits and politicians' stump speeches so regularly venerate families and so noisily bemoan their supposed demise. In the American mythology, the family is a "haven in a heartless world," a womblike inside that protects the innocence of children against the temptations and risks of the corrupt outside.[12]

Such risks have lately come to seem overwhelming. Reports mount of neglected children and abandoned children and stolen children; and mind-blowing tales are told of child sexual abuse. Scarcely a day goes by without some new account of trusted caretakers, day-care workers and babysitters, and priests—priests!—molesting children by the score; of Satanic rings in bucolic communities like Jordan, Minnesota, and Bakersfield, California; of fathers regularly accused in the course of custody fights of abusing their own small children; and of a two-year-old girl in North Carolina, dying of AIDS contracted when she was molested by her mother's boyfriend.

It is unclear whether sexual abuse has actually increased or whether, with the topic no longer a shameful secret, reporting has simply improved. It is not even clear how well founded the reports are, how often they are based not on fact but on a child's fantasy or an adult's desire for revenge. Whatever the empirical reality, their social importance is undeniable.

In an era when "family" often means working mothers and one-parent households, the attention paid to child sexual abuse evokes troubling feelings in mothers and fathers. They suddenly see themselves as failing in their obligation to their young by abandoning them to dangerous hands. And these accounts make parents especially anxious to protect their offspring. Behavior that would appear paranoid in other situations comes to seem like necessary caring when one's own children are at apparent risk.

In the minds of most people, a child with AIDS remains an

innocent. Over and over, it is said that the sins of the parent (let alone those of an unknown blood donor) should not be visited upon these children, that the disease is not their fault. But if one perceives childhood as a kind of Eden, the AIDS-afflicted child is, at once, innocent and poisoned, an Adam who cannot be extricated from the coils of the serpent. That child has been transformed, not into a "bad seed" but something much worse, a child capable of polluting the childhoods of other children nearby, a power all the more daunting because its exercise is unknowing.

It should come as no surprise that these dramas of innocence and pollution have been played out in the public schools, for schools are routinely asked to act *in loco parentis*—the bureaucracy as parent and protector against risk, at a moment in history when parents find themselves under siege. If it sometimes seems that the only thing the school can institutionalize is inequality, the hope is otherwise—that, as a place set apart, the school can institutionalize innocence by buying time, maintaining the awesomeness and remoteness of the adult world in the eyes of children.

With the advent of AIDS, playtime abruptly ceases, and the hope of preserving innocence vanishes. Whatever decision is reached about a child with AIDS, the child's schoolmates are taught a very adult lesson.

For the members of the Swansea, Massachusetts, school committee, habituated to brief and sparsely attended bimonthly meetings in the century-old red brick administration building, the evening of September 11, 1985, was an eye-opener. More than seven hundred people, almost all parents, filled the high school auditorium, the biggest meeting place in town.

The people of Swansea are usually polite in their dealings with one another, but these parents were in no mood for good manners. They demanded to know why their superintendent and their school committee had acted differently than every other school official in the entire country. Why had they allowed a thirteen-year-old boy with AIDS—a boy named Mark, known and liked by many of the people, but now fatally tainted in their eyes—to remain in school?

Why, the parents asked, had people they trusted—a school committee they had elected, most of whose members were natives of Swansea, and a superintendent who had been a fixture in their schools for nearly three decades—exposed their children to the bizarre terrors of AIDS? And why had they learned this awesome fact, not firsthand, but from TV?

The questions that night were often belligerently phrased, the meeting barely civil. These were mothers and fathers who, in their own minds, had come to defend their young.

In San Francisco and New York City, the battle against AIDS has been a Verdun, with trench lines everywhere and the dead carried daily off the field. But in much of the rest of America, AIDS came as it did in Kokomo and Swansea, a seemingly random shot from a sniper's rifle.

"Why here?" those in the heartland asked themselves, for even as AIDS sprang up in more and more places, it was still entirely unexpected wherever it appeared, the uninvited guest who upends the party. The disease struck, not the many, but a single friend or neighbor.

Debates over how to respond to AIDS have taken place in schools and offices and factories, hospital rooms and church pews, in army barracks and across dining room tables. Some groups resolve to exclude people with AIDS from their midst. They lift the drawbridge in the hope of securing a form of safety. Others have learned to live with the disease as a fact of life, much as Britain accepted the blitz during World War II as a menace to be confronted by a community together. They have also learned to live with those who have AIDS as neighbors and friends, lovers and family.

Everywhere, AIDS poses a threat. Less obviously, it offers an opportunity. And all the ways in which we respond to AIDS tell us something of value about ourselves.

Schools became the most important public institution in which Americans came to terms with their complicated feelings about AIDS. The process began with Kokomo and Ryan White in the summer of 1985. Initially, the Kokomo school officials' stance met with considerable sympathy across the country: What parent, after all, would deliberately expose a child to the risk of contracting AIDS? In the face of dread and uncertainty about a very real threat, protective measures acquire an inevitable logic.

But this instinct to protect wars against other deeply rooted sympathies, which emerged first in places like Swansea. Reaching out to strangers, caring for the sick and the dying, taking collective responsibility for ending the epidemic—such communitarian dimensions of America's response to AIDS have been just as vivid, just as real, as the strongest defensive measures.

AIDS is often talked about in terms of communities. The gay community is hard hit by the epidemic; the drug-users' community is claimed to be the most difficult to educate; the heterosexual community is said to be (or not to be) at risk. "Community" is sometimes a convenient shorthand to describe groups that may or may not ever commune. It is also used to invoke a vision of how people *should* treat one another.

Some critics maintain that to search for community is to indulge in sentimentality. They insist that the idea itself is dead— killed off by the media that bring the world into our living rooms, by the quest for self-fulfillment, or by the demise of institutions like the town meeting and the church, which once linked self-interest to the shared good. Others say good riddance to a corseting social institution that requires everyone to know, and keep, one's place.

Lost in the differing views is any sense of what actually happens once people who live close at hand join to make decisions that directly affect one another. When AIDS intrudes into our lives, fairly demanding some joint response, community comes to life—not as a static form but as a spirit that arises in decisive moments when neighbors decide the fate of neighbors.

This is one purpose the institution of public schooling has historically served. It was in American schools that racial equality acquired new meanings, and in the aftermath of busing and black power came other questions concerning sexual equality and student freedoms and fair treatment of the handicapped. School boards debated these matters; class hours were given over to previously undreamt-of topics; parents argued; organizations were formed; lawsuits were filed; state and federal officials intervened or stayed away—the entire arsenal of American political life was put on display.

So too with AIDS.

By and large, Americans are not meeting-goers. We habitually leave the running of the public schools, as we leave so much else, to the experts. Perhaps one citizen in ten votes in a school board election. Perhaps one in a thousand shows up at a typical school board session, where the buzz and hum of conversation is about a new tractor for the 4-H Club, a trip for the high school band, a new paint-remover to strip the graffiti from students' lockers.

But we get much more engaged when it comes to our own offspring.[13] One-third of the students in a recent national survey reported that their parents attend parent-teacher night at their schools, one student in five that a parent visits the classroom at least once a year, and half the students that a problem they had in school brought their mother or father to talk with the teacher. And administrators treat parents warily, seeing them as tigers fiercely protecting their cubs: one parent in three—an astonishing figure—has had a run-in with a school official, administrators report.

Superintendents and school boards are left alone to direct school affairs as long as they do generally what parents want— as long as they operate within what political scientists call a "zone of tolerance."[14] Yet quiescence does not always mean acquiescence. If an incautious school system stirs passions—by authorizing the distribution of contraceptives at the high school, say, or banning *Slaughterhouse Five*—or wounds the pocketbook by raising taxes, the popular response can be as angry and overpowering as a flash flood coursing through an arroyo.

For nearly a century, ever since superintendents undertook to rescue the public schools from lay boards dominated by what one historian of the era described as "patientless doctors and clientless lawyers," they have struggled to dam these political floods. Education is a scientific enterprise, the new breed declared; what was needed were fewer political intermeddlers and more rationally trained experts who could tame the governors and manage the bureaucracy. Progress in the schools, an 1890 National Education Report decreed, would result from the wise commitment of their management to a superintendent selected for a known ability "not merely to 'run the schools' but to devise, organize, direct and make successful a rational system of instruction."[15]

The enterprise had a kind of missionary zeal at first. As a visiting British educator named Michael Sadler observed at the turn of the century, "the American school is radiant with a belief in its mission, and it works among people who believe in the reality of its influence, the necessity of its labors, and the grandeur of its task." Even when the religious imagery became less potent, the schools retained their sense of mission; their leaders claimed to form an aristocracy of character. Today, the rhetoric of moral charisma still complements the dream of professionalism and the language of the social engineer.

The desire of superintendents to decide for themselves whether to accept children with AIDS in school, or at least to fix the terms of the discussion, is consistent with these rules of the schoolmaster's trade. Sometimes, administrators have tried to still the AIDS controversy by claiming that they have the expertise to make this decision on their own. "We are the authorities," goes the litany, "trust us." Dealing with AIDS, they assert, is a routine health matter, not significantly different from determining whether to shut the schools during a flu epidemic. "It is time to normalize AIDS," says Indiana's health commissioner, Woodrow Myers Jr., explaining why he never countenances informing parents of a child with AIDS in their midst. "We wouldn't tell them about a case of syphilis."

Decisions involving a child with AIDS have often been blanketed in secrecy.[16] "We are just following policy. Why talk about the particulars?" say the superintendents where AIDS guidelines are on the books (a majority of big-city districts).

"We are just protecting the privacy of the student," say superintendents who have quietly kept a youngster with AIDS in school—the very sentiment voiced by other administrators who have quietly eased AIDS-stricken youngsters out of the classroom, ostensibly for the youngsters' own good.

Secrecy does makes sense when it keeps the name of the child with AIDS from being made public. The trauma of a child's fatal illness should not feed neighborhood gossip or expose anyone to the ugliness of the lynch mobs that have driven children out of school and forced families out of town.

But the ambition of the school chiefs goes well beyond maintaining a decent respect for privacy. Their intent is to banish AIDS from the realm of school politics, rendering conflict about how to confront the disease as quaint as witch trials. If those who run the schools can veil the presence of AIDS, a "rational system of instruction"—and at least the illusion of an orderly life—are preserved.

Some day we may be ready to turn these matters over to the experts. But not yet. Deciding whether a child with AIDS belongs in school, like so many other questions to which school chiefs claim to have answers, has an inescapably political dimension. It is about taking not-quite-zero risks; about determining rights and, very differently, making a gift of trust; about being heard out—and about listening, too.

This is why, in cities and suburbs and hamlets as varied in their character as the country itself, parents have assembled to talk through their worries about enrolling a child with AIDS in school. The cast of characters is as familiar as the roster of players in *Our Town:* the school principal everyone calls by first name, the parent who thrills to the sound of his or her own voice, the board member eager for public notice, the doctor who knows too many four-syllable words, the lawyer on the lookout for lawsuits, the priest who quotes from the Book of Matthew, the reporter after a hot story.

It seems strange that a question as basic as the rights of children with AIDS should be decided locally. Although local control has been the byword ever since public schools first took root in the Massachusetts Bay Colony—"The Battle Hymn of the Republic" among school chiefs, as a Massachusetts state official called it—things have changed in recent years. And rightly so. If local control has all the virtues of neighborliness it also has all the vices of parochialism, the inattention to rights, and

the unwillingness to help the have-lesses that can be counter-
balanced by officials farther from the scene.

For a quarter of a century, Congress and the White House
have promoted nondiscrimination, extra help for the disadvan-
taged, and, latterly, "excellence." Fair treatment for minority
students, more equal distribution of school dollars, and securing the rights of students who are no longer docile as lambs:
these are among the issues that have pricked the interest of
judges. And the statehouses, which increasingly foot the school
bills, have been demanding a better return on their investment.[17]

AIDS policy, in sharp contrast, has essentially been left to
local sovereignty.[18] There is no counterpart to the 1954 Segregation Cases that shaped the politics of school integration—the
handful of lower court rulings, although consistently favoring
children with AIDS who want to stay in school, have been thinly
reasoned and carry little weight as legal precedent. No civil
rights legislation is aimed at persons with AIDS. Instead, there
have been nonbinding guidelines from the Centers for Disease
Control coupled with a counsel to chastity, "Just say no," from
Ronald Reagan's White House.[19]

Meanwhile, most state health and education officials have
danced a gavotte of avoidance, even—perhaps especially—
when pressed by harried school superintendents. The problem
of how to respond to Ryan White in Kokomo, and all the other
Ryan Whites, has been left to their own communities.

A county hospital chief or jailhouse warden wouldn't dream
of inviting the citizenry in, either to talk through rules about
AIDS or anything else. But public schools are different from
hospitals and prisons. We inhabit them, for one thing: one
American in four is a student, schoolteacher, or school administrator. And as freestanding institutions with their own gov-
erning boards, schools are uniquely accessible. You don't have
to hunt them down as you would, say, a city's transportation
agency. Their most important decisions are reached in the
open, in public meetings that resemble a political fishbowl.

This is where racial justice was translated into the concrete
terms of bus routes and nonracist texts, where parents have
quarreled about sex education and the teaching of creationism

alongside evolution. There is a tradition of citizen participation in school affairs, at least when something out of the ordinary is being decided, and a sense among administrators that they ought to respond to citizens' concerns, at least if they can do so and remain professionals.

Those who manage the schools describe public forums like the contentious meeting in Swansea, Massachusetts, as "information sessions," insisting that the decision to admit a child with AIDS is theirs alone. Technically they are right. But the unsweetened reality is that the people who gather in those auditoriums select, and can oust, their leaders. That fact has given a certain bite to the public conversations.

"We wouldn't have dared to hide what we were doing from the parents. Imagine the firestorm if they had found out," is the way a Chicago school official explained why the district went public in March 1987 with the enrollment of its first pupil with the AIDS virus. Even where the decision has not been disclosed, administrators have nightmares about whether, if the facts leak out (and it is very difficult to ask someone who has AIDS, or that person's brother or sister, to keep the secret), they would survive the accusation that a relationship based on trust was violated.

The influence of the community is real. But equally real is the power of leadership held by the steward of the school. While he may not have total control (and most superintendents are men), at the outset the school chief manages the story and decides who will learn what. He is the one whom reporters seek first, the one who stares into the TV camera. He plans the public forums, picks the experts, sets the format of discussion. If he is artful, he can persuade school board members and the leading lights among the teachers and townspeople to support his strategy.

The administrators have also shaped the moral tone of the discussion. It is not just their office but their deepest values that are on the line. For some, bureaucratics *are* their deepest values, "I followed the rules" their talisman. Others, scared silly, have allowed their personal bogeymen to speak for them. In the picture-postcard California village of Carmel, a superintendent conjured up an elementary school where merciless classmates would hound a sick child to misery. His aim—which succeeded—was to frighten the parents of nine-year-old Benjamin Oyler into keeping their AIDS-stricken son at home. This was an improbable conjuring, for small children would be unlikely to be so cruel if adults took the time to teach them about AIDS. Its true origin lay in the unstated fact that the superintendent was also the father of a child in what had been Ben Oyler's school.

Other administrators have successfully driven off the fear mongerers. In the Hartford, Connecticut, suburb of Granby, another nine-year-old with AIDS, Chris Barnoski, remained in class until he was too sick to attend. The Granby superintendent's pleas for reasonableness carried more weight with parents than did the message of a defrocked psychologist named Paul Cameron, who insisted that "gays deserve their AIDS" and came to town on a $1,000-a-day retainer to preach about the dangers of contagion.

There are despairing school leaders who have looked out from behind their desks at the communities they serve and concluded that, no matter what they might say, no child with AIDS could negotiate the gantlet of shame and shunning. And sometimes, as in Chicago, the mob at the gate, stirred up by the crazies of the political right, has come close to upsetting administrators' best-laid plans. But often—more often than one might imagine from the news, which feasts on burning houses—things have turned out the way the civics texts say they should. When that happens, the citizens stop concentrating entirely on their own fears and start walking in their neighbors' shoes.

The best of the school chiefs have become true aristocrats of character in taking on the challenge of AIDS. They have acknowledged the special nature of the moment: "We're making history," they would sometimes say to one another in the midst of the turmoil. They have recognized that AIDS demands both their leadership and the active involvement of parents, who become a true community in the course of deciding what will happen to one among them.

The forums organized by these administrators have been contemporary versions of the venerable New England town meetings, led not by local elders but by professional school managers—and led in a way that falls "between the coolness of rational purpose and the warmth of sentiment found in religion and magic."[20] These leaders have been able to bank on the trust they had built up with parents who, over the years, had learned that this official, this human being, would do them no harm.

The decisions about how to respond to a schoolchild with AIDS that emerge from these forums, and the deliberative way such decisions have been reached, mark a special occasion. Confronting a crisis, these public schools became the "wisest parent," a role envisioned for them long ago by John Dewey, America's foremost educator.[21] The members of these communities have made a rare gift to one of their number—and, in doing so, have given themselves the gift of their own compassion.

C H A P T E R   T W O

"No Place To Die": Kokomo, Indiana

"The City of Firsts" is Kokomo, Indiana's boast, for the town takes pride in what it has given to America. The first commercially built automobile, the pneumatic rubber tire, the carburetor, and the transistor car radio—all were developed in Kokomo, and local museums honor these inventions. But there are no markers commemorating the Ryan White case, another Kokomo first, for this is a bit of history the town would be pleased to forget.

Kokomo sits in the middle of farm country as flat as a skipping stone. Although only a handful of the local workforce in this community of 48,000 holds down farm jobs, farms define its physical geography. Roads run rigidly at right angles, refusing to make allowances even for the river that meanders across the countryside. In Howard County, which surrounds Kokomo, the names of the roads mark off the distance from downtown: 300 West, 400 South.

The moral geography, too, seems rigidly squared off. Sunday sermons in the county's more than three hundred churches eschew relativism in favor of recounting "The Tragedy of Living in Sin" and "The Blessing of Obedience." A half-century ago, isolationism flourished here, and the Ku Klux Klan has historically looked to the region for support.

While some things have changed—local Klansmen were pelted

with rocks and bottles when they marched down Kokomo's main street in 1980—the traditions of bedrock Republicanism and righteous conservatism endure. The "overpowering continuities" that generations of scholars have described in writing about nearby Muncie, the sense of "life's having gone on unaltered . . . in these big and little, clean and cluttered houses in their green yards"—these are palpable in Kokomo too. The continuities are maintained locally. When change comes, it "is something flowing irresistibly from the outside world."[1]

Kokomo is 95 percent white and mostly working class. As the litany of "firsts" suggests, the auto industry dominates the local economy. A Chrysler transmission plant and General Motors' Delco Division, a dazzlingly high tech operation with the world's biggest "clean room" for making computer chips, together employ some 15,000 workers. The Kokomo branch of the University of Indiana enrolls about 2,500 students, three-quarters of them part-time, and the Indiana Vocational Technical College, known locally as Ivy Tech, trains workers for the auto plants. Kokomo's economy has been through the boom and bust cycle of the auto manufacturers. During the early 1980s, thousands of workers were laid off, and only recently has the city again begun to share in the general prosperity.

An undistinguished county courthouse is the focal point for a faded downtown. The action is at the malls, where Sears, J. C. Penney, and K-Mart draw the shoppers. This is the land of family restaurants and bottle shops, of big front porches and lemonade, where pickups and midsize American cars, not Toyotas, fill the parking lots, and the American flag flies everywhere.

Kokomo prides itself on being a good place to raise a family. The city doesn't spend lavishly on most public amenities, but its fourteen softball diamonds, its ice skating and roller skating rinks and Olympic-sized swimming pool all testify to its concern for the welfare of its children. Kokomo's elders fret about how legally to shut down the two adult bookstores that flank the entrances to town, countering the aura of wholesomeness that is the community's biggest attraction. They fret, too, about what the Ryan White case, another family matter, did to Kokomo's good name.

Everything crucial to understanding why different communities have responded differently to children with AIDS surfaced first in Kokomo: whether the child was regarded as one of the town's own—one of us—or an outsider; whether the school leaders followed the crowd or recruited support for a possibly unpopular stance; whether, in this law-ridden age, judges spoke definitively about legal rights or ducked the question; whether medical experts soothed or intervened; ultimately, how the community came together—showing empathy or defending itself against the terrifying unknown.

In August of 1984, Ryan White entered seventh grade at the Western Middle School.[2] Earlier that summer, his mother Jeanne had moved the family—herself, Ryan, and Ryan's younger sister Andrea—from the neighboring village of Windfall to a trim house in Kokomo. For the Whites, this was really a return home. Jeanne had grown up in Kokomo, and her parents still lived there. When she graduated from high school in 1965, she married Wayne White, had a son and a daughter, and hired on as a Delco Dolly, her own gently derisive description of a woman working on the assembly line with no great aspirations to do more.

Jeanne White's story is not the Kokomo dream tale. She divorced her first husband, a high school classmate who drank too much, married Steve Ford, another hometown boy, and then divorced him in 1980. Although Wayne White still makes regular child support payments, he has vanished almost entirely from the family's life. But Ford remained close to Jeanne, even after the divorce, and it was he who became Ryan's real father.

In most respects, Ryan, a boy with a mop of sandy blonde hair, whose most remarkable feature is his enigmatic, almost Madonna-like smile, was no different than millions of teenagers. He collected GI Joe toys and comic books. His room was plastered with Max Headroom and Huey Lewis posters. He had a paper route for the *Kokomo Tribune* and rooted for the Dodgers and the Cubs. With his friends, he dressed up in camouflage costumes to hunt down imaginary enemies in the neighborhood.

But Ryan was always a little smaller and a little more fragile than most children his age. As a hemophiliac, he was forced into an early maturity, a necessary awareness of his own limits. He learned that lesson on the Little League diamond when a blow to the abdomen, which other youngsters would have shrugged off, caused severe internal bleeding and forced him to quit playing ball.

Until AIDS intruded, scientists would have reckoned that Ryan White belonged to the fortunate generation of hemophiliacs. A half century ago, there was no way to replenish factor VIII, the protein in blood plasma that helps blood to clot and that hemophiliacs cannot manufacture for themselves. Then, in 1941, scientists discovered how to separate the plasma from whole blood so that hemophiliacs could receive factor VIII without the many complications of ordinary blood transfusions.

This was only modest progress, since the plasma treatment was painful and inefficient. Patients would lie strapped to a hospital bed for hours at a time while the plasma dripped slowly from a bag into an intravenous tube. Because factor VIII is short-lived, it was hard to introduce enough of the substance into the body to do much good. As a result, even when patients submitted to treatment—and hemophiliacs often opted to ride out the pain at home—their joints would stiffen and grow arthritic from internal bleeding. Many hemophiliacs became permanently crippled, and many became dependent on the morphine administered to deaden the pain of the bleeding.

It was difficult for someone who suffered repeated incidents of bleeding to maintain even the semblace of an ordinary life. Going to the dentist was traumatic, since it was possible to die from having a tooth pulled. The protracted course of treatment meant that hemophiliacs were hospitalized for weeks at a stretch, which often prevented them from holding a steady job and forced them to go on welfare.

Hemophilia is an inherited disease that strikes only males, and young hemophiliacs had a hard time coming to terms with their inheritance. In all other respects, they were healthy boys, full of energy. They wanted to climb trees and play football. But their parents, constantly worried about cuts and bruises, tried to build a protective cocoon around their children, and school officials sharply curtailed their activities. Young hemophiliacs already on crutches or in wheelchairs because of bleeding incidents were required to attend classes for the handicapped. Although intellectually normal, they were often taught with cerebral palsy patients who had suffered mental as well as physical retardation and were given less demanding assignments than their age-mates. Treated as stupid, they often—and tragically—became so.

The development of cryoprecipitate in 1965 rewrote the script. One dose of cryoprecipitate contains factor VIII drawn from five to fifteen donors, not just one, and a large amount can be administered in a relatively small volume. The treatment is infinitely less painful, faster, and far more effective than the administration of whole plasma. Patients who had resisted being hospitalized every time they bled could now have their bleeding stopped in a matter of minutes. They could live lives that approximated normality.

When factor VIII concentrate, which reduced the plasma to a powder, came on the market in 1970, it held out the promise of almost total liberation. Now factor VIII can be kept at home, without refrigeration. Adults—even children as young as eight years old—can inject it themselves whenever bleeding occurs (or prophylactically, in the case of severe hemophilia). While this procedure is not entirely painless, for the needle puncture still stings like a blood test, it has revolutionized the lives of hemophiliacs; work and school are now taken-for-granted activities. The new medical wisdom holds that a boy with hemophilia should not be discouraged from trying almost any venture, since a speedy and reliable treatment is available if he gets hurt.

But medical science is not free from grim ironies. The reason factor VIII concentrate is so effective is that a single dose is drawn from as many as 10,000 plasma donors, which also greatly increases the risk of contamination with the AIDS virus from an infected donor. Hemophiliacs came to depend on pooled blood from an enormous number of donors and particularly, because plasma, unlike whole blood, is typically purchased, they relied on blood from the denizens of places like San Francisco's Tenderloin and New York City's Times Square. These were down-and-outers who counted on the $15 or $20 per donation to support themselves. As it turned out, a sizable proportion of these donors had AIDS due to risky sex practices and sharing of unsterilized needles.

Once the connection between AIDS and blood was evident, plasma centers, already familiar with the problems of contaminated blood from their experience with hepatitis, were quick to screen out donors from high-risk groups, particularly intravenous-drug users and homosexuals. But not until 1985, with the development of a test for the AIDS virus and a heat treatment that destroys the virus, was the supply of factor VIII rendered essentially AIDS-free. By then, however, almost every child and adult with severe or moderate hemophilia had received AIDS-contaminated blood. Although no one knew it then, in 1984 Ryan White was one of them.

When Jeanne White enrolled her son at Western Middle School in the summer of 1984, she told the principal, Ron Colby, about Ryan's hemophilia, and they worked together to plan his school day. That December, when Ryan was admitted to an Indianapolis hospital with pneumonia, she informed Colby. Blood tests revealed the devastating fact that Ryan had contracted AIDS from a tainted batch of factor VIII, and Jeanne White told Colby that news as well. "AIDS was so new then," says the principal, recalling the conversation. "I don't think that she realized the ramifications of what she was saying."

Some 2,300 students are enrolled in the four schools of the Western School Corporation—a primary school, an elementary school, a middle school, and a high school, which stand side by side among plowed fields and groves of trees in Russiaville, a half-dozen miles outside Kokomo. The school complex is the heart of the region. "When something happens in the area," says Colby, "it happens here." Western exemplifies—indeed, passes along to succeeding generation of students—the region's rooted conservatism.

The community showed its pride in its schools by raising

$100,000 when the high school band was picked to play at the Orange Bowl in 1984 and needed money to make the trip. But pride doesn't translate into routine generosity. The Western school board was dominated for years by big landowners who succeeded in keeping tax rates low, and Western still spends less per pupil than any of the other four districts in Howard County.

Students at Western's middle school, which includes the sixth and seventh grades, are generally clean-cut and conservative. The informal code of student conduct says that it isn't "finking" for a student to tell a teacher if a classmate has stashed cigarettes in a locker. Ron Colby, who organized the middle school in 1980 and became its first principal, works hard to maintain that atmosphere. "It's important for kids to have fun and to learn," he says, but fun takes a back seat to other values. "I push for them to have respect. That is the key word at this school."

Colby has lived almost all his life in Howard County. He graduated from Western High in 1959 and has spent his entire professional career in the Western system, teaching high school and coaching the defense for the football team. Broad-shouldered and burly, with black hair graying at the temples, he looks as if he could still manage an open field tackle.

"What's hardest," says Colby, "is being able to reach kids with problems at home." To the principal, "problems" translates as broken families, and "there are a lot of youngsters from single parent homes at Western." Colby often conscripts his wife, Sandy, who runs the audio-visual program, to help him out. His relationship with Jeanne White was the kind of bond that, as principal, he was after. The bond became strained at the end of July 1985, with Superintendent James O. Smith's decision to keep Ryan out of school. But Colby stayed in constant contact with the family—"Jeanne understood my feelings," he says— and well before Kokomo's opposition to Ryan's attending classes had run its course, he was working with the Whites to plan Ryan's return.

"Real honestly, I didn't know what AIDS was when Jeanne White told me about Ryan's condition, except I knew that if you got it, you died," Colby says. He set out to teach himself, over time filling six notebooks with articles on AIDS clipped from newspapers and medical journals. Colby also recalls that, when Ryan had a severe nosebleed just a few weeks before going to the hospital, he and the school nurse had been spattered with the boy's blood. The chance that they had been exposed to the AIDS virus was real enough, and terrifying enough, to prompt both of them to have their own blood tested.

Sitting in his hospital bed in December 1984, Ryan was determined to get back to school as quickly as possible. School was where his friends had always been. And he liked his academic work, particularly math; school was the one place where his ailments had not slowed him down. But during the first months of 1985, after discharge from the hospital, he was generally too sick to leave the house.

The events of that spring hinted at the troubles to come. Colby went looking for advice on how to handle Ryan's education, contacting the state's Department of Public Instruction, but got none. "Good luck," said the department's lawyer, and the Howard County health nurse and the state's Board of Health were similarly unhelpful. Meanwhile, anxieties were surfacing in the community. A teacher who had agreed to tutor Ryan at his house was warned away by her father, a doctor.

Ryan was feeling cooped up at home and missed his friends. Jeanne White called Colby late in March to ask if Ryan could come to "pizza day" in the cafeteria. On the advice of the county's health officer, Dr. Alan Adler, the principal said no.

The Whites' request was not the first time that Adler, a full-time family practitioner and Kokomo native, had dealt with AIDS—another case had appeared in the county—but the school issues were wholly new. By law, the county health officer must decide whether a child with a communicable disease can attend school, and the Indiana Board of Health had produced draft guidelines for youngsters with AIDS. Like the standards then being framed by the federal Centers for Disease Control, Indiana was poised to recommend that these youngsters be accepted in school in most instances, but that certain precautions—using plastic gloves to clean up blood, for example—be followed.

Ryan was suffering from bouts of diarrhea, and Adler felt that was reason enough not to admit him. Besides, with the state sitting on its guidelines waiting for the CDC to go first, Adler was unwilling to take chances. Why should a county health officer anticipate the state? "Because of the potential major impact, and because the state had no policy," recalls Adler, "I felt it best that he be denied."

Ryan was too ill to keep up with his classwork that spring, and Jeanne White decided that he would be better off having a normal summer and repeating the seventh grade come August. Anticipating Ryan's wish to return, Colby and Adler pushed the state health officials to publish their guidelines, submitting a lengthy list of questions about how AIDS might be transmitted, but no word came back from Indianapolis.

Western School Superintendent James. O. Smith knew about Ryan's condition from the outset but kept his distance. Smith "just sort of shrugged his shoulders," Colby recalls, when the principal brought him the news of Ryan's diagnosis. "In a case like Ryan's," the superintendent acknowledges, "sometimes the problem goes away"—to say it more plainly, sometimes the child dies. But when Jeanne White called him on June 22, 1985, to ask about Ryan's returning to school in August, Smith took charge.

James O. Smith is a paternal figure who looks like a country squire, courtly and white-haired, a man whose schools, surveyed daily, are his domain. For twelve years J. O., as he is generally called, had previously been superintendent at another rural Indiana school district. There, he had stood his ground against a group of fundamentalist parents who demanded that he rid the library of books they saw as profane. The superintendent eventually won, but it was a grueling ordeal, marked by poison pen letters and a visitation from the Klan. "Hate groups came out of the woodwork," Smith recalls.

"All I knew about AIDS was how to say it," Smith remembers, but everything he learned that spring argued for keeping Ryan White at home. Several school districts elsewhere had already opted to keep AIDS-stricken youngsters out of regular classes. In Miami, Florida, Haitian triplets with AIDS had been isolated in a separate classroom. In New Haven, Connecticut, Superintendent John Dow, Jr. had barred a youngster with AIDS from school. "Do you fire teachers [who are unwilling to teach such a child]? Are they insubordinate?" Dow asked, as if he were posing a rhetorical question. "How do you deal with parents who say 'My child must be out of that classroom'?"

Neither of these instances had caused a hullabaloo, Smith learned, so—not appreciating the persuasive power of a telegenic child like Ryan White—he saw no reason why things should be different in Kokomo.

Events of the spring made the superintendent particularly leery about AIDS. The reaction of the doctor father of Ryan's would-be tutor, Dr. Adler's decision to keep Ryan home for pizza day, and, above all, the state health department's delay in publishing its guidelines all led Smith to suspect that the authorities in Indianapolis weren't entirely certain about how AIDS was transmitted.

Keeping Ryan out was the rational decision, the superintendent concluded. "If we bar children who are not immunized, how unreasonable is it for us to keep out a child with AIDS?" While Smith sympathized with Ryan's wish to attend school as a way of maintaining a normal life, he was not persuaded that this was the right course. There were the other students to consider, after all. And "How do you treat as normal someone who is dying—especially a kid?" the superintendent wondered.

The reaction of a good friend, a dentist who had been on the school board, was the clincher. "When I asked him if Ryan should be allowed in school," Smith remembers, "he looked at me as if I were crazy. 'This is the most dreaded disease ever,' he said."

Smith talked with Western school board members, particularly with Board President Daniel Carter, a high school classmate of Colby's, an English and German teacher at a nearby high school, and the dominating voice on the seven-member panel. "You won't find anything in the school board minutes," says Smith. "These were what you could call informal executive-type sessions. You know, over coffee." But the ultimate decision, the superintendent says, was his call. "With the keys to the schoolhouse in my hand, the final say-so was going to be mine."

In the universe of Kokomo, cut off from the pathbreaking medical developments and the most up-to-date public health wisdom on AIDS, keeping Ryan out of school came, in the spring of 1985, to seem not only reasonable but obvious, almost inevitable—the professionally correct decision. In all the conversations that Superintendent Smith held during those months, including those with local health officials, no one spoke out strongly for Ryan's admission. And while the CDC in Atlanta was about to publish AIDS guidelines, it would never have occurred to the self-styled "country superintendent" to call Atlanta for advice.

In the summer of 1985, AIDS was still new and not well understood, both in Kokomo and across the country. It was only fifteen months earlier, in April 1984, that the discovery of the AIDS virus had been announced, and the properties of the virus remained the subject of intense investigation. While most scientists agreed that AIDS was spread only through blood and sperm, reports still conflicted on how the disease was transmitted and who was at risk. The virus had been isolated in minute quantities in saliva and tears, leading some to wonder whether the disease could be more easily spread. A well-publicized 1983 report in the *Journal of the American Medical Association* (*JAMA*)[3] seemed to confirm such speculations in declaring that household members could transmit AIDS to one another. That study would eventually be discredited, but for many Americans it established a framework of understanding: AIDS was, potentially, everywhere.

The media had initially ignored AIDS, then described it as a "gay plague." Now it played up any research, however tentative, that suggested that the epidemic would affect the "general population"—that, as one TV special put it, AIDS was going to "hit home." What ordinary people learned about AIDS in all the ways they usually learn about the world—from doctors and radio call-in shows, newspaper stories and coffee-shop conversations—left them confused. According to national surveys, one American in five believed that AIDS could be contracted from a doorknob or a toilet seat; one American in four was sure it could be contracted by *giving* blood. What was generally believed about AIDS was a mix of science, often misunderstood, and folk wisdom. What that knowledge spelled was danger.

Superintendent Smith's decision to keep Ryan White out of school reflected these confusions about the character of AIDS. It was also smart politics. "If I was going to generate something to give me support," he admits, "I couldn't have done a better job." And Smith needed that kind of support. Western's school board has a reputation for reversing the recommendations of school officials on everything from tax rates to new courses. The superintendent's predecessor had clashed repeatedly with board members, particularly with Board President Carter, a man inclined to speechifying. And Smith wasn't necessarily secure in his post. During the year immediately preceding his arrival, Ron Colby had filled in as superintendent. Smith got the job only because Colby hadn't obtained his administrative credential fast enough, and Colby, credential now in hand, remained discreetly on the scene.

The circumstances of Ryan White's education might have gone largely unnoticed outside the precincts of Howard County had it not been for an extraordinary event that occurred the very same week Superintendent Smith told Jeanne White that Ryan couldn't come back: on July 26, 1985, Rock Hudson announced to the world that he had AIDS.

Suddenly, AIDS was what everyone was talking about at the local diner and the barber shop. AIDS had become vivid—real—in middle America. It was a strange sort of reality, however. Rock Hudson was widely known in Hollywood to be gay, and AIDS was widely known to be sexually transmitted. But to a nation that regarded the sexual acts of gay men as unspeakable, it was inconceivable that their matinee idol had done them. The media did not link his condition to the "gay plague" of AIDS. Instead, as *USA Today* editorialized, Rock Hudson's disclosure was taken as evidence that "AIDS can reach anyone." The desire was strong to believe that something else, like a handshake or a mosquito bite, could spread the disease. No known cases of AIDS were caused by casual contact, the scientists said, correcting the 1983 *JAMA* report. Yet, when they were asked about the future, the scientists talked only of probabilities. Their listeners wanted guarantees.

It was this angle—the ubiquity of AIDS—that the Indianapolis TV reporter was pursuing when she called Superintendent
Smith on July 30 to ask about Ryan White. By the time Jeanne
White got home that day, TV cameras were planted on her
lawn, and reporters crowded around. What both sides call the
war in Kokomo had begun.

Ryan White was on all the national news shows that night,
a winsome David trying to go to school but kept out by the
Goliath school administration. "I'm pretty upset about it," he
said. "I'll miss my friends, mostly." The next day, the state's
health commissioner, Woodrow Myers, Jr., chastised the Western school officials. "If a kid is well enough," Myers said, "he
should be in school." And on August 2, with Jeanne and Ryan
White at his side, Myers held a press conference to present Indiana's draft guidelines on schoolchildren with AIDS—the very
guidelines that, for months, Kokomo officials had vainly tried
to extract. Although he acknowledged that the state board of
health couldn't force Western to reverse its decision, Myers
called on Superintendent Smith to "reconsider."

But Woody Myers had in effect set the terms of war. From
that point on, it would be the Kokomo educators and a sizable
contingent of parents against the medical authorities and the
media, the insiders resisting the world beyond Kokomo.

At their own rival press conference, Superintendent Smith
and Board President Carter stuck to their position. "We would
be negligent" to admit Ryan White with so many questions unanswered, said Carter. "Woody Myers and the state board of
health got caught with their pants down," he declared. "They
can carry out their tests somewhere else." Smith spoke of his
"responsibility to protect other students" and played up the un-
reality of the precautions that the guidelines called for. Stock-
ing rubber gloves and cotton swabs would "turn the school into
a hospital," the superintendent insisted, and only illustrated the
hazards of admitting a youngster with AIDS.

The two school officials were furious with Myers, and not
without cause. After all their pleas for help, the guidelines had
finally arrived—but only after Smith had announced his deci-

sion, and without even the courtesy of a cover letter. Instead of talking with them privately, Myers had gone public, making them look like ignoramuses who should "reconsider." Under the circumstances, backing down was out of the question.

Myers doesn't place much faith in the power of diplomacy. In July 1985, the state public health officer was just thirty-one years old and relatively inexperienced. He had been on the job for only five months, having left a junior staff position with San Francisco General Hospital and a part-time post with Senator Ted Kennedy's Labor and Human Resources Committee for what he regarded as a once-in-a-lifetime chance. Despite his stint at San Francisco General, the leading hospital for AIDS care in the nation, Myers had not anticipated spending much time on AIDS. "I figured I had two or three years before having to gear up."

Through sessions with his staff, Myers knew about the developing controversy over Ryan White but deliberately chose not to get involved. "I tried to stay personally out of this," says Myers. "I need to save myself for those things where I can have the biggest impact—not the minutiae."

"Minutiae" is not exactly how Kokomo officials would characterize their concerns in the summer of 1985, and Myers' unsympathetic attitude didn't make matters easier. "Change is a hard thing for people to do," Myers says. "The epidemic moved quickly. People in Kokomo didn't want to change." What is missing from this recital is any sense of how enormous and how rapid was the change being asked of Kokomo—and how much help they needed.

Yet, it is unlikely that even a Woody Myers with the diplomatic talents of a Metternich would have succeeded, for there was much more to the fight between Kokomo and Indianapolis than insensitivity and wounded feelings. Woody Myers was a real outsider—an exotic, in Indiana terms. He came from San Francisco; he was young and new to his position; and he was black. None of that counted in his favor. "No one here knew Dr. Myers from my pappy," says Ron Colby.

Nor were the Kokomo officials impressed with the guidelines themselves. Their pedigree was tainted, for the task force that had developed them included not a single educator. "I consider

that an act of arrogance," says Superintendent Smith. Moreover, the task force did include "people who are sympathetic to
gays," says Smith. "I guess I'm not."

Myers belatedly sent three members of his staff to visit
Kokomo, but the visit changed no minds. Carter and Smith
barraged Dr. Charles Barrett, head of the board of health's
Communicable Disease Section, with pointed questions—about
swimming pools and drinking fountains, about washing the
towels in the gym class and silverware in the cafeteria, about
coughs and cuts and sneezes. Barrett and his colleagues have a
reputation as low-keyed and even-tempered people, but to the
educators their answers sounded wishy-washy. When Carter inquired about Western's legal liability in the event that Ryan was
admitted and another child contracted AIDS, the doctors demurred—that was a lawyers' problem. Carter dismissed the
delegation as "Woody Myers' flunkies."

The absolute reassurances the school administrators were
seeking could not then, in truth, be given; the strongest evidence against the easy spread of AIDS—studies showing no
nonsexual transmission among several hundred people living
in households with AIDS patients—had not yet been published.
In the summer of 1985, most experts believed the risk that
a thirteen-year-old student would spread AIDS in school was
essentially nonexistent—far smaller than the chance of a student's being killed in a school bus accident or struck by lightning on the playground. But risks do not appear to most people
as numerical probabilities. Whether from a nearby nuclear
power plant, toxins in the water, or AIDS in school, risks usually come with some moral significance attached. That AIDS
was almost impossible to transmit casually did not undo its
stigma or satisfy the demand for guarantees impossible to be
given honestly.

The emerging medical evidence did have an impact outside
the school system, though. Alan Adler, the Howard County
health officer who during the spring had refrained from taking
a position, now concluded that Ryan should be allowed back in
school. Adler had since talked about Ryan's case with specialists
at the University of Indiana, and "all to a one said there's no

problem." But Adler would take no responsibility for making this decision—that, he believed, was a matter for the state board of health.

The *Kokomo Tribune,* the daily paper, read the medical evidence exactly as Adler now did and on August 5, less than a week after the superintendent's announcement, came out editorially on the Whites' side. During the many months that the Ryan White story played itself out, the paper ran hundreds of articles on the controversy and on AIDS generally, sometimes two or three a day.

This was a brave stand for a small city paper, where subscription cancellations and threats to withdraw advertising are taken seriously, for, as the editors anticipated, the *Tribune*'s position won it no friends. Even as people across the country wrote letters in support of Ryan White, a stream of correspondence from those living in Kokomo and surrounding villages lambasted the paper. But to Editorial Page Editor John Wiles, who has been with the *Tribune* since 1970, the paper's decision was straightforward. "From the flood of publicity nationwide, we knew that this was *the* AIDS story of the year," Wiles recalls. "We decided immediately that we had to take the lead, to establish our point of view, as a way of defusing the emotionalism that was already building up, to combat the misinformation about how you get AIDS."

The editor talked with Woody Myers. Then he contacted the CDC in Atlanta—a sensible phone call, but one made by nobody else in Kokomo. "Does this boy pose a threat?" Wiles asked. "No," he was told.

Chris MacNeil, the young *Tribune* reporter and Kokomo native who covered the Ryan White story, was not an expert on AIDS, just a general assignment reporter who had written several pieces trying to dispel popular fears that the disease could be transmitted by donating blood. Jeanne White had been talking to MacNeil for months about her problems getting Ryan back in school, and when Superintendent Smith made his decision, MacNeil was a natural for the assignment.

Because of the importance and the delicacy of the story, MacNeil's copy got microscopic scrutiny—three editors, each with more than a decade of experience, read every word. The *Tribune*'s readers didn't know of these unusual precautions, though, and to many in Kokomo MacNeil was not only a reporter but an advocate for the Whites. Soon he became a target himself. So frequent were the obscene midnight phone calls that the reporter had to get an unlisted phone number, and more than once he was shot at. MacNeil was sleeping with Jeanne White, the rumors in Kokomo went, or with the queer lawyers from the Indiana Civil Liberties Union who had volunteered to help the Whites, or even with nameless blacks living in Fort Wayne.

The level of hostilities quickly escalated, as the community mobilized behind Superintendent Smith and Board Chairman Carter. The day after the press conference at which Myers asked Western officials to "reconsider," the school board met and unanimously backed the decision to exclude Ryan; not a questioning voice was heard. About fifty of the Western teachers interrupted their summer holidays for a meeting and by a unanimous show of hands resolved not to teach Ryan in their classes unless ordered to do so by a judge.

Parents also pushed hard to keep Ryan out of school. Mitzie and Dave Johnson, whose daughter was a first grader at Western, went looking for information on AIDS, checking with local hospitals for medical guidelines on AIDS patients, and putting the same kinds of questions to county health officials that Smith and Carter had addressed to Indianapolis. What they heard was scary. "The more we looked for answers," recalls Mitzie Johnson, "the more we knew that there were none."

Mitzie Johnson describes herself as a troublemaker, someone who isn't shy about taking on the powers-that-be. Here was the right cause, the protection of her children against the possibility of death and defilement, the theft of their innocence that Ryan White potentially represented. What the Johnsons did next was as American as a political precinct meeting: they phoned all their friends and went door-to-door in their apartment complex, collecting signatures on a petition supporting the superintendent's stand from all but three of the 102 residents they talked to. As she made the rounds, Mitzie Johnson harped on the callousness of the state officials who were insisting that Ryan be enrolled in school. "The big doctors and the government officials don't give a damn about our children," she said. The parents were discovering the great potential power of the difference between "us" and "them."

In mid-August, the Johnsons returned to their phone network to organize a parents' meeting. Because Western schools are situated on a common campus, the parents of all the children, from kindergartners to high school seniors, felt their offspring were potentially at risk. Three hundred mothers and fathers, the kind of turnout not seen for years, packed Western's gymnasium to hear a local doctor and the head of the local teachers' union talk about the "inconclusive" evidence on how AIDS was spread. A more balanced presentation might have eased some fears, but neither a spokesman from the state health board nor anyone else who advocated Ryan's admission had been invited.

No one who spoke that night had a word to say in support of Ryan White's wish to return to school. "Everyone was in turmoil," recalls Larry Gabbard, whose son Chad was in Ryan's class.

Gabbard was no stranger to risk. He was an ex-Green Beret whose bronze star and other commemorations for heroism, earned during his tour of duty with the 101st Airborne in Vietnam, are annually displayed at the Howard County Library on Memorial Day. But this situation was different; it was his son's life at stake. "I got up," Gabbard recalls, "and I said, 'We don't have to have this shoved down our throats.'"

Parents who came to the meeting already anxious had their anxieties reinforced; what had begun as a discussion rapidly turned into a crusade. At the end of the session, 117 parents signed a petition to be used in a lawsuit for damages against the Western school system, should Ryan White be admitted. Now the legal question that had gone unanswered when Carter and Smith met with the delegation from the state health department had become real. And the Western officials who had actively courted parental support were locked into their position by something stronger than their own rhetoric.

"We also went to the Centers for Disease Control," Gabbard

recalls, "and asked them for all they had." But in the prevailing atmosphere of confrontation, with dispassion hard to detect anywhere, it was predictable that the CDC's *Morbidity and Mortality Weekly Reports,* hedged with the qualifiers beloved by scientists, were unsatisfying. As the parents read the material, all the unanswered and seemingly unanswerable questions only exacerbated their fears.

In an era when everything from racial integration to textbook selection winds up in the courts, it was hardly surprising that the Howard County parents gathered in the overheated gym should start thinking about a lawsuit. Nor were they the only ones with this idea. Immediately after Superintendent Smith announced that Ryan could not return to school, the Indiana Civil Liberties Union (ICLU) offered to represent the Whites in a discrimination suit.

Jeanne White was hesitant at first. "I feel I owe it to kids who have hemophilia who could get AIDS," she said. "But I've got to think of Ryan, too. I don't want to push Ryan back into school in that atmosphere." The school officials are trying to do the right thing, White added, and she hoped that they could be persuaded to change their minds.

But as community sentiment hardened, White put the ICLU in touch with the law firm of Vaughan & Vaughan, which had already filed a $10 million suit against the manufacturer of factor VIII from which Ryan had contracted AIDS. The Vaughans— father Charles R. and son Charles V.—are not the kinds of attorneys who hesitate long before going to court or who readily share the legal limelight. Their firm, located in the nearby city of Lafayette, has a reputation for fighting for the underdog; in conservative Kokomo, that readily translates into a reputation for publicity seeking. On August 8, just nine days after J. O. Smith announced his decision, the Vaughans (leaving the ICLU on the sidelines) filed a complaint in Indianapolis federal court. The Western district was discriminating against a handicapped child, the lawsuit asserted, by keeping him out of the classroom. "This is the test case for the nation," said the younger Vaughan. "What happens here will set the trend across the country. But the people in this town just want to be afraid. They are running away from the facts."

The complaint in *White v. Western School Corporation* was meant to force the court into deciding whether Ryan really posed a health threat to his classmates; unless he did, he was legally entitled to go to class. Yet Federal District Judge James Noland ducked the question of how AIDS is transmitted, focusing instead on the particulars of procedure. The law the Vaughans were invoking, the Education of All Handicapped Children Act, normally requires that those claiming discrimination go through an elaborate series of hearings, reaching all the way up the state's education ladder, before they can be heard in court. Noland was unwilling to read an exception into the statute. To Ryan's lawyers, those procedures would be a farce, because Western had already made up its mind. All the hearings could accomplish was to buy time for the school district, the Vaughans argued unsuccessfully, and time was in very short supply for their young client.

On August 26, Ryan White started the school year by joining his fellow seventh graders on a speaker phone as, one by one, his thirty classmates introduced themselves. Reporters from newspapers across the country squeezed into the tidy white two-story home where the Christmas tree, put up the previous December when Ryan's condition improved following his diagnosis, still filled a corner of the living room. Camera crews from the networks parked their vans alongside the broad front yard.

The journalists got the boy-versus-town story they were anticipating. There was Ryan, straining to hear what was going on, while the voices of his teachers drifted in and out, and the words of his classmates went unheard. The school district insisted it was doing its best by Ryan. "Any child in a homebound situation can get an adequate education," said Principal Ron Colby; besides, what other seventh grader had a speaker phone? Yet, when a reporter asked him how he liked the setup, Ryan's response was to the point. "It stinks," he said, a message that for many who heard it came to represent how Kokomo was treating Ryan White.

The next day, Ryan jetted off to New York for an interview on ABC-TV's "Good Morning, America," the first performance of what would become almost a family roadshow. Later in the year came an appearance with Elizabeth Taylor at an AIDS benefit, a trip to Los Angeles, and another all the way to Rome where Ryan got an on-the-air hug from the host of the TV show "*Italia Sera*." Everywhere the Whites went, people took to the boy with the winning smile and to his feisty mother. Ryan loved the attention. It represented support, affection even, which the boy badly needed.

And so it went, for months on end. Ryan could count his supporters in the thousands, but almost all of them lived thousands of miles from Kokomo. They filled the Whites' house with their presents, and so many people wrote to Ryan that he wound up sending xeroxed thank yous. A New Jersey songwriter composed two ballads about Ryan and pledged to donate the proceeds to a foundation named in Ryan's honor. The American Telephone & Telegraph Company and Radio Shack won some favorable publicity for themselves by installing a state-of-the-art speaker-phone system to improve communication with the school and a fancy new computer in Ryan's bedroom.

This was heady stuff for what had been an ordinary family until J. O. Smith made his famous phone call. Yet, within the precincts of Howard County there was little support for the Whites. Some help did come from the congregation at St. Luke's United Methodist Church, which the Whites attended. And Arletta Reith, a friend who worked with Jeanne White at the Delco assembly line, printed up five hundred "Friend of Ryan White" buttons so that Ryan could have a new bed.

But the church raised only a handful of dollars, and Reith sold only half a dozen of her buttons to Kokomo residents. Opinion in the town was solidly against the family. Townspeople accused Jeanne White of milking her son's plight, exploiting him for attention and money. Board President Daniel Carter carried that accusation with him to Queens, New York, where he spoke in September with parents waging their own AIDS battles. It didn't matter that Ryan's travels were devoted partly to investigating new kinds of treatment, or that the trips boosted the boy's spirits. This was just not how sick people, victims, were supposed to behave.

The White family, only recently resettled in Kokomo, found itself largely isolated. Although Jeanne White's parents and her ex-husband Steve Ford were often around, most of Ryan's friends stopped coming by, and, when some subscribers complained, Ryan dropped his paper route. His younger sister, Andrea, a national champion roller skater, was heckled in school by her classmates. "I walk into Denny's restaurant," said Jeanne White, "and people just whip around and stare like we're from Mars."

It was the reporters who stayed with the story month after month—particularly Chris MacNeil from the *Tribune* and Carrie Jackson Van Dyke, an Indianapolis TV reporter—who became the family's new friends. During all the time they spent together, Ryan developed a teenager's crush on Van Dyke, who acknowledges that she "got closer to Ryan than reporters are supposed to get."

Although Ryan was hospitalized twice in the fall of 1985, he kept up his schoolwork, doing creditably in every subject except social studies. Meanwhile, the long process of determining whether he had a legal right to be in school had begun. The first stop, a "case conference" chaired by Middle School Principal Ron Colby, was held in mid-September. Jeanne and Ryan White and lawyer Charles R. Vaughan looked on as the conferees reached the generally anticipated decision to keep Ryan home. After staying mum for several weeks, Superintendent Smith, also as expected, upheld the decision.

On the national scene, those who favored allowing children with AIDS to attend public school were winning new support. At the end of August, the CDC had issued its long-awaited guidelines. Like the Indiana standards, they called for admitting youngsters with AIDS to school unless they were acutely ill or prone to misbehavior.[4] In Queens, New York, thousands of parents who had organized a boycott against school admission began to resign themselves to the fact that a child with AIDS would attend school someplace in New York City, at least until a court reviewed the issue. And in the village of Swansea, Massachusetts, that September, townspeople acceded to the wish of another thirteen-year-old boy with AIDS who wanted to stay in school.

The events were known in Kokomo, but by this time the

Western School Corporation had little inclination to rethink its position. The school officials had become heroes in their home town because of their stand, had the active backing of teachers and parents—and faced the threat of a lawsuit if they reversed themselves. Risks bring not just fear, but also a sense of power when people see themselves united against a deadly foe.

Those who participated in the Western school conference acknowledged that it was important for a child to spend time with youngsters his own age. But it was more important, they said, to defend against the dangers posed by AIDS. Besides, admitting Ryan might actually be illegal. The point was technical but important: a 1949 Indiana quarantine statute required a health certificate before any child with a communicable disease could be admitted to class, and no such document was at hand.

The Vaughan firm, representing Jeanne and Ryan White, immediately appealed Western's ruling to the Indiana Department of Education, and a hearing was set for November 1. The attorneys talked confidently in public but, as the younger Vaughan recalls, "I was ready to give up on the case." The firm was already financially in the hole. Its business was suffering. And, says Vaughan, "I felt that the hearing officer would find that Ryan shouldn't be in school, because everything had gone against us." Jeanne White, worn out and flat broke, also was on the verge of abandoning the fight.

It was Ryan who changed their minds, Ryan who kept insisting that he wanted to go back to school more than anything else. "In the car on the way to that hearing," Vaughan recalls, "he looked at me and said, 'Don't worry. Some day they'll learn that we were right.' When I heard that, I turned to Jeanne White and said, 'Now *he's* the client.' The kid who was supposed to be the weakest had become a source of strength."

The day-long Indianapolis hearings included testimony from Dr. Donald Fields, Ryan's Kokomo physician, who until then had stayed out of the school dispute, county health officer Adler, and Dr. Charles Barrett, the communicable disease expert with the Indiana Board of Health. All agreed that it made medical sense for Ryan to be in school. Western school officials didn't rely on any experts of their own. They talked instead about how impractical it would be for Ryan to attend class, pointing out, for instance, that only a single nurse served both the middle and high schools. And they argued that, under Indiana law, the fact that Ryan had a communicable disease meant that he had to stay home.

Nearly a month later, Hearing Officer Kathleen Madinger Angelone, a private attorney, reached her decision: it was legally "inappropriate" to keep Ryan out of class. To the teenager, who had spent much of that month in the hospital and had lost thirty pounds, it was exciting to think that he might finally be getting back to school. "It's a great birthday present" for Ryan, Jeanne White told reporters.

No one was really surprised when Western announced that it would appeal Angelone's order to the state Board of Special Appeals, the last step up the administrative ladder. At a press conference called to explain the school board's decision, School Board Chairman Daniel Carter lit out after the media for playing up "photogenic" Ryan White while ignoring the crucial legal niceties of the case. Carter insisted that Angelone had "totally ignored the law in her findings." And he lambasted Health Commissioner Woody Myers for his "malfeasance. . . . When a public official presses us to break the law, we welcome the lawsuit."

Yet for all the outrage, Angelone's decision was a turning point. When Stephen Jessup, Western's attorney, went looking for expert witnesses on AIDS transmission, he began to realize just how many doctors were lined up against Kokomo. Jessup tried desperately to hire an expert who would say that Ryan's attending school posed a threat to his classmates and to his own health. But most of the doctors Jessup contacted strongly disagreed with Kokomo's position, and the handful who didn't were under considerable pressure to remain silent.

Jessup did find one physician associated with the CDC who agreed to testify but backed out when ordered to do so by the CDC, and, Jessup reports, a New York City doctor was told that he would lose his prestigious hospital job if he took up Kokomo's cause. "We began to realize that the only people we could get to come would get us held up to public ridicule," the school lawyer recalls. "We could get [right-wing fanatic] Lyndon LaRouche's personal physician or a guy who wrote a newsletter in Chicago and who was feuding with the American Medical Association, but that was it." So Western went with its old arguments: not enough was known to be sure that Ryan couldn't spread AIDS, the state guidelines were unworkable, and no health certificate had been issued.

On February 6, 1986, the state board issued an oddly legalistic ruling for a case that had stirred such fierce passions. Angelone was unjustified in making a medical determination that Ryan could attend school, it said, scoring one point for Kokomo. But the board also concluded that Western should seek a medical certificate from Dr. Adler, the Howard County health officer. Once it was issued, Ryan had to be admitted.

Superintendent Smith and Board President Carter still believed that they were right and talked about carrying their fight back to the federal court. But the Western school district had already sunk over $100,000 in the cause, and its lawyer, Jessup, believed that the district didn't have a prayer. He persuaded Smith and Carter that they had won at least a technical victory and should now back off. They reluctantly decided not to appeal.

Dr. Alan Adler still had to produce the medical certificate. For months he had thought that Ryan should be admitted to school. But believing was one thing, putting himself on the line was something else. On February 13, he reached what he calls "the single biggest decision that I've ever had to make" and issued the precious piece of paper. Six months after the ordeal had started, it seemed as though the story was finished and Ryan White would be returning to school. "You'll be watched all the time," Adler told Ryan during the medical examination he gave the boy. "You'll really need to behave yourself."

Middle School Principal Ron Colby had anticipated the ruling. When he had chaired the case conference in September, the principal says, he had voted to keep Ryan out of school because "I was concerned, not about sneezing and things like that, I had progressed beyond that point, but about the possibility of an accident such as blood spilling." During the fall, though, the principal read more about AIDS; what he learned left him doubting that Western was right.

In December, after Angelone's ruling, Colby had set up a conference call with Dr. Martin Kleiman, the specialist who cared for Ryan at Riley Children's Hospital in Indianapolis, Jeanne White, and School Nurse Bev Ashcroft. Colby and Ashcroft quizzed Kleiman about Ryan's condition, and about what the state's guideline precautions would mean in practice. "That conversation convinced me that we could handle Ryan," says Colby. After that, when the principal talked to reporters, he was less a defender of the district than a voice cautioning against hysteria.

While Smith and Carter were still fulminating, Colby started planning the details of Ryan's return. Teachers, janitors, and cooks were briefed. Sixth and seventh graders got a lesson on AIDS in their science classes, and first aid kits were distributed to all classes. Bleach, rubber gloves, gauze squares, disposable washcloths, and alcohol swabs: everything Superintendent J. O. Smith had pointed to in ridiculing the state's guidelines back in August was now standard equipment. To allay anxieties, Jeanne White agreed to precautions well beyond those the state suggested. Ryan would have separate utensils and use a separate bathroom. He would not go to the gym, swim in the pool, or drink from the hall fountain. Nightly, the entire building would be fogged with a disinfectant.

A heavy winter snow blanketed Kokomo the moring of Friday, February 21, Ryan White's first day back, and millions of Americans watched on TV as a thin boy, bundled in a parka, was driven off to school. While reporters massed at the middle school waiting for Ryan to arrive, Ron Colby had his wife Sandy go in the front entrance of the school, video camera in hand, as a decoy. The ruse worked; when the TV crews followed Sandy, Ryan was whisked quickly through the side entrance.

Many of Ryan's classmates had seen him only on television.

"They didn't shy away from him," said Ryan's health teacher, Ruth Dougherty. "It was like he was the new kid in school." When Dougherty asked him how he liked his first day back, Ryan answered, "It's great, it's great. It gets so boring at home looking at the four walls."

Things at the middle school were not entirely peaceable, though. Almost half the students had been kept home by protesting parents, and a handful of picketers paraded outside the building. Nor were the parents ready to go along with Western's decision to abandon the fight. Just hours after Ryan's first day back in over a year, he was ordered out of class. The parents, still battling, had won an order from a state judge to keep Ryan home until the court could hear the case.

During the long course of the administrative hearings and appeals, the Western parents had never wavered in their opposition to Ryan's being in school. At first, some of them had admitted they were puzzled by contradictions in the evidence on how AIDS was spread. But as outsiders kept pushing for Ryan's return, in a way that called the community's good name into question, public puzzlement ceased. In the minds of these parents, it had become Kokomo against the world of armchair moralizers who, after all, didn't have to put their children's lives at risk. It was time to circle the wagons, to use the image frequently offered in Kokomo. To raise questions in such an atmosphere was to risk accusations of being a less than good—less than loyal—neighbor.

The week after Hearing Officer Angelone ruled against the district, seventy-five people turned out for a strategy session at their familiar meeting place, the Western gymnasium. The gathering of this group, which now called itself Concerned Citizens and Parents of Children Attending Western School Corporation, was as purposeful as a quilting bee. "There is no negotiating with AIDS," the parents' lawyer, a onetime policeman named David Rosselot, informed them. Talking about AIDS was yesterday's business; the task at hand was planning legal tactics to keep Ryan out. The week of Ryan's scheduled return, and out of earshot of the press, Principal Ron Colby organized his own meeting, but it was not a success. "Some of the parents, maybe ten of them, kept shouting us down. We didn't win them over."

As the day of Ryan's return approached, the parents stepped up their campaign. Several hundred people crowded into the gym for a meeting to orchestrate the boycott. Seven students from the 360-pupil school had already been pulled out, but parents who asked about transferring their youngsters to other school districts if Ryan remained in class learned, from those who had already tried, that it was too late in the year to switch districts. The only other option seemed to be to set up their own school.

On Wednesday, February 19, two days before Ryan was supposed to be back in class, Rosselot filed a petition in the Howard County court on behalf of three middle school students and their parents. The lawsuit relied on an obscure provision of Indiana law specifying that no one with a communicable disease could attend school or even appear in public. At the Friday afternoon hearing, the unhappy parents and students testified that they wanted Ryan out of school.

Among those present was Larry Gabbard, the much-decorated Vietnam vet. "I had many restless nights thinking, 'Am I doing the right thing?'" he recalls. "But I feel like I can go into a restaurant, and if there's someone there I don't want around, I can leave. My boy didn't have that right. He came home shaking from the mental pressures of being in class with Ryan." Gabbard didn't believe the reassurances of State Health Commissioner Myers. "I wouldn't use Woody Myers for my veterinarian. . . . When there was one person killed from Tylenol in Chicago, Woody Myers pulled Tylenol off the shelves immediately. With AIDS, you had so many people dead, but Myers wasn't willing to wait and be safe."

The county judge who heard the case, Alan Brubaker, was not particularly sympathetic to the litigants' cause. "You're not going to convince this court by having a group of parents parade in and tell me what they read in the *National Enquirer*," Brubaker informed Rosselot when he filed the legal papers.

Indeed, the judge seemed persuaded by the testimony of the doctors, who reiterated what by now had become scientific commonplace: there was no evidence that AIDS could be spread in the classroom.

But medical facts alone couldn't decide the case. Even though Brubaker criticized the 1949 Indiana law as "antiquated . . . and not a reflection of the needs of our society," the law was reason enough to keep Ryan home, the judge ruled, at least until its applicability could be more fully explored.

This was the verdict that Kokomo had been waiting for. Never mind Brubaker's harsh comments about the statute; the law was on their side. "It should never have been up to doctors and health officials. There's a state law against it," said Dave Johnson. The judge's ruling vindicated their belief that Ryan White had no business being in school, and the packed courtroom erupted in cheers when Brubaker delivered his message. A few parents left with tears in their eyes.

As Marcia Rosselot, whose husband had argued the parents' case, emerged from the courtroom, she defiantly flashed a thumbs-up sign. Kokomo had won. But outside Kokomo, that picture, carried on the nightly TV news, reinforced the sense of this heartlands town as a heartless place.

A few weeks earlier, in the Indiana community of Hobart, a teenager with AIDS had been ordered out of school and then run out of town by classmates who made his life intolerable. He had to "fight his way in and out of the house," said the father of the fifteen-year-old boy, whose name was not made public. The Whites, too, had been the targets of similar nastiness. On local radio talk shows, Ryan was vilified as a faggot and a queer. The family's car was pelted with eggs and its tires slashed. Much scarier, someone fired a bullet through the living room window.

Events at the courthouse—the decision and the cheers—only made things harder. To Ron Colby, who had sought to ease Ryan's path back to school, "It was the worst day of my life." The principal had come to court with Ryan and Jeanne White and Dr. Alan Adler. He remembers hearing the applause from the crowd: "We went out the back way. It turned my stomach.

Everything we had worked for, everything crescendoed up and I thought, 'Why the hell, why is it worth it?'"

For the Concerned Citizens group, though, it was a time for celebrating. When Judge Brubaker, who had issued the decree temporarily barring Ryan from school, ordered the group to post a $12,000 bond, they raised the money overnight with an auction in the school gym. Seemingly everyone in town chipped in with something. The Ford parts store where Dave Johnson worked donated $6,000 worth of parts, and a local tanning salon planned a "tan-a-thon." Televisions, refrigerators, stoves, and beds were all put on the block. A Pete Rose collector's plate raised $60, and a Hummell collector's bell sold twice, each time for $100—the original buyer donated it back to be resold. The auctioneer, Dick Bronson, host of the radio talk show on which Ryan had been slandered, promised to hold an auction for the Whites too, if they agreed to drop their fight.

To the parents, it didn't matter that out-of-town writers of letters to the *Kokomo Tribune* blasted the event. "What gives you the right to destroy this boy's life," one reader wrote. "I hope the people involved with this auction have a disaster such as this hit them and have to stand alone." "A grade-B western showing a lynch mob scene," declared another reader. The parents felt, as one of them told a reporter, that they were fighting for their "most precious commodity—their children."

Judge Brubaker's order only increased the pace of legal maneuvering. Charles V. Vaughan had been galvanized by the scene at the courthouse. "From that point on," said this pistol of a lawyer, "there was no stopping me." Vaughan first went back to the federal court, which had kept jurisdiction over the case when it ordered the Whites to pursue administrative remedies. But once Western had decided not to appeal the administrative ruling, that lawsuit was legally dead. This was now a new case that depended entirely on state law, and Vaughan would have to pursue it in the Indiana courts.

Concerned about the massive publicity in Kokomo, and about the prospects of getting a fair hearing there, Vaughan asked for and got a change of venue. Judge Jack O'Neill in Clinton

County, located to the west, would hear the case, which was set for April 10. But things were moving far too slowly for the aggressive attorney. He was tossed out of the Howard County court clerk's office after a shouting match with the bureaucrats who weren't producing a transcript quickly enough for him.

Although Superintendent J. O. Smith and Board President Daniel Carter had helped the parents group every way they could, providing a place to meet and offering neighborly encouragement, the Western School Corporation was nominally a defendant in the lawsuit. Yet even if the court ruled in Ryan's favor, as Western's lawyer, Stephen Jessup, anticipated, the Kokomo parents would not blame the school, the school officials believed. Western had done its best for them.

As the TV cameras camped outside, the Clinton County courthouse was filled with parents hoping for another victory. But even before the crowd had settled in their seats, Judge O'Neill announced his decision: "The preliminary injunction is dissolved." Ryan could go back to school.

Ryan leaped up and hugged his mother, as a half-dozen friends and members of the family, all wearing "Friends of Ryan White" buttons, gathered around them. Vaughan called Colby, who said: "Bring him in. I want him back in school." An hour later, when Ryan walked into Western Middle School, Ron Colby's arm was around his shoulder.

Now it was the Kokomo parents' turn to be mad. They resented the publicity that portrayed them as hicks, or worse. "We're all kind of angry that it has turned around to where we're the bad guys," said Leslie Wells, whose thirteen-year-old daughter Kari attended Western Middle School. Stephen Daily, the young mayor of the town, lapsed into obscenity when he was asked about Kokomo's image. "I don't give a flying shit about what the people in the rest of the country think," he told a *Fort Wayne Journal-Gazette* reporter.

The accusations of meanness stung. "I know of no one who is against Ryan," a parent wrote to the *Tribune*. "We all feel compassion, for he is an innocent victim of circumstances. But we are just as concerned about our own loved ones, and if you were in our shoes, you wouldn't act any differently." "We haven't forgotten Ryan here," wrote another mother, "and we don't need criticism from outsiders who haven't walked in our shoes. I've lived in Kokomo for many years and find it disgusting that we should apologize to anyone and especially out-of-staters for the fact that we have decent parents who will do anything possible to protect their child from an incurable, life-taking, communicable disease."

Yet for all that the Western parents claimed that those who disagreed with them hadn't "walked in their shoes," hadn't tried to understand their fears, these fathers and mothers never put themselves in the Whites' place. They insisted that their vision of being a good parent was the only valid one: if their child had AIDS, they would keep him home and try to make his last days happy. No one seemed capable of comprehending Ryan's desire for an ordinary life as a seventh grader or his dislike of being branded a victim and stored out of sight. Because almost no one in the town ever argued publicly for Ryan's point of view, the call to empathy—to consider how Ryan must feel— came only from strangers. The appeals only made townspeople angrier and more stubbornly defiant.

Immediately after Judge O'Neill's ruling, there was talk of a legal appeal. Parents resented the fact that, as Larry Gabbard said, they had never really had their anticipated day in court. They felt that their point of view, the facts they had marshaled, and the sentiments that gave force to those facts, had not been taken seriously—that *they* had not been taken seriously. They had been ordered to give up something they believed in without ever having had a chance to argue, without really knowing why they had lost. But the legal wrangling ended at the Clinton County courthouse because the parents were too drained, emotionally and financially, to keep going. Ryan White was back in school to stay.

Not that the parents of Kokomo were surrendering entirely. Twenty-two sixth and seventh graders were pulled out of

Western Middle School to form the Home Study School, housed in Russiaville's old American Legion Hall. "Ryan's a tragedy and we don't need any more," said Charles Byer, one of the new school's organizers. "The evidence may suggest a lot of things in the short term. We're worried about the long term."

These parents saw themselves upholding a proud American tradition of dissent. But the Home Study School did not invoke a venerated way of life, as did the schools the Amish had provided for their children, despite state objection, for many years. It was a gesture driven by antipathy, on the model of the private academies Southern whites opened after public schools were integrated. The Kokomo parents hired two teachers to instruct their children in the basics. And Western risked charges that it was siding with these families by allowing the youngsters to keep their rented school texts and giving the teachers its curriculum guides. "J. O. Smith was very, very helpful," says Larry Gabbard.

At the end of the term, the Home Study School closed for good. The tensions of the year had stirred up hard feelings among the organizers. Come August, Kokomo parents who remained anxious about their youngsters' welfare could send them more cheaply to another Howard County public school district. The others were resigned to returning their children to a school in which Ryan White was enrolled.

It was, finally, the end of a long seesaw battle, and Ryan was momentarily healthy enough to enjoy it. He would ride his bike around town for miles and sometimes stayed up until midnight, even on school nights. He talked about going out for the track team, about some day becoming a lawyer like the Vaughans. But victory for Ryan did not mean acceptance. For the balance of that school year and during the year to come, he remained a stranger in Kokomo.

From far away came only praise and honors. Olympic diving champion Greg Louganis invited Ryan to a national championship meet in Indianapolis and presented him with his winning medal. Rock star Elton John flew him to Disneyland. And Ryan got his biggest wish of all when Johnny Carson asked him to appear on the "Tonight" show. The outside world—some of it—also took the lesson of Kokomo to heart. Parents living in other towns that had their own AIDS-afflicted children, their own Ryan Whites, vowed to behave differently.

At Western, though, Ryan was no hero, and few proposed to treat him with more sympathy. One day in May, health teacher Ruth Dougherty conducted a class exercise demonstrating how to clear an obstructed windpipe. When students teamed up, only Ryan and a timid girl were left.

Adolescents can be, all at once, as hypersensitive as the princess in the story, "The Princess and the Pea," and as cruel as the youngsters in *Lord of the Flies*. What Ryan got, when he enrolled in the fall of 1986 as an eighth grader at Western High, was a dose of the cruelty. "My classmates backed away from me and called me names," Ryan recalls. He had to learn how to "ignore everything."

Incident piled on incident. A souvenir mirror that Jeanne White had bought Ryan during their trip to New York was swiped from his locker, and the locker was spray-painted with the word "butt-fucker." Classmates regularly drove by the Whites' house yelling "fag." A girlfriend who used to call him regularly while he was sick suddenly stopped talking to him altogether. Ryan was very much alone.

Long after Superintendent J. O. Smith gave the bad news to Jeanne White that Ryan couldn't attend school—long after the hearings and the lawsuits and the national publicity—very little had changed in Kokomo. School Board President Daniel Carter is still waiting for Woody Myers, the state health commissioner, to apologize. Smith continues to be convinced that, if only the media hadn't butted in, Ryan would have stayed on homebound instruction and none of the controversy would have happened. Long after the event, there were still heated discussions on radio call-in shows about why Ryan never should have been allowed in school.

The old fears about AIDS persist. Dave Rosselot, the parents' lawyer, is still talking about how mosquitoes spread AIDS. Mitzie Johnson is still worrying about the "two percent of what

the medical community knows that the public doesn't see." And
J. O. Smith remains scared of being in the same room with
Ryan while he is coughing.

The Kokomo contretemps did make a decisive impression on
the Indiana Board of Health, which had previously done little
about AIDS. In response to a flood of requests, Woody Myers'
staff developed what are among the nation's best educational
materials on AIDS, and in July 1987 Myers was named vice
chairman of President Reagan's panel on AIDS.[5]

The events in Kokomo also led the Board of Health to press
successfully for a change in the state law that had given the
judges such fits. Under legislation adopted in the spring of
1987, the state health director now has the final say on whether
a child with AIDS stays in school. A dozen inquiries were made
immediately after the law was passed, but at Myers' insistence
none were publicized. "We have no obligation to inform the
community when a rational public health decision has been
made," says Myers. "We have to desensationalize AIDS, take it
out of the realm of the unusual and bizarre."

To Woody Myers, whose office has turned out AIDS materials by the truckload, to "desensationalize" AIDS means "mas-
sively educating the public." But that education has not taken
hold in Howard County. There, resentment prevails, and the
community remains closed off. It sees itself as having come
under siege by outsiders because it tried to do right by those
who lived there.

When Superintendent Smith and School Board President
Carter argued their cause elsewhere, their message was generally not well received. At a national superintendents' conference in the spring of 1986, Smith debated Jack McCarthy, the
superintendent in Swansea, Massachusetts. At almost exactly
the same time that Kokomo was being traumatized, McCarthy
had persuaded the townspeople of Swansea that a thirteen-year-
old boy with AIDS could safely stay in school. A year earlier,
Smith reminded his professional colleagues, the conventional
wisdom among superintendents had been to keep such children isolated, a view that some other school chief later endorsed. But on this day, the superintendents in the audience

were all on McCarthy's side. In January 1987, when Smith appeared in Wilmette, Illinois, a Chicago suburb that had decided to admit an elementary school child with AIDS, he encountered a blizzard of criticism for his defense of Kokomo. "I was set up as the hick," Smith ruefully acknowledges. That summer, Ron Colby spent several weeks huddling with administrators in Arcadia, Florida, where he tried to deliver a different message, that a child with AIDS need not pose insufferable problems. But in Arcadia, as in Kokomo, passions partly stirred up by the administrators themselves could not readily be contained.

Initially, it was the school officials, Smith and Carter, who launched Kokomo on its course and, when they were attacked, they became caught up in roles they had scripted. But the two men were not only speaking their own minds. In a place like Kokomo, where everyone knows everyone else's business, the distinction between school board members—even superintendents—on the one side, and ordinary citizens on the other, is exceedingly fine. The decision made by Smith and Carter perfectly caught the local sentiment; people in the community quickly made the decision their own. The fact that outsiders saw things differently only hardened the resolve of parents who, more than anything, wanted to manage things for themselves.

Kokomo's school officials ran into trouble when they allowed this community sentiment to define their position. Eventually, their effort to rally popular support made their leadership depend entirely on the consent of the citizenry. Gone was any pretense that they were acting as rational men making a considered judgment on the merits; by the winter of 1985–1986, they were behaving simply as politicians. The families of Western had found solidarity around the theme of exclusion: that is why, when the court eventually rejected their position, they had nothing, and no one, to fall back on.

While the district's leaders found themselves defending a policy that scientific evidence was making increasingly hard to defend, Principal Ron Colby was keeping his own counsel, learning more and more about the disease. Because he did not grandstand, Colby could alter his judgment about the risk posed by

Ryan White without paying too heavy a personal price. But the appeal to populism by the district's leadership made it much harder for parents in Kokomo to accept the school district's shift in position—harder to agree that a judge's ruling had suddenly made it all right for their children to be in the same school as Ryan White.

The *Kokomo Tribune* did challenge the prevailing sentiment but, for all its efforts at detailed and balanced coverage, was derided along with the rest of the media. The fact that the *Tribune* had recently been sold to the Thomson syndicate made it seem more like a carping carpetbagger than a respected local voice. "I think that the media made up things to sensationalize it," says Mitzie Johnson. "They wanted to make it bigger than life." "They were an incitement," says Colby, yet the only specific instance the principal cites is the headline that appeared the day after Superintendent Smith called Jeanne White, which declared—correctly—that Western had "barred" Ryan from school.

Although some community leaders agreed with the *Tribune*'s position, they chose to remain quiet. Had Dr. Alan Adler spoken out, people in Kokomo might have listened, for the county health officer is well regarded in the town. Adler believed as early as August 1985 that Ryan should be in school, but he remained out of the picture. Nor was he the only medical officer to stay away from what he scorns as the "political" treatment of the issue. No doctor with expertise on AIDS became usefully engaged in Kokomo: Woody Myers admonished, rather than trying to educate, and Ryan's own physicians were conspicuously silent.

The same story, of doctors avoiding the political arena, had been told in the 1950s and 1960s, during the controversy over the fluoridation of drinking water. Even though all the major medical groups had declared support for fluoridation, doctors retreated when they came to realize that their word would not be accepted as gospel. They could not stomach the notion that their proofs were treated as just part of a political debate.

When the Western school district was making its initial decision on Ryan's enrollment, national authorities still disagreed to some extent about the AIDS risks. Small wonder, then, that politics-shy physicians stayed out of the limelight. But by the time the parents took their fight to the state court, the scientific case for Ryan's admission looked irresistible: then, a doctor who could acknowledge the Kokomo parents' fears while carefully desensitizing them, explaining the lack of scientific evidence for those fears, might have made a difference.

The default of leadership was not just a problem of the doctors. When the Whites went to federal court in August 1985 to seek Ryan's readmission, a less literal-minded judge could have concluded that, in a case where days were precious, legal rights should not be sacrificed to procedural niceties. But James Noland used the procedures laid out in the federal law to avoid the issue. A more aggressive state trial judge might have decided, when the parents brought suit in Howard County in February 1986, that the Indiana ordinance they relied on to keep Ryan White out of school was so inconsistent with modern state law as to deserve no respect from the bench. But Alan Brubaker, too, stayed silent. For almost a year, not a single widely respected individual in Howard County—not one—was willing to answer the Mitzie Johnsons and the Larry Gabbards.

Five people in Howard County had died from AIDS by 1988, and several other cases had been reported. But to listen to the talk in Kokomo and Russiaville, it is as if Ryan White—and AIDS itself—was only a bad dream, a momentary disruption of the continuities of a way of life untainted by the bedevilments of our times. Woody Myers' AIDS education materials go unused by the Western School Corporation. The county's public health nurse keeps the brochures entitled *AIDS and Homosexuals* in her desk drawer and waits for people to ask for them. Superintendent Smith, expressing openly a view that many in Kokomo hold privately, believes that if "the homosexuals had stayed in the closet," AIDS would never have come to Kokomo.

In June 1987, with Ryan once again seriously ill, the Whites moved away. They bought a bigger house on the river, in the nearby town of Cicero. The money for their new home came

from the rights to an NBC television movie on Ryan's life—
more of Jeanne White's exploitation of her son, in the minds
of the citizens of Kokomo, and another unhappy "first" for
the town.

But it was Ryan, not Jeanne, who most wanted to leave Kokomo, just as it was Ryan who had wanted to continue with his
case even when his mother was ready to quit. Ryan knew he was
dying. In a *People* magazine cover story that August, he said as
much. "I didn't want to die there," Ryan had told his mother. "I
really didn't want to be buried there."

CHAPTER THREE

ORDINARY HEROES: SWANSEA, MASSACHUSETTS

For most of its 300-year history, the southeastern Massachusetts town of Swansea, population 15,000, has been a placid backwater, a detour off a highway leading nowhere special. So little known was the community even in its home state that when Swansea made news in September 1985, the *Boston Globe* pinpointed its location on a map, giving it the kind of treatment usually reserved for exotic places like Dar es Salaam.

But on the evening of September 11, 1985, cameramen and reporters were everywhere, waiting for the hastily called public meeting that would earn Swansea its footnote in the history books. Floodlights illuminated the flat brick facade of Joseph Case High School. Camera tripods were dug into the lawn, and helicopters from Boston's TV stations hovered overhead. Reporters buttonholed Swansea residents heading into the high school auditorium—a standing-room-only crowd of more than 700 was packed into the town's biggest meeting place. At the edge of the light stood a group of high school students, shouting at the newsmen to "go home . . . leave us alone."

The media anticipated the kind of confrontation that plays well on the eleven o'clock news. Two weeks earlier, Swansea's school superintendent, John McCarthy, had told Mark, a thirteen-year-old boy with AIDS—his last name, though generally known among townspeople, was not published during the controversy—that he could return to Case Junior High School with the rest of his eighth-grade classmates.

At the time, only the school committee members and Mark's teachers were informed of his condition. The hope was to protect the teenager's privacy, the superintendent said, but as word slipped out, parents with children at the junior high demanded to know why Mark was allowed in school. Just five weeks before, Kokomo Superintendent J. O. Smith had cited the risk of contagion when he barred Ryan White from the classroom. Now Swansea Superintendent McCarthy was urging a very different course, one that would make Swansea the first community in the country knowingly to enroll a child with the dread disease.

The parents of Swansea had the same doubts about Mark that the Kokomo parents harbored about Ryan White. They wondered whether it made sense to invite a carrier of this twentieth-century plague into their junior high school, even if he was also the friendly and scrupulously polite boy many of them had known for years.

Swansea was neither the first nor the last town to act out this drama. There would come, famously, Queens, where thousands noisily protested New York City's decision to admit a youngster with AIDS; Arcadia, Florida, where the Ray family's house was burned to the ground; and less-publicized places like Ocilla, Georgia, and Atascadero, California. But Swansea distinguished itself as a community of ordinary people who, in extraordinarily difficult times, were better than they had to be.

Out-of-town journalists reached for the cliché of the tight-knit New England village when they reported on the events in Swansea. Yet Swansea is really an aggregation of little villages, French-Canadian and Portuguese and Yankee, largely cut off from the outside and from one another. Although the map shows Swansea in Massachusetts, the town is psychologically so far from the metropolis of Boston that it might as well be on another planet. The old Yankee contingent that ran the town for centuries remains well-off but over the years has become a minority. Since World War II, Swansea has been mostly working class; the nearby mills and factories of grim Fall River and reviving Providence are the biggest employers.

While registered Democrats outnumber Republicans two to one, Swansea politics is hardly liberal. When a subsidized housing project, Smoke River, was being built in the early 1970s, Swansea residents were up in arms over the prospect that outsiders—poor and maybe black—would leave Fall River and move into the neat tract homes, changing what they called the town's character. A handful of black families did come to Swansea but remained largely invisible: it was a noteworthy event when, in 1985, a black student played Hardcastle in the high school drama society's production of "She Stoops to Conquer."

Long before tax reduction became fashionable, Swansea had embraced the politics of less. During the 1960s and early 1970s, a proposal to build a badly needed new high school was regularly voted down at the annual town meeting. Proposition 2-1/2, the Massachusetts tax-cutting initiative, won overwhelming local support when it appeared on the ballot in 1978. Swansea's representative in the state legislature was a social conservative whose concern about the spread of AIDS was his stated reason for voting against a gay-rights bill that came up one week after the open forum on Mark's admission.

Though there was hope that the Boston Patriots would locate their football stadium in Swansea, it was built closer to Boston instead. Not until a mall opened in 1976, years after Swansea voters had grudgingly paid for an exit from the highway, did the town acquire anything resembling a main street.

Swansea residents measure themselves, somewhat defensively, against the more prosperous neighboring towns of Somerset and Seekonk, which spend considerably more on schooling and have a higher average level of education and a lower crime rate. Somerset fattened its tax base when the New England Power Company built a plant on the shores of Mount Hope Bay. All Swansea got, townspeople lament, is the soot and the ruined view.

Anyone who wants to understand America must first understand baseball, Jacques Barzun once said, and that aphorism perfectly fits Swansea. It has not only a Little League but also an unaffiliated baseball league for boys and a girl's softball league. The baseball diamonds are lovingly manicured, and when money for maintenance ran short one year the Little Leaguers quickly raised $1,000 by soliciting contributions door to door. A great deal of gossip is exchanged and business transacted by parents watching their young Tigers and Lions. Political careers in Swansea often begin with administrative jobs in Little League; that is how four of the five people serving on the Swansea school committee in 1985 got their start.

Baseball happened to be Mark's passion. Since he was seven, Mark had been a shortstop and pitcher, good enough to be described by his coach as one of the dozen or so best players he had managed in fifteen years. In a town where many families know one another through long-standing webs of relationship—one member of the Swansea school committee went to school with Mark's mother, another had been a friend of Mark's father since high school—Little League was how Mark became known. "Like a politician," school committee member Gene Rutkowski observed, "Mark had a good base."

In the spring of 1985, Mark began tiring easily. He would lose his breath after an inning in the field, his weight dropped, and he ran dangerously high temperatures. Because Mark is a hemophiliac, the family had always carefully monitored his medical progress, but these symptoms were new and alarming. Laboratory tests confirmed what his parents had feared. From a tainted batch of factor VIII, the blood clotting product he depended on, Mark had developed AIDS. The family was shocked into numbness, said Mark's mother, Dale, "as if we were handed a death sentence."

By late summer, though, the crisis had passed. Mark was playing ball again, and Dr. Peter Smith, the specialist who saw him regularly, felt that he was ready to begin school. Dale wondered whether it made sense to put her son through that kind of pressure. "They're all going to make fun of him and think

he's contagious," she fretted. But Mark wanted to go back, and
Dr. Smith was all for it.

Over the years, the family had learned to trust the advice of
this self-effacing physician who happens to be the region's leading pediatric hemophilia specialist. Smith works closely with
local pediatricians and gets high marks from professional colleagues as someone who contributes far beyond the call of duty.
It was the desire to be useful that hooked Smith on medicine.
He had read Albert Schweitzer's *Out of My Life* as a teenager
and determined that he too would be a medic in the African
bush, "but then I figured out that we can do our work in our
own backyard."

It was very important, Smith thought, that Mark be treated as
a normal child—not for his sake alone but also because of the
precedent that would be set. Smith is an unabashed advocate
who "preaches the gospel" about the rights of hemophiliacs as a
"labor of love." If Mark were kept out of school by this new disease, he believed, all the gains hemophiliacs had made over the
years would be jeopardized. If this fight were lost—if Kokomo
became the exemplar—then "the whole country could start
discriminating."

On August 20, barely a week before the school year began, Dr.
Peter Smith telephoned Harold R. Devine, principal of Case Junior High School, and reported Mark's condition. Devine immediately contacted Superintendent McCarthy. Together they
handled the issue, McCarthy making and defending the decision
to admit Mark, Devine putting a business-as-usual face on the
turmoil that engulfed the junior high.

McCarthy and Devine are both Irishmen and natives of
Providence, Rhode Island, but there the similarities end. Jack
McCarthy is short and stocky, with the bearing of a winning
football coach, which he was, a blunt man used to speaking his
mind and getting his way. "I don't usually back off," he says. "I
don't know why, really. I just never have."

For thirty years, McCarthy has worked his way up the ladder
in the Swansea school district, from teacher to principal to assistant superintendent. In 1975 he took over as head of a riven

school district that had hired and just three years later fired a leader brought in from out of town. In a place where full membership comes only after generations, McCarthy thinks of himself as an outsider. But he enjoys deep reservoirs of trust in Swansea; it seems that every adult in town had English teacher McCarthy or played under coach McCarthy.

McCarthy stitched the district back together. Over time, he was able to convince the school committee, whose membership became less penny-wise, and the annual town meeting, which sets the budget, to give him the dollars needed to upgrade the educational program.

Ron Devine came to Swansea in 1971 after managing the often grueling effort to desegregate the public schools in Providence. He is a fastidious man—"You'll never find a speck of lint on Ron's blazer," McCarthy jokes—more formal in manner than his boss. As principal at the 653-student junior high, Devine had to surmount considerable opposition in converting a conventional school, with seven forty-two-minute periods and constantly ringing bells, into a less factorylike institution whose educational program is designed with the characteristics of emerging adolescents in mind.

In the formal curriculum at Case, the periodic table of elements has been banished in favor of what the principal calls "exploratory learning," including everything from an introduction to foreign languages to survival cooking. The implicit curriculum encourages students to "take and accept responsibility," to go beyond their personal preoccupations—no easy business for adolescents—and look at things from what Devine calls a humanistic perspective.

Superintendent McCarthy had faced the press before, once when an overzealous undercover police officer had shown local TV stations videotapes of Swansea high school students smoking dope, and again when the driver of an oil truck fell asleep while making a delivery at the junior high and allowed oil to overflow into Mount Hope Bay. But neither these episodes, nor the normal run of memo-writing and conciliating that fill a small town superintendent's time, prepared him to deal with a problem as big as AIDS.

When confronted with the specter of AIDS, other super-intendents have run for cover, unwilling to offend jittery parents or deliver ultimatums to rebellious teachers. But Jack McCarthy, described by those who work with him as having a highly developed and strongly felt sense of values, was impatient with what he saw as a default of leadership. "I figure they pay me to make decisions," he says.

The superintendent spent the week after he learned of Mark's condition reading everything about AIDS he could get his hands on and asking questions of the country's leading pediatric AIDS experts. He spoke at length with Dr. Peter Smith, who explained that AIDS could be transmitted only by being introduced directly into the bloodstream. When he called the federal Centers for Disease Control in Atlanta, where a statement about the education of children with AIDS had been in preparation for months, Dr. Martha Rogers, who heads the CDC's program on AIDS and children, advised him to keep Mark in school.

The CDC's guidelines, hurried into print at the end of August because of what had transpired in Kokomo, used the familiarly hedged language of medical science. "Based on current evidence, casual person-to-person contact as would occur among schoolchildren appears to pose no risk." But its conclusion dropped all the qualifiers. With a handful of specified exceptions—habitual biters, for instance—"these children should be allowed to attend school."

What the experts told him, McCarthy said, meant that, medically, "It really wasn't a hard decision at all. I just did my job. I don't see how it could have gone any other way." Yet the superintendent felt the heaviness of the responsibility he was assuming. "I prayed that I was right," he says. "I prayed a lot about it."

McCarthy went looking for help from state officials, with mixed results. While the CDC was working out its guidelines, a Massachusetts task force, including representatives from the state's public health and education bureaucracies, had been struggling for months to develop an AIDS policy of its own. They had been stymied, largely because the state's education commissioner, John Lawson, didn't want to take responsibility for what he regarded as entirely a health problem. Eventually, McCarthy extracted a letter of support from the Education Department's staff attorney.

The superintendent found a less hesitant ally in Dr. George Grady, the state Health Department's chief epidemiologist. The lack of bureaucratic consensus didn't keep Grady from inventing policy on the spot, for he is not shy about sticking his neck out. "The junior high school student you describe does not present a risk to the public health," Grady promptly wrote McCarthy.

It was not "compassion for the downtrodden," Grady recalled, that prompted his unequivocal response. "If I thought that child was a risk, I'd say 'no way.' I don't believe in minority rights in that sense." Two decades of experience working on viral diseases such as hepatitis, whose patterns of transmission are basically similar to those of AIDS, had convinced Grady that admitting a child in Mark's condition to school was the right course.

Superintendent McCarthy's real challenge was to make his decision to keep Mark in school stick. The first hurdle was the five-member Swansea school committee. Two of the committeemen had earlier heard through the Little League grapevine that Mark had AIDS, but they hadn't anticipated that he would want to return to school. All had the same instinctive reaction: "No way."

"When it comes to your children," says Committee Chairman Bob Paquette, "hey! that's your entire life." But Paquette recalls how McCarthy persevered: "Let's not jump the gun," the superintendent insisted. "Let's investigate." As they carried on their own conversations with the AIDS experts in Atlanta and Providence and Boston, they began to see things differently.

The composition of Swansea's school committee reflects the insularity of the town. Four of its members were Swansea natives (the fifth was born in Seekonk); only one, a high school shop teacher, had a college degree; all were men. One had just been through a messy divorce, which he suspected might well mean defeat in the next election.

The committee members were acutely aware of the potential

for trouble in Mark's case, aware too that they might be in way over their heads. As they struggled to think through their concerns, they also thought how special Mark was, "ten years above himself in maturity," as one of them said. And they recalled children in their own lives who had needed help. "I never even thought about special needs till I saw what happened to my nephew, who became paraplegic after a car accident," said Russ Howarth. "I'd want the same opportunity if it was my kid," Chairman Paquette said. "You have to give everybody some freedom."

After talking it out, the school committee members were more than willing to let the superintendent make the decision and take the heat. Jimmy Carvalho, who describes his tenure on the school committee as partly an ego trip, was eager to claim some public credit for the stance Swansea was taking, but the school's lawyer, John Lucey, persuaded him to let McCarthy speak for them all. Having a single spokesman, Lucey argued, could keep the press from distorting their words and might just keep them out of court. The superintendent, characteristically, made the point more bluntly. "If you open your mouth, you're on your own."

On August 26, the day before school opened, all the teachers who would have Mark in their classes were summoned to a special meeting. McCarthy, Devine, and Smith were there; so was Mark's father, apprehensive about how those who taught his son would handle the news. For two-and-a-half hours, the teachers, caught unaware, pressed Dr. Smith for information.

Like the teachers in Kokomo, their initial feeling was that it was a bad idea to allow a mysterious and fatal virus into their midst. Some resented the pressure placed on them and the fact that they had no choice. ("You have a choice," Devine would later inform the most obdurate teachers. "You can consider another career.") One teacher worried about whether her own medical condition, as a cancer patient whose spleen had been removed, made her particularly vulnerable to AIDS.

Dave Gibeau was the most vocally angry person in the room. "I didn't like Smith. He was blaming us—me personally—for not accepting the situation. It was the medical profession that was screwing things up, though. Different places did different things. I told Smith, 'When you guys get your act together, when all the evidence points in the same direction, then I'll believe you.'"

Gibeau also had a more personal reason to be upset. He was the father of a daughter, then just five months old, and feared that his wife wouldn't let him touch his own child. "Is there any chance—one-one millionth of a chance—that I could give AIDS to my daughter?" he asked, and when Smith wouldn't give him unequivocal assurance, Gibeau responded: "If I'm in that school and I bring AIDS home, it's like child abuse."

Over the next few days, though, almost all the teachers reconciled themselves to Mark's presence. Smith's talk changed some minds. He spoke with "reverence and believability," said Lynn Sullivan, the cancer patient. Sullivan was reassured by her own doctor; besides, she knew Mark well and "anybody that good can't be that bad." Another teacher, Paul Krupa, recalled that "the meeting allowed us to talk out our fears, like cafeteria food, water bubblers, his spit and sweat and what if he fell down the stairs and bled. After you absorb it all, you have to begin to trust someone. It was slow and painful, but finally you reasoned that fear was not grounded in fact."

Mark's condition quickly became known among all the teachers in the school, for a junior high faculty lounge is no place for secrets, and a meeting of all the school's teachers was held later that week. Again, Dr. Smith explained to anxious teachers how AIDS is transmitted. This time, some who had been at the earlier session acted as therapists to defuse the fears of their colleagues.

Lynn Sullivan recalled how important it was to appear in control of her feelings in front of the students. "Dear God," she prayed, "no matter what I'm thinking, don't let it show on my face." As the teachers pulled themselves together and went about their vocation, McCarthy crossed his fingers that this would end the controversy. All along, he hoped to preserve Mark's privacy and the school's well-being by keeping the news from leaking out, for the superintendent was particularly troubled by the possibility of what he called "another Kokomo."

But as Ron Devine pointed out, there was really no way to keep this story under wraps. The only question was how to influence its telling.

"One important decision was to frame everything narrowly," says Devine, "to neutralize the perceptions of AIDS as linked to gays and junkies sharing needles. We emphasized that here was a responsible thirteen-year-old victim who through no fault of his own became infected with a deadly disease. It would have been a whole different set of circumstances with an eighteen-year-old homosexual."

To a man, the school committee members say they would have reached the same decision if Mark had been gay. Perhaps so: during the debate over Mark's fate, concern about homosexuality never surfaced publicly in Swansea, as it did in Kokomo. But Swansea is not especially tolerant toward gays, and some in the community blamed homosexuals for Mark's illness. "My wife says that gay people caused AIDS and hurt Mark," said one of the teachers at Case. "They should be punished." To Dave Gibeau, AIDS was just a "disease of tolerance."

During the first week of school, reporters from the *Providence Journal,* the leading daily in the area, were tipped off that a child with AIDS was attending Swansea's junior high. But when the newsmen contacted the school district they got a flat "No comment," and without confirmation their editors were unwilling to run the story. "In the newsroom, sometimes the buzzword of the public's right to know automatically controls, and there's not enough attention to the real impact on real people," says medical reporter Irene Wielawski. "This time, though, the normal routine just stopped. Everyone saw the potential power of the press to have a tragic impact."

Superintendent McCarthy delivered the same message more personally to another *Journal* staffer who kept pressing for confirmation. "If you publish this, God help you for what you are going to do to this kid."

The dilemma for reporter Wielawski involved more than one child's emotional well-being. "Did I have a right to participate in

keeping a secret from the parents of other children whose lives might be affected?" she asked herself. Wielawski thought hard about how she would feel if she were a parent in Swansea. At a party that weekend, she asked some friends how they would react if a child with AIDS were in their youngsters' class. "They're all Gene McCarthy-type liberals, but this was different: they all said they'd fight."

"Swansea was an astonishing story to chronicle," recalls Wielawski. "AIDS exploded the deepest fears of a society. . . . People were being asked to put the most precious thing they have on the line in the interest of compassionate behavior." Until that time, the *Journal* was not in the forefront of AIDS coverage. It had run one article on a female prostitute with AIDS who refused to stop streetwalking, another on an alcoholic gay hustler on the streets after having been kicked out by his family and by the YMCA. "They were the only people with AIDS who would speak to me," says Wielawski, explaining why she had picked such inflammatory characters to write about.

Providence had a dozen AIDS cases in 1985, almost all gay men, but the gay community was furious at the paper. Understandably so: earlier that summer, in an editorial opposing a city gay-rights ordinance, the *Journal* had condemned homosexuality as "a psychological disorder."

The AIDS-in-school story was treated very differently. The *Journal,* as well as several other local newspapers and a Providence TV station—all had gotten similar anonymous leads—refrained from aggressive journalism. They hoped that, by holding off, they could help keep Swansea from becoming another Kokomo. (For similar reasons, they later decided not to reveal Mark's last name, even though it was widely known in Swansea: the name was "not newsworthy," and publication might hurt the family.)

This journalistic reticence vanished when the *Spectator,* a local weekly, broke the news on September 4 in a circumspect piece about "one child in town with AIDS," age and sex unspecified. The article began with an editor's note that read: "Because of the nature of the following subject and a natural tendency to react strongly, we ask that you read the following story in its entirety."

That afternoon, the phones at the Swansea administration building began ringing nonstop. The following day at 2:00 P.M., Superintendent McCarthy, flanked by Swansea school attorney John Lucey and the school committeemen, held a brief press conference. He handed out a one page statement confirming the barest facts and then refused to answer any questions.

The timing was ill-chosen, though, for the junior high school, barely a hundred yards down the road, was just letting its students out for the day. As children headed for the buses that would take them home, cameramen and reporters chased after them, cornering youngsters in the parking lot, shoving microphones in their faces, and asking them how they felt about having a classmate with AIDS.

Most of the students had no inkling of Mark's condition and were terrified by the insistent intruders. Looking out the schoolhouse windows, teachers saw the children being assaulted. Suddenly, the situation was transformed: the beleaguered community was under siege by unfeeling outsiders. "A feeding frenzy for sharks," school attorney Lucey called it and quickly phoned the police. "These guys are endangering our children," Lucey told them, and the TV crews were escorted, none too gently, off the school grounds.

During the next week, as the press camped out across the street from the junior high, Devine struggled to keep the school itself safe from the probing cameras. Each day he disappointed the reporters by telling them that everything was normal at Case. And while the anonymous tips to the media came from two men who identified themselves as teachers at Case, those teachers still opposed to Mark's attending school retreated into silence. Almost the only voices to be heard on the record were those of the administrators, saying as little as possible, and McCarthy's supporters in the community.

At corner stores and baseball diamonds and church halls, though, everyone was talking about Mark. A dozen parents took their children out of school as soon as they heard the news. More were angry that they had had to find out about something that so directly touched their lives by watching the six o'clock news. Many were incredulous. They thought of AIDS as something that happened to *those* people and not to themselves. It wasn't fair, they told one another, that Swansea should suddenly be a fishbowl everyone else was staring at.

"I got so scared," said Colette Hrojcaj, whose daughter was a junior high student. "It had seemed so remote. Now it's like 'Oh, my God! in my town, my child's class, my child's classroom.'

"I was so outraged. God, is the kid drinking out of my daughter's bubbler? All I had been seeing on TV was the leprosy of the '80s. I didn't send my child to school the next day. I was so alarmed. I guarantee you that the first day everybody heard, nobody was saying, 'Hey, that's great.'"

An open meeting for all the parents had become a necessity, but McCarthy held off, setting the date for a week later. He hoped that, once the initial shock subsided, parents would learn from their pediatricians, and from newspaper accounts of the spread of a disease that until then had gotten no local coverage, that Mark posed no danger to their children. The pediatricians were indeed helpful. Several had called their colleague Peter Smith and asked whether there was anything they could do. Coincidentally, school committeeman Jimmy Carvalho's son went to the same Swansea doctor as Mark. "Do you think I'd go home to my kids if there was a danger?" the pediatrician told Carvalho.

At the junior high school, Devine never called a mass assembly, for that, he said, would be "playing with the emotions of adolescents." Instead, he left it to the teachers to answer students' questions whenever they came up during the school day. The technique worked, and Mark's classmates became his most vocal supporters. They told their parents not to worry, that they had learned in school that AIDS wasn't contagious like chicken pox. Several of them even asked to be transferred into his classes.

It helped that Mark was popular, that he was an honors student who didn't brag about how smart he was, a solid kid who always seemed more grown-up than his years, a baseball nut who had collected every Topps baseball card issued since 1979. And because Mark was an eighth grader, his classmates, the biggest youngsters in this grades-six-through-eight school, could keep younger kids from mouthing off.

What was most remarkable was the maturity with which these twelve- and thirteen-year-olds handled the most serious moral question most of them had ever encountered. "Eighth graders can deal with—control—their feelings," Devine had observed, and was confirmed when, on a TV interview several weeks into the term, a half-dozen of Mark's classmates fielded a reporter's questions.

"It was a real serious problem that we had to think hard about and make a decision about. We made the right decision," said one. "It wouldn't feel right if he were home, if he couldn't communicate with his friends. He belongs here, it's his home. He has a right to an education just like we do. He shouldn't be shut out." Another classmate added her plea for empathy. "Think of it like if you were in his position—how would you feel?"

Parents in Swansea talked about how proud they were of their children, how grown-up they had become. And as they listened to what their own sons and daughters were telling them, they were reintroduced to their own compassion.

The town forum scheduled by Superintendent McCarthy was billed as an informational meeting, not an occasion for deciding anything, but McCarthy and Devine knew they needed the community's backing. The superintendent looked to the institution of the town meeting as his model. In Swansea, such meetings have been held each spring for nearly three centuries, historically deciding everything from the building of a church to a division of land. While the day-to-day business of Swansea is now conducted by a board of selectmen, the single most important public issue, the pocketbook question of the town's budget, is determined at this annual gathering of the citizens.

A century ago, James Bryce declared in *The American Commonwealth* that the town meeting "is the cheapest and the most efficient [form of local government]; it is the most educative of the citizens who bear a part in it."[1] In the intervening decades the town meeting had become more a relic than a democratic reality in Swansea, sparsely attended except when new taxes were on the agenda (then, the old-line WASP families would pack the hall to vote the measure down). But on this night, a ritualized way of bringing neighbors together offered the residents of Swansea a familiar setting in which to air their unfamiliar concerns—making it, for once, "not only the source but the school of democracy," as Bryce had grandiosely opined.

Much to the regret of Jimmy Carvalho, the self-styled egoist who wanted to appear on the stage, the school committee members were seated in the front row of the auditorium. (So was the thirteen-year-old son of the state epidemiologist, who was eager to hear his father speak; and several TV stations, surmising that this must be the youngster with AIDS, ran his picture that night.)

Peter Smith drove up from Providence, as he had three times before, far more unsettled now at the prospect of facing hundreds of fretful parents. Smith talked about how this boy, his patient, was a threat to no one, how forcing him to stay home, even if ostensibly for his own good, was killing with kindness. "I tried to empathize, to respond directly to all the concerns," Smith recalled. "If you take people's questions seriously, you won't turn them off. If you argue, people stop listening."

The state epidemiologist, George Grady, turned out to be a tall, distinguished-looking man, as perfect for his part as if sent by central casting. He explained how much was known about the way AIDS spread from one person to another, laying out the research that made him confident that Mark presented "zero risk" to his classmates. "There's never been a case of child-to-child transmission, and we've had five years. . . . In Kokomo, people were saying 'We're frightened . . . this child shouldn't be in school . . . we don't care what you doctors think.' But we do know a lot about this disease; it is paralleling other diseases in how it's transmitted. There is no mystery."

Superintendent McCarthy detailed how he had reached his decision and why, to maintain confidentially, he had said nothing about it publicly. "I saw no need to twice jeopardize a victim—and no need to socially isolate a student." Curtis Hall, a state education department representative who talked of his "thirty-four years in public education," added his endorsement. "This town must stand proud."

There was an edge-of-the-chair tension in the air as people

strained to make sense of what they were being told. The school officials and the doctors who had a hand in admitting Mark were asked why they hadn't waited for more definitive medical answers, what precautions were being taken to keep the water cooler and the silverware in the cafeteria from being contaminated, what the high incidence of AIDS in Belle Glade, Florida, signified, what the data showed about "parent-sibling contact." Over and over, parents wanted assurances that the presence of a child with AIDS posed no risk to their own children.

Those who made the case for admitting Mark to the townspeople of Swansea had a clear sense that, whatever the outcome that evening, history was being made. That is why the school district arranged to have the meeting preserved on videotape. Yet when the last question had been asked, and the meeting ended after nearly three hours, they weren't sure who had carried the day.

Some parents had spoken out for "the rights of this child" and exclaimed about what a proud night this was for the town. "You want guarantees—you can't even guarantee your next breath," said Toby Donley. "Put yourself in that family's situation. They need compassion." But there were also enough angry outbursts that at one point the usually unflappable Ron Devine, whose concern for the proprieties got him selected as moderator of the Seekonk town meeting and who was presiding at this session, had to plead with the crowd to maintain "civil order."

"Whoever was responsible for keeping this from us should face charges," yelled Terese Fagundes. Henry Santoro, speaking with a thick Portuguese accent, his face a perfect depiction of the pain he felt, practically begged the doctors to "guarantee me that my daughter, she will not catch AIDS. It seems like a circus here but we are talking about a life—I've lost two children. If she dies, will you take the responsibility?"

Grady delivered what few other medics have been willing to issue: an assurance that stunned the audience with its directness. "If you can guarantee me 100 percent that your daughter will never shoot drugs or have sex with another person, then I can guarantee you that your daughter will not get AIDS."

The TV news shows got the confrontation they anticipated

when Leonard Cabral, a mechanic and father of four, stood up and, shaking his fist for emphasis, shouted that "letting this boy in school is like leaving a kid going around with a gallon of gas and a match." McCarthy responded: "You have four children, I have six. I share the same concerns. Six months from now, I could be dealing with an issue involving your children. I hope you'd feel that I'd be as fair with your child as I am being here."

Cabral kept up the attack. "It's my daughter, my son. You have no right to do this without telling me." And the superintendent, barely containing his own anger, replied: "I can't let parents decide on the basis of fear and hysteria."

Cabral stalked off. "It's a whitewash," he told reporters.

As people drifted out at the end of the marathon session, the school committeemen mingled with the crowd to judge its mood. They weren't disheartened by the number of hostile comments because they knew the speakers personally—knew how much impact their words would have on their neighbors. And they recalled that Leonard Cabral had a vendetta against McCarthy for firing him from his job as school bus driver.

When the committee reassembled for the post mortem, Chairman Bob Paquette sounded confident. "They're with us," he announced.

The marathon meeting was not the end of the matter. Although some minds were changed that night, others remained unreconciled to the decision. Robert Cook had pelted the doctors with pointed question about AIDS transmission, often citing chapter and verse from the CDC's *Morbidity and Mortality Weekly Reports* (*MMWR*), and he was unhappy with the answers. "I was just trying to get Grady to open up to the people." Cook was offended by what he saw as Grady's overconfidence: "'I'll bet $100 that no one catches AIDS in school' [Grady had said]— What kind of answer is that? . . . I work for the government and I know the tactic. The people I work with try to bluff the public with knowledge all the time."

Cook organized a small contingent to call on their state representative, Philip Travis. Although Travis shared the parents'

misgivings, he could offer them no encouragement. Out of respect for McCarthy, whom Travis had known since his school
days twenty-nine years earler, the legislator was unwilling to
push too hard. Moreover, the state education department had
informed him that any child kept out of school for fear of contracting AIDS would be treated as truant.

As it turned out, not a single youngster was permanently
withdrawn from Case. Parents heard only defiant responses
from their children when they proposed sending them to private schools. "You can drop me off in the morning," said one
eighth-grade girl, "but I won't be there when you come to pick
me up." Another girl did go to a nearby Catholic school for a
few days. But when she was told that, in order to remain there,
she would have to take the AIDS antibody test and could not
tell anyone she came from Swansea, she returned to Case.

The mother who had talked about taking legal action at the
community meeting, Terese Fagundes, spent three days at the
baseball field. She collected eighty-nine signatures on a petition
urging McCarthy to reverse his stance, almost as many as in
Kokomo. But, unlike in Kokomo, this petition signing didn't
blossom into an effective organization of angry parents.

Fagundes had no experience at organizing, and no help, for
no one else wanted to get involved. Fagundes kept her own
daughter out of school for three days. But after checking the
cost of sending her elsewhere and giving some thought to how
her children had gone to Swansea schools their whole lives, she
let her daughter return.

Teacher Dave Gibeau, still scared for his infant daughter,
stopped complaining when he got his long-sought transfer to
the senior high school. One of the junior high shop teachers,
Tom Slowe, vainly protested to McCarthy when he found out
that Mark would be in his class. The superintendent tried reasoning with Slowe but blew his top when the shop teacher said it
was a matter of fear, not facts. "Fear is what led the Nazis to kill
the Jews, it's what led the Romans to kill Jesus," McCarthy
thundered.

What troubled Swansea's school officials most was the prospect
of a lawsuit. At a time when so many questions of educational

policy wind up in court, their concern was not misplaced—indeed, judges have had the decisive say in a number of communities, including Kokomo and Queens.

By the time of the community meeting, attorney John Lucey was confident that the district had the law on its side. He hoped to keep the very idea of a lawsuit out of people's minds, to convince them that AIDS was a medical question to be settled by doctors, not judges. A few days after the meeting, several parents did consult Jeffrey Entin, a local attorney, about the possibility of litigation. Entin told the parents that it was not morally or legally right to go off on a crusade without giving the schools a chance to work things out. Besides, his wife taught at the junior high; as Entin wrote in a letter to Superintendent McCarthy, he was unwilling to bring the tensions of the teachers' room into his home. When Entin decided not to handle the case, the idea of a lawsuit faded away.

Within a matter of weeks, those who opposed McCarthy's decision had lost interest in pushing their cause. "One real strong objector could have made the opposition cohesive," says attorney Lucey. But the opponents were isolated from one another—those talking about a lawsuit were not the people meeting with their state representative—and no one ever tried to bring them together. Even if they had joined forces, it isn't clear that they could have found common ground. What strategy would satisfy both Robert Cook, given to citing the CDC reports, and Leonard Cabral, the man with a flair for incendiary metaphor?

The very niceness of the town seemed to stand in the way of a prolonged fight. Living in Swansea doesn't require that you like everyone, just that you get along more or less peacefully; too many people know each other's cousins or grandmothers, attend the same church or have children on the same Little League team, for long-standing animosities to be tolerable. It's not that people are routinely intimate with one another—Swansea is too big, and too private, for that—but that personal reputations, once acquired, are not easily remade. With no room for compromise on the AIDS question and little enthusiasm for challenging a superintendent who, almost everyone believed, had the best interests of their children at heart, people retreated.

Mark's family felt that they were the ones in the fishbowl, their lives the object of community curiosity. They were entirely unprepared for the role. "We're so normal," Mark's mother Dale said, almost plaintively, and in fact their lives sound like something straight out of "Ozzie and Harriet," a story set in the troubled 1960s and 1970s but with the innocence of an earlier time.

Dale was a hometown girl who met Jay, a college boy from Fall River, when she sneaked into a college mixer held at the Venus de Milo Restaurant. They were married in 1969 after Jay graduated. Jay began teaching history and religion at a nearby Catholic junior high, while Dale worked at a local bank. Mark was born three years later, and the papers on their first home— a brand-new house in Smoke River, the development whose construction had provoked such hostility—were signed while Dale was still in the hospital. Dale made that house the prettiest suburban dream on the block and stayed home to take care of Mark. It wasn't until their second child, Scott, was born in 1975 that she started working nights as a salesperson at Sears.

Their families have always been close, geographically and personally. Dale's mother and stepfather are just a block away, and her brother lives next door. Jay's brother is across the street, his sister lives in town, and his parents moved to Swansea from Fall River. Though family members see a lot of each other, "feelings aren't something we talk a lot about," says Jay.

"It was hard enough dealing with Mark's hemophilia," Dale recalls, "with all the fears about what happens when he gets cut and bleeds." They learned to handle those fears, to be comfortable with Mark's passion for baseball; eventually they even bought him the dirt bike he had been pleading for. Mark's physical vulnerability was one reason that the family did so much together, that they had never spent a night apart until Mark had to go into the hospital. "I worry that I kept a leash on him," says Dale. Maybe, too, that vulnerability helps explain why Mark was so shy—the boy who always got "A"s in conduct.

"At the beginning, when the doctors told us he had AIDS, all I did was cry, cry, cry," Dale remembers. "I was in shock. Sometimes I'd go into a store and pretend that I wasn't even me, that I was someone else." Some of the things being said about Mark—"never to my face, though,"—made Dale angry. She was particularly angry at Leonard Cabral. "We've known him so long, you'd think he'd have a little compassion. We're not strangers. He should have realized that we wouldn't do anything to hurt his children."

While Dale stayed home with the boys that fall, Jay went, never speaking up, to all of the meetings that concerned Mark, including the community forum. He was livid at the parents who signed the petition demanding Mark's removal from school. "I'd just like to see those names," he says, still furious long afterwards.

At the town meeting, one woman called on Dr. Smith to "walk us through the next year of this boy's life." Smith demurred—who could confidently predict anything about the course of AIDS? Jay, sitting silently in the next row, felt as if he was watching his own nightmare displayed in full view of everyone.

That very night, Mark was taken back to Rhode Island Hospital. He was suffering not from AIDS but from a painfully infected ankle joint that resulted from the kind of internal hemorrhage common among hemophiliacs. During the eight weeks that he spent in the hospital, Mark had to undergo three operations. Dale stopped working at Sears, and Jay quit his second job to spend more time with his son. Mark's classmates sent him a balloon-a-gram reading "Hurry back, Mark." The grandparents and in-laws pitched in; and so did a group of parents, most of them strangers, who called themselves Friends of Mark.

Among those at the town forum who had spoken out most strongly on Mark's behalf was a parent named Susan Travers. "Everything in life involves a risk," she had said. "Buses, day care, everything. What's important is that we have to support each other."

"I have three children," Travers told a local reporter shortly afterwards. "My oldest son goes to school with Mark. I have a relative whose children received blood transfusions at birth. And, I often think, but for the grace of God it could have happened to any of them."

Travers also had a more personal reason for wanting to get involved. Her brother is gay, and at one point she had kept him away from her children out of fear that he might have AIDS. Subsequently, she changed her mind—"Family is too precious to cut off like that," she said—and that experience made her realize how important it was that Mark not be exiled by the community.

After the meeting, Sue Travers and two of her neighbors enlisted the help of thirty women to make dinners regularly for the family while Mark was in the hospital. Friends of Mark also organized a benefit dance, which was held just after Mark left the hospital in November and raised over $10,000 from townspeople and local groups. A huge banner reading "We Miss You, Mark" hung from the wall of the community center, and Tora, a local rock group, gave up a well-paying gig to play for free at the benefit. "He lives right down the street from where we practice," said bass player Augie Pimental. "If I was dying from something like that I'd hope someone would help me." Mark's classmates, many of whom had not seen him since his hospitalization, turned out to welcome his back.

Mark, who had been depressed by the tension during the first weeks of school, was overwhelmed. "This is the only place in the country where this is happening, isn't it, Mrs. Travers?" he asked. At home, though, Mark didn't talk much about his illness. "We didn't dwell on it," says Dale. "He said his prayers every night. They were long ones, too; he had a lot of religion in him."

The fact that a boy named Mark who happened to have AIDS returned to school, read *Macbeth* in English class, learned how to bake a yellow cake in cooking class, and won the science fair with an exhibit on the wonders of the human eye, went unreported in any newspaper. Sue Travers became something of a celebrity, going on a Boston TV talk show to speak about the choice between fear and caring that any person—any town—can make. She was going to "put Swansea on the map," Travers said.

McCarthy, Devine, and Smith were frequently on the road, speaking to groups of school board members and school administrators and doctors. At a statewide meeting of school board members that winter, Swansea's committeemen, conspicuous in their work clothes, stood down those who thought children with AIDS should be kept home. "You don't have your facts right," said Chairman Paquette. "It's not so scary." There was talk in Swansea of a TV docudrama, and Jay, Mark's father, started writing a book, entitled *Mark*, about the family's experiences.[2]

A half-dozen Massachusetts towns confronted the AIDS issue during the 1985–1986 school year. In the Boston suburb of Framingham, the school committee initially voted to keep out a child with AIDS, but later reversed itself. The most telling arguments were those of a committee member who had been in a Nazi concentration camp; after initially voting to exclude the child, she had come to recognize the parallels between her personal history and the isolation of a child with AIDS. In the Boston neighborhood of Brighton, supporters of political extremist Lyndon LaRouche tried to stir panic among parents, as they would again in other locales. But in Massachusetts, every child with AIDS was allowed to attend school. Swansea's experience—recounted by state epidemiologist George Grady, who was a visible figure in the most contentious of these controversies—helped convince people that their children, too, would not be in jeopardy.

The advent of this plague, the biggest event in each of their lives, was a test of character for everyone involved in the decisions. In Swansea, ordinary people grew to heroic proportions during those heady days, and when they opened their mouths they spoke heroic sentences. Later in the year, at the annual town meeting, the citizens gave their nearly unanimous approval to a million-dollar renovation of Case Junior High—an acknowledgement, many believed, of the exemplary job Principal Ron Devine had done.

School Superintendent John McCarthy was chosen Swansea's citizen of the year. "He lit a candle that dispelled the darkness of fear and ignorance," the citation read. "Swansea can always be proud that one of their own took this step forward in the best tradition of the people of the United States of America." Both houses of the Massachusetts legislature, as well as the statewide superintendents' association, added their commendations. McCarthy is proud of those commendations, which are prominently hung in his office. But he doesn't see himself as a hero. "Hell, the kid is the hero."

Fifty-three children, out of 367, were absent from the junior high in Kokomo, Indiana, on the day in April 1986 when Ryan White finally won his court case and returned to class, and a few days later the parents of twenty-two of them set up their own school. When nine-year-old Benjamin Oyler, who had been kept from attending school in Carmel, California, because he had AIDS, died in July 1986, his father said that the banishment had been the most painful thing for his son to deal with. "It's pretty sad that there aren't more understanding hearts."

Swansea inhabited this same moral universe and might well have responded similarly. The town is not, after all, distinguished by its liberalism or a reputation for tolerance; nor is residence restricted to saints. What was known about AIDS was no different in Swansea than in Kokomo or Carmel. The difference was in how that knowledge was used.

In Kokomo, Superintendent Smith and Board President Carter did not try to look beyond the newspaper accounts about AIDS. They fixated on the unknowns: the six percent of cases of unestablished causes, the finding of the virus in sweat and saliva, the fear that mosquitoes could transmit AIDS. In Swansea, McCarthy, Devine, and the school committeemen, on the phone for hours with the AIDS experts at the CDC, took away another message: scientists were essentially certain that only direct blood-to-blood contact would transmit the infection.

And the school officials in the two communities did not share the same sense of mission. While Smith in Kokomo was cresting the wave of scared parents and teachers, and Carter was taking refuge behind the threats of lawsuits and literal readings of anachronistic laws, McCarthy and Devine in Swansea concentrated on one child's tragedy. Evidence in hand, they looked for what lawyer Lucey called "the high road," a way to show that, even without ironclad guarantees of safety, the people of Swansea could still keep Mark among them. Parents in Swansea, educated by their own school officials—and by two strong-willed and effective doctors who had no counterparts in Kokomo—came down on the side of hope. "It was like during the hurricane," recalls Jimmy Carvalho, "when everyone pitched in to help."

Years after the events of September 1985, Swansea residents still talk proudly about what they accomplished, yet at the time the consensus appeared as fragile as their grandmothers' china. Most parents started out fearful, and some remained fearful after the forum. Names were gathered on a petition to bar Mark from school, as in Kokomo, and the idea of a lawsuit was bruited. If Mark's identity had been publicized, the national media, always keen for a good photo opportunity, would have been hovering, and that would have made the work of reconciliation harder.

Swansea was lucky, of course, but much more than luck was involved. McCarthy and Devine kept things together. They were not newcomers, but men the townspeople were accustomed to relying on. Faced with an out-of-the-ordinary problem, they behaved like true professionals. As Committee Chairman Paquette said, "They earned their salaries that month." McCarthy and Devine found out the facts. Then they asked committeemen and parents to accept the miniscule, but more-than-zero, risk that Mark's presence in school represented—to recognize that such risks are a part of life and to offer the affected family the solace of community.

Reaching out in empathy is not something we are called upon to do very often, because our public lives usually proceed on the tracks laid down by laws and bureaucracies. AIDS, however, throws our lives off track—the right actions are no longer obvious, and communities must deliberate about them. Parents in Swansea were understandably fearful in the face of an ominous new disease. The question they faced up to was whether the scary disease warranted renouncing the person who contracted it. In Kokomo, the idea of safety counted above all else. In Swansea, people decided that rejecting a thirteen-year-old boy—*this* thirteen-year-old boy—was too high a price to pay for an uncertain purity.

Mark and Ryan: the differences between these two thirteen-year-olds—more precisely, the differences in how they were known to their neighbors—shape the telling. Mark, in Swansea, remained an innocent, even in the face of his own death, and everything he did made Swansea proud. In a community that values rectitude, Mark's family stayed cloistered within the town; and townspeople, even those opposed to Mark's presence in school, honored the family's wish for privacy by conspiring to keep Mark's identity secret.

Rectitude also matters in Kokomo, and the Whites made themselves strangers when they went public. They had no real choice, if Ryan was to have any hope of being in school, but the family was excoriated for bringing a plague of outsiders upon the town. Ryan White, TV star and globe-trotter, was no longer an innocent—when Mark wrote Ryan a long commiserating letter, he was treated as just another well-wisher in the endless stream and received a xeroxed form letter in reply. This worldliness made it easier for Kokomo to turn its back on Ryan; only among outsiders did his plight generate much loving-kindness.

In Swansea, Mark became the boy-hero that Superintendent McCarthy calls him. But he was a quiet hero who did not want to show his face to the world, which is why Kokomo's, not Swansea's, was the AIDS story broadcast across America.

In Swansea, Mark came to his junior high graduation ceremony on the last day of school in June 1986. He had been home with a fever for several weeks but was doing better and wanted to see all his friends before summer vacation. The graduation featured a slide presentation of the highlights of the year, accompanied by the kind of songs meant to stir strong feelings. The slides showed a teacher demonstrating, unsuccessfully, how to ski; boys putting on too-big shoulder pads in the locker room; the cast of the school's production of *Annie,* including the girl who had refused to attend private school, running through their numbers. They showed Mark, too, hamming it up in a fake moustache and straw hat during a French class skit.

Lots of students were crying, for the pictures and the music were telling them that this period in their lives was over. Ron Devine had one last surprise for them. He called Mark to the front of the auditorium and presented him with the Principal's Award, as the student who exemplified the spirit of Case Junior High School. Mark's classmates gave him a standing ovation.

The summer of 1986 was a normal one for Mark, a whiffle-ball-playing, dirt-bike-riding summer. Its highlight was a day at Fenway Park with the Red Sox, his team. This was deluxe treatment—limousine, box seats, a trip to the dugout before the game—and Mark was in heaven. He had been given a video camera, paid for with some of the money collected by Friends of Mark, and he spent hours chronicling the minutest doings of his family, including the attempted housebreaking of a new puppy, Chipper.

One night, soon after he had begun ninth grade in September, Mark complained about his breathing. He had an infection, the doctors said, but would be all right. By the end of the week, though, Mark was in St. Anne's Hospital and, the following Monday, he was transferred to Rhode Island Hospital and placed on a respirator. His parents and his brother stayed with him around the clock.

"If anything happens to me," Mark told Scott, "you can have my baseball cards." And to his parents Dale and Jay he said: "I should just die so that it would be easier for you."

Early on the morning of October 26, 1986, a year and a half after contracting AIDS, Mark Gardiner Hoyle died. Only after his death was his name made public.

More than 200 people gathered for the burial service at Mt. Hope Cemetery. Throughout the service, the Hoyles kept their feelings in tight check. When the prayers ended, Dale gave Scott a cluster of rainbow-colored balloons; and as he released the string, a sharp wind launched the balloons into the brilliant blue sky. After Mark's family left the burial site, classmates plucked flowers from the bouquets that blanketed the brass casket and carried them away to remember their friend.

That week, the flags outside all of Swansea's public schools were flown at half mast.

Passion Play: New York City

If there were some way to reach the best moral and spiritual instincts of all concerned, the problem would be simple. That's where the total answer lies to everything. All the philosophers, through all the ages have said precisely the same thing: The single best rule for the intelligent conduct of life and society is "love." The perfect answer. Unfortunately, however, that is plainly too much to ask.

Mario Cuomo, *Forest Hills Diary*

The announcement, issued just forty-eight hours before the opening of school in September 1985, was as meager on the specifics as a John Doe bulletin. A second-grade child with AIDS, unnamed, would be attending classes in a public school, also unnamed, somewhere in the vastness of New York City, the largest school district in the United States.

The vagueness of the notice was a deliberate attempt by the city's bureaucrats and politicians to defuse a charged social issue through delicate handling, to understate the message by relying on the deadening language of routine. But the strategy, like so many others tried by those responsible for managing New York City's AIDS policy, had its own perverse consequences. By publicizing the fact of admission while insisting that the child remain anonymous, city officials invited limitless dramas, unconstrained by the specificity of—and the possibility of empathy for—a real youngster in a real school.

Here was no focused anxiety but a license to panic that reached far beyond the few known facts of the case. Signs carried in street demonstrations and rhetoric shouted in overheated meeting halls pilloried the gays, drug users, and sinful Manhattanites charged with blame for the spread of AIDS.

Here too was an occasion for local politicians energetically to oppose the admission of the unnamed youngster, even as an earlier generation of local politicians had opposed racial integration of the schools—and for much the same reasons. In part, this was a matter of beleaguered locals taking on City Hall, an act so familiar in New York as to be almost instinctive. But demanding that children with AIDS be kept out of school was also a way for the ambitious to get ahead in the sharp-elbows roller derby that is New York City politics.

This drama was played out in front of the klieg lights, with reporters scribbling and camera crews recording every public moment. The actors were fully aware that, as one school official put it, "the whole world is watching." The whole world seems always to be watching when the setting is New York, whose fabled self-absorption is regularly translated into a national obsession by the networks and newsmagazines headquartered in the city. This attention raised the ante by making New York's drama not only interesting to itself but precedent-making as well. "New York City ought to be able to handle AIDS better than Oshkosh, for chrissakes!" exclaimed one of the leading figures in the story, confusing Kokomo with Oshkosh—a completely understandable slip from a New Yorker's perspective.

As the school year began, a lawsuit brought by unhappy locals challenging the city's decision relocated the theatrics inside a courtroom. AIDS remained very much a political question; indeed, the Republican candidate for mayor made it a central theme of her campaign. But the framework of a lawsuit served to keep the histrionics in check, and out of the welter of examined and cross-examined evidence an education on the issues emerged.

It is almost dreamily naive to imagine that lawyers, masters of obfuscation, could act as educators, or that any judge, let alone one so opinionated as the judge who presided over this case, could be schoolmaster to the city. Yet that is more or less what happened: the events in the courtroom muted the street dramatics and helped New Yorkers come to terms with the presence of AIDS in their public schools.

By the fall of 1985, when the school controversy broke, AIDS was a depressingly familiar specter in New York City. Approximately one-third of the nation's AIDS cases were to be found there, far more than in any other city in the United States. AIDS had become not only a health crisis but a volatile political issue as well. City officials, foremost among them Mayor Edward Koch, were savaged for their fecklessness in the face of this new epidemic. Critics charged that the mayor was fearful that rumors of his homosexuality, which had dogged his entire political career, would be revived if he took the AIDS epidemic more seriously—a charge Koch dismissed as character assassination. "Nothing could be more vile," he insisted. "Regrettably, in our society . . . one technique used to slander an individual is to simply accuse that individual of homosexuality."

"I do not exaggerate when I say that New York is unique in the history of human kindness," Koch had proclaimed in his inaugural address, but no one would suspect this from the city's response to AIDS. Unlike San Francisco, where the incidence of AIDS was also high, New York had devoted almost none of its own resources to the disease. Activists regarded the city's health services as too busy warring over bureaucratic prerogatives to notice those who needed help. They saw its politicians, who for years had blocked a gay-rights bill, as too homophobic to support organizations such as the Gay Men's Health Crisis, which had taken on what otherwise would have been a public responsibility.

In New York City, where strangers are forced together in inevitable and impersonal daily intimacies, fear of contagion may have been especially palpable, like the city's "polio panic"

decades earlier. Whatever the reason, from the outset of the
epidemic AIDS had evoked deep and sometimes irrational anxieties among New Yorkers.

Newsweek's 1983 cover story on AIDS had featured accounts
of New Yorkers afraid of catching AIDS in the subway. Now,
with the news that matinee idol Rock Hudson was dying of
AIDS, panic became pandemic—"a kind of disease in itself,"
the *New York Times* reported. Phone calls to the city's AIDS
hotline increased exponentially, and as the director of the hotline noted, "People don't seem to be absorbing the details that
might reassure them, but instead are picking up on details that
might terrify them." News coverage in certain quarters nurtured the terror. "AIDS Now A Top Killer In City," blared the
New York Post, the tabloid that thrives on scandal and sensation.

Only absolute assurances could answer panic, but absolutes
were not—could not be—forthcoming from the authorities.
While city officials declared that, from everything that was
known, AIDS could be spread only by intimate contact, many
New Yorkers, never inclined to trust officialdom, remained
unpersuaded.

It was the issue of admitting children with AIDS to public
school that brought these tensions fully into the open in late
August 1985. But an important, if little-noticed, preview had
come a month earlier. When the city's Health and Hospitals
Corporation decided to house adult AIDS patients in a nursing
home in the Neponsit neighborhood of the borough of Queens,
the neighbors went to war—and won.

It is hardly a coincidence that Queens became the focus of
both AIDS battles. "Only the dead know Brooklyn," Thomas
Wolfe once wrote, referring to that borough's cemeteries, and
only airline passengers and New York Mets fans know Queens,
population two million, New York City's bedroom. It is, to a
large extent, a borough of tidy two-story homes faced with asbestos shingle or permastone, built thirty or forty years ago
as the first suburb for many who saved up just enough to leave
behind the crowded and increasingly menacing precincts of

Brooklyn and the Bronx. Queens is also the borough of Lefrak City, a forest of blank-faced apartment blocks that reinvents urban blight.

Compared to the rest of the city, Queens is well-off and white, though many of its recent migrants came from Puerto Rico. It is highly politicized, with activist homeowners' associations as familiar and as intrenched as crabgrass. Its politics are conservative by New York standards, particularly on social issues. When TV producers looked around for a place to situate that archetypal bigot Archie Bunker, Queens was a natural. Republicans—not of the silk-stocking variety either—occasionally get elected here, something unheard of in most of New York City. No Marquis of Queensbury rules govern local campaigns, where appeals to clannishness are routine, and racist fear-mongering is not unknown. Reform is an unvoiced word, and political business is done on the basis of who you know and, sometimes, what you are prepared to pay.

On a major Queens thoroughfare, a sign points "To the City," meaning Manhattan—meaning, too, all the evils of the urban underlife associated in the popular imagination with New York. Queens thinks of itself as an "outer borough," relatively free from the taint of the inner city. Its residents have fought, with some success, to preserve a separate integrity against what they regard as attempts by City Hall to turn the borough into a dumping ground for problems generated elsewhere. They have fought, too, against ideas—the moral rightness of school integration and the cultural legitimacy of homosexuality, for instance—which are taken as an assault on a way of life that is as vulnerable as it is highly prized. Several neighborhoods have been able to beat back proposals to build massive public housing projects whose occupants would have been preponderantly black and poor; indeed, one such campaign gave Mario Cuomo, then a local lawyer, his political start.[1] Such tales become the stuff of legends in the homeowners' associations and political clubs, emboldening the residents to resist the next incursion.

Neponsit is an especially insular community in this insular borough, a sandspit not easily reached from the mainland. It is an enclave of large frame homes and manicured lawns, some distance from the subway and the urban miseries to which the subway leads. Neponsit's pride and joy is its beach, effectively preserved for its own residents by a law that bans on-street parking. When residents were told, in July 1985, that in a matter of weeks the Health and Hospitals Corporation was planning to move adult AIDS patients to the Neponsit Health Care Center, a partially vacant nursing home, they were already orgainzed to fight, and the organization remained intact for the subsequent battle over the schools.

In 1985, there had been more AIDS cases in the borough of Queens than in forty-four states of the union. In the minds of the Neponsit residents, though, AIDS was not their concern. It was a problem for "the Village"—Greenwich Village, the center of New York's gay community. Neponsit had already taken on the gay community, demanding that city officials ban nudity on a neighborhood beach where gay men congregated. In Neponsit AIDS patients would be regarded as twice-contaminated.

The plan for housing adults with AIDS in a local nursing home had Neponsit in a panic. "People wouldn't go into a supermarket if there was an AIDS patient there. They were that afraid," recalls Joel Gerstel, who chaired the local community board. One longtime resident of the nursing home fretted: "We are going to start being treated like we have the bubonic plague, and with the AIDS people coming, we might wish we had the bubonic plague. The bus drivers, the cab drivers, they say they won't pick us up anymore. Your restaurants and the stores—all of them tell us they don't want us coming in if there's AIDS here."

A local delegation asked for and quickly got a meeting with the city's top health officials. In the stately Blue Room of City Hall, the Neponsit spokesmen complained to a squadron of city bureaucrats that the plan lacked proper medical precautions. They complained more loudly about the presence of AIDS patients in a residential neighborhood, where they could spread the disease. And they objected to the city's announcing the plan as an accomplished fact, without troubling to educate the community about the disease.

Victor Botnick, the mayor's top health adviser, tried to soft-pedal the delegation's anxieties, but Joel Gerstel put a quick stop to that. "I said to Botnick, 'Very honestly, we didn't come all the way in here on a hot summer day when we could be sitting on the beach to listen to you bullshit.'"

The city officials promised only to keep listening and to provide information to the local residents. But when Botnick asked Gerstel to hand out the city's brochures on AIDS at the next community board meeting, Gerstel replied: "You've got to be crazy. You want to hand them out, you come and hand them out. I don't want to be strung up."

At a packed community meeting on a muggy July night, residents demanded that the city abandon its housing scheme. The mood was fierce—"like a lynch mob," one participant recalls. "We don't want the community to be contaminated," shouted Bill Sampol, a local Republican politician, and the crowd yelled its approval as TV cameras whirred. Joel Gerstel announced "We will use any method at our legal disposal to prevent AIDS patients from coming to this facility." Days later, on July 30, several residents of the village sued the city to stop the plan.

The suit in *Connolly v. Koch* had little legal basis—the principal claim was that, under state and city law, an environmental impact statement was required—but recourse to law was really only a means of buying time. At that, Neponsit was successful. The judge who initially heard the case, Harold Hyman, quickly granted the request for a temporary restraining order against the city, refusing even to hear the city's witnesses before issuing his order. Fear of contagion, not concern for legal niceties, powered Hyman's decision. "Like most of us, he didn't know much about the disease at that time," his long-term law clerk, Stuart Spitzer, recalled.

A full-dress hearing was conducted the following week before another judge, Joan Marie Durantee. During the month of August, while Durantee pondered her ruling, tensions mounted. Mayor Koch, heckled about Neponsit while politicking at an

Irish Festival in Queens, angrily shouted back: "Are you so mean-spirited, so without compassion, that if these people need help you're going to throw them out? If it was your son or your daughter, would you want them cast on the street without care?"

But Koch was worried about the impact of Neponsit on the mayoral primary set for early September, and the involvement of another major player, Donald Manes, the Queens borough president, heightened the pressure. At the City Hall meeting with Neponsit's delegation that preceded the lawsuit, Mayor Koch's delegate, Victor Botnick, had called Manes a "lying sonuvabitch." Botnick insisted that despite Manes's disclaimers, Manes had been told months earlier that AIDS patients would be moved to Neponsit. The accusation infuriated Manes, who demanded that the mayor abandon the plan. Since Manes could turn out the votes Koch needed to roll up the big victory margin he was after, what he said mattered.

Complaints also came from an unexpected quarter. Gay groups, whose criticisms of the city's inaction had prompted the proposal in the first place, voiced their own objections to shipping AIDS patients into alien country. When Archbishop (soon to become Cardinal) O'Connor announced, days before the primary, that the archdiocese would provide housing for AIDS patients, Koch had his out. At a hasty news conference, held as he was rushing from City Hall to get a haircut, the mayor declared that the Neponsit plan was history. "What is the sense of having people in the Neponsit area on pins and needles—that's the wrong expression—when in fact we're not going to be using the facility because of the Cardinal's generous offer?" Was the mayor responding to pressure from the voters? reporters asked. "What do I care how you characterize it?" Koch replied.

By then, the Neponsit story had been superseded by the headline-grabbing possibility that a child with AIDS would attend public school. But the Queens setting was familiar, as were certain members of the cast of characters in the two dramas. Grace Goodman had a hand in arguing both the nursing home case and the schools case for the city. Sam Granirer, a local politician who spoke out against the nursing home plan, chaired the community school board in Queens that brought a lawsuit

to keep a youngster with AIDS out of the classroom. The case
was heard by Harold Hyman, the same trial court judge who
had ruled so quickly in favor of the Neponsit neighborhood
group and against the city.

The very idea that a child with AIDS might attend school
came as a surprise to New Yorkers when it was first aired, in an
announcement issued by the mayor's office just twelve days before the opening of school. In fact, officials from the Board of
Education and the Health Department had been struggling for
half a year to shape a policy. These officials tried to define
AIDS entirely as a public health matter, to be resolved by professionals. "We weren't going to do this by votes," said one high-
ranking school administrator. That approach didn't play well
on the streets of New York.

Authority to manage New York City's public schools, a mam-
moth organization encompassing nearly a million pupils and a
hundred thousand teachers and staff, is uneasily divided between the central Board of Education, led by its chancellor, and
thirty-two community school districts, each with its own board
and its own superintendent.[2] In theory, the central board is legally responsible for matters of "city-wide impact," while the
community boards are supposed to attend to local concerns.
But the dividing line is far from sharp, and controversies, including court cases, are the norm. "We're in court when we
keep the schools open in inclement weather, we're in court
when we open the schools on Passover . . . we're in court when
we close an annex to a school," says Joseph Sincenti, who as
deputy chancellor was in charge of day-to-day operations for
the entire system during the AIDS controversy.

School decentralization was initiated in 1970 out of the widespread distrust of the bureaucrats at 110 Livingston Street, the
Brooklyn headquarters of the system. Though it was black
neighborhoods in Manhattan and Queens that pushed hardest for decentralization, in no borough has the distrust been
greater or the disputes with the chancellor's office fiercer than
in Queens. "When the Board of Ed installed new coal furn-

aces that turned out not to have decent emission controls, two Queens districts were in court and had won their case before a Bronx district with the same heating problems even knew what was going on," boasts Joseph Lisa, who had represented Queens in the New York State Legislature and more recently in the City Council.

In these squabbles over power, the key players are well known to one another. Sincenti, who regularly used his authority to overrule Queens community boards, was nonetheless highly regarded by most local board members, and he returns the compliment. "The relationships are professional," he says. Sincenti is, by self-description, a "survivor" in the administrative infighting that has accompanied decentralization. His boss, Chancellor Nathan Quinones, was looked upon as a survivor too. Passed up several times for the top job, the career bureaucrat was finally appointed chancellor in 1984—but only after his predecessor was forced out for mismanaging his personal finances and after Mayor Koch's first choice for the job, Deputy Mayor Robert Wagner, was turned down by the state because he lacked the requisite educational credentials. Quinones had a reputation as a fair-minded manager, if not as a high-powered educational leader.[3]

Uniquely among big city school districts, the New York City Board of Education relies on the city's health department, rather than on its own staff, for health care. That arrangement generates predictable controversies, with the Board of Education regularly demanding more school nurses from the Health Department, the Health Department responding with pleas of poverty, and community school districts blaming both bureaucracies for what they consider inadequate care.

During the contretemps over AIDS in the schools, the Health Department was headed by Dr. David Sencer. An epidemiologist by training, Sencer has spent almost his entire professional life in public health, including seventeen years at the Centers for Disease Control. Though city officials lauded Sencer as the quintessential professional, and the *New York Times* praised his "pragmatic" approach to AIDS, he was a figure of some controversy. As CDC director in 1976, when a nationwide swine flu epidemic threatened, Sencer had recommended vaccinating the entire populace on a crash basis. That policy proved to be an expensive fiasco, for the virus was far less virulent and the logistics of mass inoculation far more complicated than projected. When a few people developed Guillain-Barre syndrome from the vaccine itself, the program was called off. A year later, Sencer had left the CDC. He has "no regrets," Sencer insists, speaking about how he handled the swine flu threat. "I would do it the same way again with the same facts." After a brief and unhappy stint in private industry, Sencer was named to the top job in the New York City Health Department.

Extracting a policy on AIDS and schools from two bureaucratic behemoths, the Health Department and the Board of Education, was no easy task. Sencer tried to initiate a meeting with Chancellor Quinones during the spring, but it took months to get through. Even when a joint working group was established, institutional loyalties and personal jealousies kept getting in the way.

That spring, real differences of opinion existed among working group members on the key question: Should children with AIDS be allowed in regular classes? From the first, Sencer and his chief adviser on pediatric AIDS, Dr. Polly Thomas, favored admission because they were persuaded that the disease was not easily transmitted; the CDC staff, with whom the Health Department officials were in contact, had reached a similar conclusion. The Board of Education's top health officer initially resisted the idea but was eventually won over by the force of the evidence.

There was no disagreement about the need to keep the identity of a child with AIDS secret from everyone in the school system—the children, the teachers, the principal, even top-ranking administrators. On several occasions during the previous year, when a mother had told a school principal that her child had AIDS, the youngster was immediately sent home. In one instance, a student was expelled because his mother's *boyfriend* had contracted the disease. These stories could have been taken to demonstrate the importance of educating school administrators about AIDS. But the lesson the city officials extracted was very different: identification inevitably means ostracism.

As the new school year approached, the AIDS issue moved up the chain of command and into the realm where politics often regulates policy. "It would have been very easy for us to say, 'Well, given what we don't know about AIDS . . . why deal with all the hysteria it will cause out there when you're dealing with one or two children?'" Sincenti notes. "But instead we said [to Sencer], 'Tell us the right thing and we'll deal with all those problems.'" Sincenti saw New York as "setting the precedent for the rest of the country. Never mind that we catch all the flak. We're doing the right thing."

Mayor Koch's office was in daily contact with Sencer on the handling of the AIDS issue. Koch's aide, Victor Botnick, voiced strong concerns about the possibility that AIDS might easily be spread by children in school; also, the upcoming mayoral primary made everyone jittery. As it turned out, Mayor Koch also had an opinion on the subject, but the health and education officials did not feel obliged to shape a position to suit the mayor's preferences. To a remarkable extent, they were left on their own.

Not one word about the policy that was taking shape was passed along to the community school boards during all these months. Lack of unanimity among the officials crafting that policy was one reason. "It made no sense to wash our dirty linen in public," says Sencer. While Deputy Chancellor Sincenti acknowledges that "it would have been better in terms of process" to talk through the issue, advance notice would also have made it easier for the opposition to mobilize. "Things would have been difficult," he adds, with pardonable understatement. Sam Samuels, who as personal secretary to Queens Borough President Donald Manes knew City Hall well, describes how the city bureaucrats viewed their antagonists. "There is a tendency among a lot of the city's agencies that deal with these types of problems to think 'They're never going to say yes, they're going to scream, and therefore the only option we have is controlling the amount of time that that screaming is going to go on. If we tell them three days ahead of time, it's three days of screaming;

if we tell them two weeks, it's two weeks; if we tell them a month, it's a month.'" In the estimation of the senior staff, it was preferable to announce the decision on AIDS at the last possible minute, framing it as a clear-cut matter of public health, rather than invite hostility.

Immediately after the August 27, 1985, announcement that youngsters with AIDS might—conceivably—be allowed to attend school, the anticipated opposition began to materialize, but on a scale much bigger than anticipated. The fight was orchestrated by two districts, 27 (which includes Neponsit) and 29. Both are located in Queens, both are ethnically mixed and predominantly middle class (though 29 has pockets of poverty), and both have taken on the city before, on issues ranging from snow closings to racial integration. Between them, they enroll approximately 50,000 students. Just forty-eight hours after the city's declaration, the two community school boards voted unanimously to keep any child who had AIDS out of school. District 27's resolution went so far as to exclude a student living with someone who had AIDS.

It was the Neponsit nursing home fight that had energized Sam Granirer, chairman of the District 27 board. In the struggle over school policy, Granirer became the loudest voice for the opposition—"the man of the hour," *Newsday,* a widely read daily, called him—a natural leading man in the enchanted theater of the news. Just thirty-three years old, this well-off businessman with the year-round tan was marked as a comer in city politics. He had worked on Jimmy Carter's 1980 campaign—signed photographs of the ex-president were prominently displayed in his office and his home—and he made no secret of his own ambition to get elected to Congress. Granirer and his ally on the board, James Sullivan, also knew the seamier side of politics. A few years earlier, a *Newsday* article had noted that Sullivan had asked contributors to one of his fund-raisers to make out their checks to "cash," and Sullivan's campaign literature had nurtured fears that "Black Militant Extremists" were poised to take over the school board.

During the dispute over Neponsit, Granirer had gotten the crowds worked up by speculating, improbably, that entire families—including children whose parents had AIDS—would be moving into the nursing home. "We will take a stand in the school district," he promised. Granirer had no use for Health Commissioner Sencer—"a horse's ass," he called him—and he had a firm belief that "arrogant" city officials were forever abusing the people of Queens. On August 29, Granirer called a meeting of the board. He made sure the press knew that AIDS was the agenda and that he, Sam Granirer, was personally challenging 110 Livingston Street.

"It was like maybe there was no news that day, you know, and every TV guy was there. That one meeting was like the blowout, it was like a spark was ready to be lit." There was Granirer with his wife and kids on the front page of the *Daily News*. That night, he appeared on Ted Koppel's "Nightline." Koppel's first question was: "Mr. Granirer, are you a politician?"

"We're just very concerned about the health and welfare of all children in the district," Granirer maintained. Chancellor Quinones countered that the Board of Education would overrule any community board decisions that were inconsistent with the systemwide guidelines. "Fear is not going to be the factor by which we will separate children."

The chancellor hoped for "an accommodation. . . . Otherwise it's going to be a witch hunt. Nobody will be a winner." But no one really was in an accommodating mood. The very next day, Health Commissioner Sencer, flanked by Mayor Koch, Chancellor Quinones, and James Regan, President of the Board of Education, stood on the steps of City Hall to announce that children with AIDS would not automatically be excluded from school. A panel representing different perspectives on the issue would recommend to Sencer whether any of four New York City children known to have AIDS should attend regular classes.

Sencer acknowledged the "understandable" fears of parents. And he recognized the "theoretical concern" about modes of AIDS transmission other than through semen or blood: that was the chief reason for creating the panel, rather than automatically enrolling a youngster with AIDS. The city's policy mirrored the CDC guidelines, which had been made public the previous day; Sencer had known the content of those guidelines for months.

It was Queens versus City Hall on AIDS, in a replay of Neponsit, and once again spokesmen for the community held firm. Sam Granirer insisted that District 27 would "stand by our resolution" and threatened to take the city to court.

Claudette Webb, president of the District 29 board, also vowed to fight. Webb, a black woman who had recently been picked to chair a racially balanced board, managed to combine raising a family and holding down a hospital job with a long history of local activism. During the nursing home dispute, she said, people in the neighborhood were asking, "If they were putting patients there, where else would they [put them]—and were children involved?"

Another board member, Delores Grant, remembers that she "called the Disease Control in Atlanta and asked them could they guarantee us that . . . if the AIDS child had a nosebleed and the teacher had to wipe it up, or the child had a cut, would another child contract the AIDS. They said they were still researching it. They couldn't give a definite answer. If a child drank out of another child's glass and the child had AIDS, would the other child contract it through the saliva? They said they were still researching at that time. . . . Everything was still research, research. They said they couldn't give answers. So we brought this back to the meeting, and had the doctor there, and it was still research."

Concern about the "gay plague" also shaped opinion in Queens. "All we knew was that AIDS was generated through homosexuals," said Grant. "I think they have glorified the homosexual. Homosexuals should not be an example for children, they shouldn't be an example for anybody." Grant believed that city officials were more fearful of contagion than they were letting on. "Why else would they be closing the gay bathhouses, if they weren't scared that a gay person could infect someone who wasn't gay?" Grant wondered, discounting the possibility that the city was interested in protecting gay men themselves.

At a raucous school board session in the city's most self-consciously democratic district, where seemingly everything is put to a vote, the District 29 parents declared that they would boycott the schools if children with AIDS were permitted to enroll. "Join us in standing in the schoolhouse door" to keep any child with AIDS out of school, said Grant, unknowingly borrowing the decades-old cry of diehard Southern segregationists. The crowd answered the call by shouting "Keep our kids home Monday."

Mayor Koch seemed to be on the verge of bowing to community sentiment. On September 1, two days before backing off on the Neponsit nursing home plan, Koch told reporters that in his opinion no child with AIDS should attend public schools, and predicted that the expert panel would agree with him. "I don't believe you're going to have any kids with AIDS ending up in the classroom." Koch also had his doubts about whether confidentiality could be maintained. "The other kids are going to know immediately. The kid is going to be shunned. . . . Why would a parent expose a child to that?"

Although Koch acknowledged that current research showed AIDS could not be casually transmitted, "I'd rather err on the side of caution." Besides, contact in the schoolhouse was not entirely casual. "You want to be bitten by someone with AIDS to be the guinea pig to determine whether it's transmittable [that way]? I doubt it."

All this was just "good common sense" to Ed Koch. But to Sencer and the others who had been struggling to keep a lid on the issue, it was Koch doing one of his patented loose cannon routines. As things turned out, the panel of experts disagreed with the mayor—and got their way.

On Saturday, September 7, only two days before the first day of classes, the panel announced its recommendations in the four cases, which Sencer speedily approved. Two youngsters would receive instruction in the hospital where they were confined; one child whose identity had been made known the previous year would get home instruction to avoid "potential social discrimination."

But one child diagnosed with AIDS, a second grader who had done well in school for three years while the disease was in remission, would remain in class. Just one additional fact about the child was made public: as in the other three cases the panel reviewed, the youngster's mother was an intravenous-drug user who had passed along the disease *in utero*. This was a curious item to make public, since it enabled opponents of enrollment to associate the child with the sins of the mother, to label her as one of "them." No further details were released—not the name of the school the child was enrolled in or even the borough where the school was located. No one in the school system, including Chancellor Quinones, was told the child's identity. "We have no danger" and therefore no need for such specifics, Quinones said. All that was known was that somewhere in New York City a child known to have AIDS would be a public school student.

Inside city government, everyone professed to be delighted. Sencer and Quinones praised the panel. The panelists themselves—Polly Thomas, Sencer's pediatric AIDS adviser; Suzanne Michaels, a Health Department social worker; Agnes Green, president of the United Parents Association; and Rosalyn Oratz, the Board of Education's nominee and a principal in District 27—viewed their work as a triumph for rationality. The panel had spent less than an hour on each case, reviewing the history of each child and talking by phone with the children's doctors. "The critical piece was that it was a health issue," Oratz recalls. Agnes Green, the parent representative, thought the decision to keep a youngster with AIDS in school was an easy one. "I've been very convinced that the disease is not casually transmitted. . . . The problem is an adult problem, and I don't think it's appropriate to visit [adults'] problems on children."

Mayor Koch, who had anticipated and plainly hoped for a different outcome, nonetheless complimented the panel for acting with "great responsibility and good judgment." While campaigning that Sunday, the day before the beginning of the school year, Koch was the picture of calm; gone were his personal worries about AIDS. "This child is no danger—no danger—to other children. You can panic if you want to but I hope you won't." The fact that Koch's rivals in the Democratic primary had criticized the mayor for his statements on AIDS may have prompted his shift.

Queens was not the picture of calm, however. At a news conference the preceding Wednesday, three days before the panel's decision, the elected board leaders of Districts 27 and 29 had called for a "moratorium" on enrolling children with AIDS. Searching for a headline, they flew in Daniel Carter, president of the school board in Kokomo, Indiana. Kokomo had made national news with its decision to keep Ryan White out of school. Carter made news again when he lambasted Sencer and Quinones as being "overconfident, cavalier, even casual" in their approach to AIDS.

That performance was too much for the city's top officials to stomach. Although administrators in districts throughout New York City were reporting that parents were troubled about AIDS, in no neighborhood other than the two Queens districts was there such a rush to judgment. At a private meeting the next day, Quinones and Sencer—"all the heavy hitters," as Granirer remembers—tried to persuade the two rebellious districts to back off. But Claudette Webb, president of the District 29 Board, warned that a boycott was coming. "We have a lawyer," Granirer added, "We're going to court Monday morning."

Webb and Granirer were true to their word. On September 7, the District 29 Board called for a boycott until the location of the child with AIDS was revealed. Webb was also irate about how the city had kept its deliberations under wraps. "Everything they are calling hysteria is simply legitimate parents' concern. . . . This did not have to come to the eleventh hour. . . . They are steamrolling over us."

The District 27 Board launched its lawsuit against the city the same day. At the packed board meeting, Granirer stood up, hugging his nine-year-old and his eleven-year-old, playing on the feelings of the angry parents and their distrust of "downtown" like a virtuoso. "These are my two children," Granirer said. "I worked very hard to get them to this age. And I don't want any bureaucrat at 110 Livingston Street telling me I have no right to protect these kids." The crowd went wild. "They rallied around me like you wouldn't believe," recalls Granirer. "Everybody clapped. It was like a gyration of warmth."

On Monday, September 9, the opening day of school, the AIDS boycott was the big story. Not that the numbers were so spectacular—an estimated 11,000 students stayed home, barely one percent of the citywide enrollment and all concentrated in the two Queens districts. But the streets of St. Albans and Rock-away and Ozone Park, villages in the heart of Queens, turned into a carnival of death. Draped across the doorway of one elementary school was the sign, "Enter At Your Own Risk." Parents carried placards saying, "Our Children Want Grades, Not AIDS" and "Stop the Lies." Some signs linked AIDS and homosexuality: "Close The Bathhouses" and "Don't Let Koch Sodomize Us." Mayor Koch sounded almost apostolic when he commented: "It is sad, but I understand what the parents are seeking to do. They are demonstrating their sadness. But what are we to do with a child, cast it into the river? No, that is just not what we are going to do."

As the nightly TV news shows transmitted these pictures to the nation, the children became news sources, their fears of other children rendered into a kind of folk wisdom. Youngsters bore a coffin through the streets with a scrawled message: "Is This Next?" A ten-year-old girl told a reporter that the identity of the child with AIDS should be made public "so we could stay away from the kid."

At noon on the same day, in the Queens courtroom of Judge Harold Hyman, a different and ultimately more significant drama was beginning. Districts 27 and 29 had gone to court, seeking a temporary restraining order to keep the child with AIDS out of school; the School Boards Association, represent-ing all but two of the other districts, joined the suit.

The evidence on AIDS was too "inconclusive" to risk the lives of children, argued Harry Lipsig, an attorney who had been litigating personal injury cases for over half a century. AIDS was "the Black Plague of the 1980s," said Lipsig, and to admit a child with the disease was "a rash act." New York City's Corporation Counsel, F.A.O. (Fritz) Schwarz, Jr., began to respond, but before he could manage a single sentence, Judge Hyman, obviously angry, started shouting and wagging his finger in Schwarz's face.

"Judge, don't raise your voice and don't point your finger at me," said the usually unflappable Schwarz, "or else we are not going to manage to deal with this problem in a rational fashion." It is a rare gesture for a lawyer to insist on courtroom decorum—and a brave one, too, since an irate judge could respond with a contempt citation—but this time it worked. Immediately, Hyman cooled off. He denied the boards' request for a temporary restraining order and scheduled the full hearing to begin three days later.

That first week of school, it was the boycott and the picketing and the meetings, not the legal maneuvering, that commanded the most attention. Every night saw meetings, rallies that turned into passion plays; events took on the character of civic rituals, as people found themselves swept up in a sense of solidarity and collective importance usually missing in urban life. A thousand parents, sometimes more, packed auditoriums. They talked about spreading AIDS through nosebleeds and vomiting, through shared sandwiches and chewed-on pencils. They chanted "Two, four, six, eight, no AIDS in any grades."

Local politicians played to the crowds. At one meeting, City Councilman Lisa declared ominously: "This is not meant to scare you—but leading medical researchers throughout the world truly believe that this epidemic may well be the most serious epidemic in recorded medical history." State Assemblyman Frederick Schmidt proclaimed: "There is no medical authority who can say with authority that AIDS cannot be transmitted in school. What about somebody sneezing in the classroom? What about kids who get in a fight with a bloody nose? They don't know!" The crowd was on its feet. Cried Schmidt: "We should not experiment with our children!" Through it all, Sam Granirer remained the star, the man everyone loved to quote. He and his District 27 colleagues held press conferences, sometimes two a day. At one such session Marvin Aaron, the district superintendent, protested: "I don't want all the medical experts telling me 'Don't worry.' I'm worrying." A half-dozen camera crews and three times as many reporters were regularly there to document it all.

The specifics of the coverage varied widely. Local TV stations assiduously balanced quotes from city officials with clips from the streets. The *New York Times,* which had been solidly behind the decision to admit the youngster with AIDS, labeled what was happening in Queens "uninformed hysteria, not reasoned dissent," while the *New York Post* loudly took up the cause of Queens. *Post* news stories featured banner headlines declaiming "It Can Be Spread By Biting," "The Crisis That Has Divided The City," and "AIDS Children Need Loving Support—At Home," and its columnists delivered diatribes against gay men for bringing the tragedy to the city. "AIDS is almost entirely a disease caught by men who bugger and are buggered by dozens or even hundreds of other men every year," wrote *Post* columnist Norman Podhoretz.

Meanwhile, efforts to settle the dispute were underway behind the scenes. Sincenti, the deputy chancellor, awakened Claudette Webb with an 11:00 P.M. phone call the Sunday night before school began with promises of new information and a plea to stop the boycott. A delegation from District 29 did meet with Sincenti, Chancellor Quinones, and Health Commissioner Sencer on Monday afternoon but left unimpressed. Besides, it was too late for peace. "Even if I wanted to call off the boycott, I couldn't stop the parents," Webb told the officials.

Sam Granirer used his political connections to try making a deal. He contacted Fritz Schwarz and asked him to arrange a meeting with Mayor Koch—"decision-maker to decision-maker. . . . I knew he was pulling the strings on this deal," says Granirer. At 7:30 on Thursday morning, four days after school began, Granirer and George Russo, a colleague on the board, showed up at the back door of Gracie Mansion, the mayor's official residence. Koch, Schwarz, Quinones, and Sencer were all there.

"Television star, here he is," Koch said by way of greeting. "I've seen you more on television the last three days that I've seen the co-anchor on Channel Four." Granirer turned to Russo. "I love this. This is my cup of tea."

But when it came to doing business, there was no deal to be made. Koch proposed setting up a blue ribbon AIDS panel, to be chaired by Granirer; in return, District 27 would abandon the court case.

"We can't do that," said Granirer. "The kid has to come out. Otherwise, if I go back to these screaming people, they'd go bananas. They'd say, 'You sold us out.'" Koch and his advisers were not willing to give up what they had just won in court. "I'll see you in court at 10:00 A.M.," said Granirer.

In the 1,973 cases that, by his own count, Judge Harold Hyman has heard during his years as a New York trial judge, no one has ever doubted for a moment who was the boss in his courtroom. "You don't have to respect me," he tells lawyers who appear before him. "Respect the robe."

"I've always been opinionated," says Hyman. Stuart Spitzer, the judge's clerk for nearly seven years, calls him a disciplinarian. "Hard-driving," "intense," and "tough"—always tough—are how lawyers who have argued cases in his court describe him.

Hyman began practicing law more than half a century ago, and his entire professional career as a lawyer and a judge has been spent in Queens. He is well connected with the local lawyers (in Queens, smart litigants make it a point to use local lawyers) and political clubs. Hyman relishes the big cases he has heard since his election to the court in 1975: the murder trial of two lesbians who killed one of their husbands; the multimillion dollar civil suit in the aftermath of an explosion in the American Chicle Company factory. "That case was called and, all of a sudden, 400 people packed into a courtroom ready for trial."

From the outset, Hyman knew that the AIDS case would be an attention-getter. So many reporters and spectators showed up for opening arguments that the judge switched the hearing to a bigger courtroom. The lawyers gave hallway interviews after every session, as reporters badgered them to interpret what had taken place. "This case was really about educating the people of the City of New York," Hyman says. The AIDS case was also about educating Harold Hyman. Corporation Counsel Fritz Schwarz, searching for just the right words, describes

Hyman as "a man very much of his place and time. He had old-fasioned views about gays and blacks and women." Particularly gays. During breaks in the hearing, "He would make snide comments about the anatomy of gay males," recalls Health Commissioner Sencer.

Judge Hyman makes no secret of his fears about AIDS—fears that prompted his ruling in the Neponsit case, fears that were apparent when he shouted down Schwarz on the very first day of the case. "When I started out," says Hyman, "my heart said to me, 'Don't let the kids go to school at all. This may be very contagious.'" Hyman's niece, a New York City school-teacher, had told him, "Uncle Harold, if you decide this case the wrong way I'm going to quit the school system."

During the trial, Hyman grilled the city's witnesses with the fervor of a prosecuting attorney. And his predilections sometimes surfaced in apparently offhand and off-the-wall comments. While questioning the director of the city's AIDS program, he posed a possible scenario: "Suppose you've got a homosexual, he is reported to you, he's on his last leg. Don't you have a right for the safety of the general public to keep that man off the street, even though he may not be contagious merely by speaking to him or looking at him. But he is shown as a homosexual to go out into that same field to commit the same homosexual act? He can infect 150 more people within 150 days. . . . Now you've got his name, you've got his address, and yet the Department does nothing about picking this person up and seeing to it that he's either quarantined or something." The *Post* hyped the mention of quarantine. "Lock Up AIDS Victims: Judge," proclaimed the page-one banner. If Judge Hyman believed that diseased adult AIDS patients should be jailed, how could he possibly accept the city's position on children with AIDS?

To his credit, Judge Hyman was willing to acknowledge that he knew very little about the disease. "I'm not a doctor. I'm not a researcher. I have no knowledge in this area," he said during the trial. "This is going to be a tough decision to make, so I'm trying to learn, and that's why I'm asking these questions."

"We considered filing a motion to disqualify the judge," says

PASSION PLAY

117

Schwarz. "But the lawyers in the office who knew him said he tends to come out in a fair-minded way. And unlike some judges, he is not biased against the city." The Corporation Counsel heads an office of nearly 600 attorneys who do the legal business of the City of New York, and rarely does he try cases himself. But after the courtroom confrontation that first day, a moment caught in a photograph in the *Post* captioned "Schwarz Admonishes Judge," he decided to handle the trial. "There was a great chance that the judge would decapitate anybody else. And to be honest, another reason was that I thought an enormous injustice was potentially going to be done here. It excited me both morally and professionally to use my professional skills to try preventing that."

Schwarz thinks a lot about doing what is right, which is partly why he is the one figure in the Queens AIDS controversy who is universally admired. But he doesn't let his sense of the rightness of things degenerate into self-righteousness. Although his family is old money—in New York, F.A.O. Schwarz is *the* toy store—his style is old-shoe. Schwarz drove a beat-up old car to court, rather than riding in the chauffeured limousine his position entitled him to, and his go-to-court suit was off-the-rack and wrinkled.

Civil rights was Fritz Schwarz's first cause. As a law student at Harvard during the early 1960s, he led the picketing in Cambridge directed at Woolworths, one of the chains that refused to serve blacks at its lunch counters in the South. After a year in Nigeria, helping that new nation develop its legal system, he became a litigator with Cravath, Swaine and Moore, one of New York's premier law firms. He has been in and out of the government ever since, working on everything from brutality toward blacks in South Africa to the U.S. government's intelligence operations.

The AIDS case was so important, Schwarz says, because principles as well as individual rights were at stake. "It was a classic instance when undoing an individual injustice served a larger goal. If you go back to cases like the Scottsboro boys, who were individual victims of mass hysteria back in the 1930s, the dominant motive was helping some guys who are about to be strung up. But in that case—like this one—you also see the society's attention being drawn to those injustices."

Early on, Schwarz decided against treating the case in narrowly legal terms but to use it as a vehicle for informing New Yorkers about AIDS. That is why he never challenged the school districts' legal right to bring the suit, despite the fact that, because no one knew where the child was attending school, no one knew whether these districts were directly affected. Schwarz relied on the reporters to keep the story on the air and in the newspapers. He counted on the claque of Queens parents who showed up, day after day for six weeks, to relay to their neighbors what was being said in the courtroom. "Fritz conducted the city's defense more as a legislative hearing than a trial," recalls Assistant Corporation Counsel Grace Goodman, who had handled the Neponsit case and who worked with Schwarz on the Queens lawsuit. Entire days were devoted to hearing evidence of doubtful legal relevance, including detailed testimony about the nature of the blood system.

Judge Hyman was willing to go along with that strategy. So was Robert Sullivan, who together with his partner, Harry Lipsig, handled the case for the Queens school boards. "The judge, the city and myself, we all discussed that this trial was educating the public." But Sullivan had in mind a different kind of education. He was eager to expose the deceitfulness of the bureaucrats and the politicians who had determined New York's AIDS policy.

Bob Sullivan was born just four blocks from the Queens courthouse where the case was tried. He is the kind of lawyer you want on your side in a personal injury suit—quick on his feet, passionate in his arguments, blessed with a gift for resonant rhetoric. Paperwork bores him, he says, but he thrives on courtroom theatrics because "you get to do the Perry Mason thing."

It was Roy Innis, head of the Congress for Racial Equality, who put the District 27 board in touch with Sullivan's firm. "Lipsig might want to do this for nothing," said Innis, who was planning a run for Congress and who thought he could earn some political capital from the AIDS case. Innis showed up at

Sam Granirer's daily press conferences to claim credit for leading the fight against City Hall.

Sullivan doesn't handle a lot of *pro bono* work—"I'm no crusader," he says—but the AIDS case got his adrenaline pumping. Beginning the Sunday morning before school started, when the call came from Granirer and Russo, he worked around the clock, reading up on the law and tracking down witnesses. Finding people willing to testify wasn't easy. Several leading authorities on AIDS begged off. Sullivan's leading witness, Dr. Arye Rubenstein of New York's Mt. Sinai Hospital, a nationally prominent pediatric AIDS specialist, refused to appear voluntarily. Although he questioned the decision to send the child with AIDS to school, Rubenstein explained that he was unwilling to do anything that would make the child's life harder. Sullivan subpoenaed Rubenstein and put him on the stand without first interviewing him, an almost unheard-of gamble for a trial lawyer. But the move paid off. "I can't give assurances [that admitting a child with AIDS is the medically prudent course]," said Rubenstein. "The data are not in yet. There is more to know."

The six-week trial was a battle of the experts.[4] The school boards relied on four doctors, Rubenstein foremost among them. The city conscripted eight M.D.s, including the Director of Infectious Diseases at Sloan-Kettering and the Chief of Pediatrics at St. Luke's-Roosevelt Hospital, as well as David Sencer and Polly Thomas from the Health Department. Seemingly every aspect of AIDS was up for grabs: the nature of the risk, the adequacy of what was known, the credibility of the experts, and the fairness of the city's decision making.

The picture of elementary school life that comes across in attorney Sullivan's questions is one of children playing in an ocean of bodily secretions. What if children share the same glass or prick themselves and share blood in blood brother rituals, Sullivan wanted to know. What if they drink from the same water fountain or come in contact with vomit on the floor or urine on the toilet seat?

To the Health Department, these were remote contingencies. Commissioner Sencer declared: "We have assigned a level of risk to transmission by saliva to be so minimal that it does not have a practical implication." But while the doctors used the familar medical language of probability—"reasonable certainty," "infinitesimally small"—Sullivan wanted assurances. "The odds aren't that great but I'm a parent . . . and a parent isn't much interested in odds."

The city's witnesses introduced a wide range of evidence to show that AIDS is not easily transmitted. They maintained that the AIDS virus could not readily be transmitted by saliva or tears because it was present in only minute amounts in these fluids. And they discussed research concerning the fragility of the AIDS virus, which quickly perishes outside the body.

The most important data came from just-completed studies demonstrating that individuals in prolonged, close, but nonsexual contact with persons with AIDS, such as family members and health care workers, did not contract the disease.

In August 1985, the Centers for Disease Control had reported on a study of over 1,700 doctors, nurses, and lab technicians: none had contracted AIDS through other-than-anticipated modes of transmission. And at a meeting in early October, several weeks into the trial, members of the CDC staff had presented details of five more directly relevant studies, covering 230 relatives, brothers, sisters, and parents, of individuals with AIDS or AIDS-related complex (ARC). In not a single instance was there evidence of infection with the AIDS virus, despite the fact that half the households shared dishes and glassware and, in one AIDS household in twelve, toothbrushes had been shared.[5]

The school boards' witnesses read this same evidence differently—as not proving that AIDS could be transmitted *only* through blood and semen. "When all is said and done," said Dr. Jose Giron, Chief of Infectious Diseases at Flushing Medical Center in Queens, "we are dealing with a situation that doesn't have all the data." The argument implicitly centered on a familiar legal issue: What was the burden of proof? While the city's case focused on the evidence taken as a whole, Sullivan—and Judge Hyman too, judging from his questions—proceeded on the assumption that if a single case of AIDS being transmitted other than through semen or blood was identified, no child with AIDS should be allowed in school.

"We make our decisions on the basis of knowledge, we weigh risks and benefits . . . and we take appropriate action," said Sencer. The commissioner, who in his long public health career had never testified in court, found the trial "hard work. You sweat on the stand." Sullivan tried to discredit Sencer by taunting him about his role in the swine flu vaccine affair. "What happens if four months from now you are as wrong as you were in 1976? . . . I don't want to watch on '60 Minutes' two years from now when Mike Wallace grills David Sencer about the fact that he was wrong this time."

For their part, the school boards insisted that scientific knowledge about AIDS was actually far more limited and disagreements far more significant than the city's experts acknowledged. "The differences are not with respect to scientific matters but are . . . philosophical," argued Sullivan.

During the 1970s, it was the intellectuals of the left who advanced a critique of the entire institution of medicine as a profit-driven "medical-industrial complex" run by experts who monopolized control over our bodies.[6] In the age of AIDS, distrust of the medical expert cuts across the political spectrum.

The very fact that an entirely new and devastating epidemic could emerge cast doubt on the prevailing expectation of steady, rational medical progress. As William McNeill writes in *Plagues and Peoples:* "A world where sudden and unexpected death remains a real and dreaded possibility in everyone's life experience makes the idea that the universe is a great machine whose motions are regular, understandable and even predictable, seem grossly inadequate to account for observed reality." Such a world invites a kind of magical thinking more typical of premodern societies, where events cannot be tamed by reason because they are understood to be caused by devils and saints.[7] AIDS, a disease that stymied the scientists, evoked this primitive thinking in the modern world.

Concerning AIDS, the scientists have been caught in a classic double bind. They cannot readily offer guarantees, since guarantees are not a language in which science traffics. And if they venture definite-sounding claims, the false scientific assurances

of the not-so-distant past make them appear less credible. With
Bhopal and Chernobyl and Love Canal etched in contemporary memory—with the closer-to-hand, newly discerned
dangers posed by that toxic dump down the street, or by the
asbestos that insulates the home furnace or, more intimately
still, by the Dalkon Shield IUD—a deep-seated suspicion exists
about what the experts say about AIDS, a hard-to-erase worry
about a possible "Big Lie" of modern science.

What the scientists have asked for, after all, is faith—since
the particulars of what they achieve are too complicated for
most of us to comprehend for ourselves—and faith once un-
dermined is not readily revived. "Why should we believe the experts when they tell us you can't get AIDS from a drinking
glass?" runs the argument of the skeptics—an argument heard
frequently in Judge Hyman's Queens courtroom. "Sure, that's
what they are saying now. But look at how they misled us about
the safety of blood transfusions during the early 1980s; in ten
years, they'll be saying something different."

It was New York politics, at least as much as philosophy, that
Sullivan focused on in making his case. The theme he developed was familiar: arrogant New York City bureaucrats at "that
terrible monument called 110 Livingston Street" and the Health
Department were bullying the citizenry. The attorney, joined
by the judge, took out after Sencer and Chancellor Quinones
for the way the schools' AIDS policy was developed. "If you'd
had those guidelines earlier, you would not be in the courtroom
today," Hyman lectured the chancellor. While Quinones acknowledged that city officials had been "regrettably tardy" and
had underestimated the volatility of the issue, Sencer responded
that "you needed the scientific information that was being developed over the spring and summer" at the Centers for Disease Control before policy could be made.

Sullivan also criticized the procedure followed by the city's
AIDS panel. "They lied to us. This was no decision-making
group at all but a rubber stamp for Sencer," the attorney insisted. "[Nobody] else had an opportunity to overrule him or

even to discuss it with him." And when it came to light, midway through the trial, that the child at the center of the controversy was a girl who might not have AIDS at all but a less serious AIDS-related condition, the city was made the target of ridicule by many who mistakenly assumed ARC is less infectious. "School Girl AIDS Fiasco," read the *New York Post* headline.

Corporation Counsel Schwarz emphasized the rule of law in his closing argument, delivered late in October: no statute authorized the city to exclude a child with AIDS. To keep such a youngster out of school would endow public fears with the force of law. For his part, Sullivan insisted that the novel situation wasn't plainly covered by the rules, and he hammered away at the city's bungled handling of the affair. The school board's lawyer asked that the child be kept home, or at least that school officials be informed of her identity so that they could care for her and her classmates.

Sullivan's understanding of the risks posed by allowing a child with AIDS in school had evolved during the course of the long trial. He had taken on the case convinced that the Queens school boards were right. Now he wasn't so sure. Even as he was making his final arguments, Sullivan now says, "Forty percent of me thought the kid should go to school, forty percent of me thought the kid shouldn't go to school, and the other twenty percent didn't know what to think."

But Bob Sullivan believes in the adversary system as a way to get the facts out, and that system had assigned him a role. "I did the best that I could to keep the child out of school. Somebody had to stand up and be a mouthpiece to get this opinion expressed."

Fritz Schwarz worried that Sullivan had done too good a job. "Everyone was sure that we were going to lose," he recollects. And many people believed that the city *should* lose. At a dinner party at Gracie Mansion that Schwarz attended during the trial, Mayor Koch queried his guests on the issue. Almost everyone at the table, including Rupert Murdoch, at the time the publisher of the *Post,* thought that the city had made the wrong decision. An opinion poll conducted by the *Daily News* and WABC-TV showed that 55 percent of New Yorkers didn't want children with AIDS in school. It was Judge Hyman, however, who several months later would have the final say.

The AIDS case remained a media staple throughout the trial, and debate on the issue persisted outside the courtroom. At nightly meetings during the first week of school, the leaders of the AIDS rebellion were pressed for news by anxious parents. They reported on the doings in court, on the meeting with Quinones and Sencer, on the bargaining session with Koch. Parents picketed the courthouse and kept their children out of school in noticeable though diminishing numbers. Yet by week's end, with 7,000 students still boycotting classes and no sign of a concession by the city, the strain on working families was beginning to tell. When Sam Granirer brought his own children back to class on Friday, he effectively signaled the end of the boycott. The following Monday, things inside the schools were back to normal.

The AIDS controversy also continued to be the stuff of political gamesmanship. Four TV cameras and twenty reporters, a much bigger turnout than City Council members are accustomed to, appeared as Queens Councilman Walter Ward introduced a city ordinance barring any child with AIDS from the public schools. It hardly mattered that the council had no legal jurisdiction. This was matchless publicity for Ward and his Brooklyn colleague, Noach Dear, an outspoken enemy of gay rights who took the opportunity to lambaste homosexuals. "See what happens when you advocate this behavior?" said Dear. "Now you have AIDS."

School officials at 110 Livingston Street, who had been caught unawares by the intensity of the reaction, belatedly began to educate teachers and students about AIDS. There would be AIDS information in all intermediate schools and high schools, Chancellor Quinones announced, and more attention paid to teaching about safe sex and drug abuse. Health precautions were put in place, as each classroom was equipped with a supply of alcohol-dipped cotton swabs, and school custodians were provided with rubber gloves. One day in mid-October, classes ended early in each of the city's 900 public schools so that teachers and staff could watch a ninety-minute documentary on AIDS. The hope, said Quinones, was "through education to reduce the levels of anxiety."

Not everyone was convinced. Sam Granirer felt that the film, featuring a question-and-answer session with David Sencer, was "too one-sided, and I know from talking to people [in Queens] that it changed very few people's minds." Granirer's own fears had been reinforced in a conversation with Dr. Lionel Resnick, who had worked with the nation's best-known AIDS researcher, Robert Gallo, at the National Institutes of Health, and who was one of the districts' witnesses at the trial. "Sam, I can't go on television and say this because the world would crucify me. But I'll tell you something. I work with the virus every day. If I ever got the virus, I would leave my wife and family."

In Queens as elsewhere in the country that fall of 1985, AIDS ceased for a time to command the public's attention. Though Republican mayoral candidate Diane McGrath took out after Koch for his stand on AIDS, the voters weren't listening. By an overwhelming margin, they returned the mayor for a third term in Gracie Mansion.

On February 11, 1986, AIDS and schools became once more the subject of headlines. Judge Hyman surprised a great many people by coming out on the side of the city.

"The court of public opinion" is one thing, the judge wrote, but "the law" is something else. "Although the court certainly empathizes with the fears and concerns of parents, . . . it is duty bound to objectively evaluate the issue of automatic exclusion according to the evidence gathered and not be influenced by unsubstantiated fears of catastrophe."

Judge Hyman's nearly 100-page opinion in *District 27 Community School Board v. Board of Education* accepted the evidence that there is essentially no risk of AIDS being transmitted in the schools. This was reason enough to allow a youngster with AIDS in class: it was unrealistic to demand that the city establish that there was "no risk" before contemplating admission.

Not only was the city's policy permissible, it was legally required, Hyman ruled. To follow the course proposed by the Queens districts and exclude all children with AIDS would violate the federal Rehabilitation Act, since these children were legally handicapped and for that reason entitled to the safeguards of that law. It also would deny them their constitutional guarantees of equal protection: under the districts' proposal, only children who displayed the symptoms of AIDS would be kept out, while the far greater number who had been exposed to the virus, and who were equally capable of transmitting the disease, could continue attending school.[8]

The opinion offered a novel reading of the law and a venturesome one—in Kokomo, two judges had ducked the same questions. What the equal protection logic confirmed was that the Queens parents' hopes were misplaced: the fact that many other children infected with the AIDS virus, unknown and for all practical purposes unknowable, were already in school meant that the virus could not be banished and purity restored by the expedient of raising the drawbridge.

Lawyers on both sides credit Stuart Spitzer, Judge Hyman's clerk, with changing the judge's mind. Spitzer's reading of scientific studies on AIDS in preparation for the trial had made him less fearful than Hyman. The two men talked every day about what transpired in court, and the clerk prepared questions with which the judge could pepper the next day's witnesses. But it was the experts themselves, says Spitzer, who really turned Judge Hyman around. The judge himself says: "When I found out that AIDS could not be transmitted by casual contact, my fears about contagion went up in smoke."

Hyman thought well of the city's medical experts. But Sencer and Quinones, the two key decision-makers in the city bureaucracy, were another matter entirely. As Corporation Counsel Schwarz observes, Hyman came to understand the city's decision making in dramatic terms, with Sencer and Quinones rendered as "the guys wearing the black hats." The judge himself, in recalling the trial, says that he found their activities "distasteful," that on the stand they were "mealy-mouthed" and "evasive." Hyman was particularly critical of the panel that

Sencer appointed to make recommendations on the four youngsters with AIDS, describing it as a "packed house, which got its
information over the phone. [Sencer and Quinones] did what
they wanted to do." The judge made no secret of his hostility.
When he wasn't grilling Sencer, Hyman pointedly turned his
back on him.

This animosity spills over into the opinion, which is as much a
political text on wise decision-making as a judgment on the legal
merits. Hyman found no violations of the law in the way Sencer
and Quinones went about making their determinations. But
their behavior "bespeaks the hostile attitude historically displayed toward community participation since the inception of
the decentralization process," he wrote, echoing the views expressed by Bob Sullivan in the courtroom and Sam Granirer
and Claudette Webb in the community meetings.

City officials operated with "a notion that they knew what was
best and would make all the decisions for everyone's good. Believing this, they acted in imperious fashion . . . behind a cloak
of secrecy." While they followed the law to the letter, they
"missed the spirit of the law . . . the notion that officials govern
with the consent of the people and that the people have the
right to know what these officials are doing."

"It is these public officials themselves who predictably, although unwittingly, let loose the forces of anxiety and fear,"
Judge Hyman insisted—his harshest charge. "Had the public
officials involved trusted the people," this case might never
have had to come to court.

"Trust the people." That is an unfamiliar and not entirely
welcome counsel to school officials, who habitually try to transform value-laden political questions into technical problems.
The best-known instance concerns race, and the analogy to
AIDS is telling.[9]

Even after the Supreme Court's 1954 ruling in *Brown v. Board
of Education* striking down deliberate segregation in the South,
civil rights groups elsewhere had a hard time persuading school
administrators that race belonged on the public agenda of their
schools. Discrimination is not a political matter, came the response, but a highly complicated educational concern to be

settled by the experts. The school chiefs were hostile to the idea of deliberate racial integration for much the same reason: it amounted to social engineering, they said, not education. Even a racial census, it was claimed, would turn children into the guinea pigs of an ill-conceived social experiment.

Beginning a decade after *Brown,* public schools would undertake racial censuses as a matter of course—indeed, as a matter of national law. Neighborhood schools were opened up to those living elsewhere, avowedly to improve their racial mix, and pupils were bused so that blacks and whites living in segregated enclaves could be taught in the same classroom. Wholesale curriculum changes were made to end blacks' status as the "invisible men" in the textbooks. In New York City, where the sought-after integration came to almost nothing, vociferous—and ultimately successful—demands were subsequently made for decentralized, and black-controlled, schools. But it was the courts, and even more importantly the reform-minded school boards, not the superintendents, who usually framed these policies. The school chiefs' insistence that race was an illegitimate item for the political agenda of the schools—indeed, that schools shouldn't even *have* a political agenda—often forced them to the sidelines.

In 1985, as Judge Hyman acerbically pointed out, New York City had tried to treat AIDS in a comparable manner, as a health question suitable for the authorities, entirely outside the bailiwick of politics. But AIDS cannot be contained in this way—not yet, anyhow. Taboos about sex, passions about family, conceptions of justice, hostility toward gay men and drug users, distrust of authority, all contributed to molding the context in which the people of Queens responded to the news of a single AIDS case in the schools.

This is why disputes over how to cope with a child who has AIDS have regularly been blood-on-the-floor donnybrooks, not white-gloved debates over the niceties of the scientific method. There is no technical way to settle all the concerns that AIDS has raised, no reason entirely to trust the educators and the doctors to answer questions that remain cultural as well as scientific in character.

The drama was over, and New York City, fittingly, had its precedent, the first significant judicial ruling in the nation on AIDS in schools. Fritz Schwarz was delighted, while Bob Sullivan characterized the ruling as a "defeat for the people of Queens." But to the consternation of some of those whom Sullivan represented, he acknowledged that the decision was "legally correct." There would be no appeal.

The ruling set another kind of precedent. In defining AIDS as a disease that did not demand discrimination as part of its treatment by the body politic, it domesticated the epidemic, making it fit for the norms of law and common decency. Had the judgment gone the other way, the force of law would have been placed behind the power to turn children into pariahs. The impact of such a ruling would have reached well beyond the public schools to color the responses of other social institutions. As Harold Jaffe of the Centers for Disease Control points out, "The schools' decision to be extra safe [if endorsed by a court] could be cited by employers and hospitals that want to bar people with AIDS."

Perhaps trusting the people, the idea in which Hyman placed his hope, would eventually have led Queens residents to accept a child with AIDS in their schools. After all, this has happened in places where neighborly sentiment and adroit leadership have moved people, in the face of irreducible uncertainty, to make a gift of their own trust. But in New York City, the legacy of animosities and antipathies renders this kind of statecraft especially difficult.[10] It is, all too often, the people versus the experts, 110 Livingston Street versus the district boards, a war of all against all. A successful political settlement—the Swansea story recreated in Queens—would have taken a remarkable effort, led by bureaucrats with greater popular credibility and politicians with a firmer grasp of principle than the AIDS controversy evoked. It might also have needed the presence of a child as well known and loved in his community as Mark Hoyle was in Swansea. But the fact that, through the months of controversy in New York, there was no known child—just a statistic—exactly reflects the reality of urban anonymity. What transpired in Judge Hyman's courtroom was only a second-best solution. Under the circumstances, however, second-best doesn't look at all bad.

Several years after the Queens case had receded into history, the underlying patterns persisted. Queens was still writing the textbook on shady provincial politics—its chief executive, Donald Manes, committed suicide in the face of corruption charges—and offering new lessons on the cost of insularity. Howard Beach, a community situated in District 27, had entered the national vocabulary as a synonym for bigotry when a gang of white teenagers chased a black man, whose only crime was his presence, to his death on a highway. Nor had education about AIDS become part of the curriculum in the Queens public schools. "Teachers can't stand up in front of a class and explain it to children," said Delores Grant from District 29. And Grant worried that instruction about AIDS would somehow make homosexuality legitimate, even exciting, to impressionable teenagers. "You could get a child that might want to experiment because it might have sounded interesting. It's important to teach children that that's not the right life-style."

City Hall was still being reviled for its handling of the AIDS epidemic, a problem that could partly be traced to Mayor Koch. In late 1987, the mayor easily weathered a *Village Voice* article describing an affair with a gay man he allegedly had a decade earlier. But Koch has continued to take as many different positions on AIDS as there are days of the week: in the spring of 1987 he endorsed explicitness in the content of AIDS-related sex education, then reversed field with the first hint of adverse reaction, coming out foursquare for abstinence.

New York's failings are more significantly attributable to the power of the bureaucratic fiefdoms within the nation-state that New York City imagines itself to be. It is within those bureaucracies that the fate of children with AIDS is lodged.

The expert panel set up by Health Commissioner Sencer in 1985 has continued to pass on requests for admission to school. It has been buttressed by a second panel comprised entirely of doctors, created in the wake of the embarrassment accompanying the disclosure that the child whose admission sparked the Queens controversy might not in fact have AIDS. The court and the public have disappeared from sight; enrollment determinations are entirely in the hands of the professionals. As a consequence, the rights that Judge Hyman wrote about, the individual's right to education and the political right to public discussion, mean much less.

The facts of one AIDS case, which slipped through the net of secrecy in which the system is enmeshed, tell a troubling story. A nine-year-old black girl, in good health but diagnosed as having AIDS, was placed in a pediatric unit of a city hospital in the fall of 1985. The only reason she remained hospitalized in the spring of 1987, when an article in the *New York Times* described her situation, was that city officials were unable to find a foster home for her. The child's mother, a heroin user, contracted pneumocystis pneumonia and could not keep her. No one else wanted a nine-year-old with AIDS.

One day, shortly after the girl was admitted to the hospital, her mother failed to make a promised visit. The youngster threw a tantrum and, in a rage, bit a nurse. Although the incident was never repeated—indeed, the girl became a favorite of the nurses—this single episode led the AIDS panel to keep her out of public school. Only in 1987, nearly two years after the bite, was she allowed to attend.

During repeated reviews of the case, psychiatrists offered conflicting evaluations of the youngster's ability to behave properly in a regular classroom. They acknowledged that many children in the New York City schools were less stable than this girl, but wondered whether the single episode of the bite meant that she was still too emotionally unbalanced to be trusted.

Although the child's caseworker said that she worried about the unnamed girl all the time, no one ever talked about mobilizing support to get the youngster back in school or about going to court to secure her legal rights. In fact, no one in a position to do any of these things even had an inkling of what was occurring. Like the several hundred other children with AIDS in

New York City, one in three of whom are abandoned by their mothers at birth, the girl's identity has remained known only to a handful of people within the system.[11]

This secrecy, of course, is supposed to protect her privacy. But the reality is that the rules of confidentiality have imprisoned her. And no one outside the circle of the well-intentioned professionals who process these cases knows how many similar untold stories there are in New York City.

BURIED FEELINGS: OCILLA, GEORGIA

It was money troubles that brought Marcella Jackson into the Ocilla, Georgia, office of the Federal Housing Administration in November 1985. The twenty-three-year-old black woman, who had lived much of her life in and around the rural south Georgia town, had always paid her bills on the dot. She wondered whether she could convince these officials that this time she had good reason—a very good reason—for not making the monthly payment on her federally subsidized home.

"I've been out of a job taking care of my daughter," Mrs. Jackson told her loan officer. "She's in the hospital with AIDS."

Within hours, the news was out. A town like Ocilla, population 3,400, keeps few secrets. And the just-revealed circumstances of Marcella Jackson's life were extraordinary news in a place where AIDS was thought of, if it was thought of at all, as a judgment on New York and Atlanta.

Yet in a matter of months, the people of Ocilla would be on intimate terms with the AIDS epidemic. Soon another case of AIDS was reported, then another—the total mounted to at least half a dozen, with rumors of more surfacing regularly. Reporters covering the story cracked mordant jokes. Question: What's the first sign of AIDS? Answer: Ocilla, one mile.

It was the school superintendent, Rudene Gentry, who took the lead in ferreting out the AIDS cases, and what passed for an official response in Ocilla came from the schools. Children related to people with AIDS were taken out of school and tested to see if they too had been exposed to the virus. Epidemiologists from the Georgia Division of Public Health showed up to educate and investigate. Reporters came to poke and pry.

Not many months after her visit to the FHA office, Marcella Jackson lost her one-year-old daughter to AIDS. But her oldest child, six-year-old Ndebe*, became the center of controversy. The boy, when tested, turned out not to have been exposed to the virus, and so posed absolutely no risk of transmitting AIDS. Yet this news did not allay fears or deter Ocilla's school officials from keeping Ndebe out of school for nearly four months, readmitting him only under powerful pressure and then only under unique conditions: Marcella Jackson had to abandon her right to live with her own son.

"Life is simply more glandular in the South than it is in the rest of the nation," writes Marshall Frady. "Southerners tend to belong and believe through blood and weather and common earth and common enemy and common travail, rather than belonging, being, cerebrally. The tribal instinct is what they answer to."[1]

It is not the new South, the land of condos and corporate headquarters, oil money and go-go banking, that Frady is talking about, but another South entirely: the broad farm belt, tobacco and cotton country that sweeps from the Atlantic coast of Georgia clear across to Texas, a region less well-off by any economic indicator than the rest of the South, more abidingly rooted in traditions that reach back to the days of the first colonial settlements.

A brochure put out by the local chamber of commerce is snappily optimistic: "No longer a sleepy little town, Ocilla, Georgia is wide awake with ideas and enthusiasm for what's happen-

---

*Ndebe is a pseudonym to protect privacy. His real name has not appeared in print. His real last name, also never published, is that of his natural father.

ing next." It is difficult, though, to find even a hint of vitality in
Ocilla, situated in hardscrabble farm country eighty miles south
of Macon. Ocilla's one landmark is the nearby museum on the
site where Jefferson Davis was captured by Yankee troops in the
waning days of the Civil War, and its only excitement is the annual sweet potato festival.

Local residents affectionately call Ocilla a "two red-light
town," though traffic is seldom heavy enough to give the lights a
workout. The only nightlife is at a twenty-four-hour fast food
place, an Edward Hopper painting devoid of customers at
10:00 P.M. The merchants on Ocilla's short main street have successfully kept out the chain stores, so when townspeople want
more than a loaf of bread, they head to the mall in Fitzgerald,
seven miles away across the Ben Hill County line.

A mobile-home plant, Ocilla Industries, has a thousand workers and a listing on the New York Stock Exchange, and several
grain mills attest to Ocilla's role as the market town for Irwin
County. Yet the unemployment rate remains well above the
Georgia average, and more than a third of Ocilla's residents,
twice the statewide average, live in poverty. So desperate is the
need for jobs that when a noisome chicken-rendering factory
considered relocating in the county, Ocilla officials decided to
hold their noses and actively court it.

"Ocilla is a God-fearing, loving, compassionate community,"
says Emory Walters, a lawyer and businessman who looms large
on the local scene, and this isn't just Fourth of July talk either.
Conservative values and habitual respect for authority go hand
in hand in a town that sells no liquor and whose elementary
school principal keeps a paddle by his side. Civic pride, religious conviction, an ingrained sense of hospitality to one's own
kind: these are the aspects of life in Ocilla, the ties of "common
earth and common enemy and common travail" so familiar as
to be taken for granted, that give the townspeople a sense
of place.

There are really two Ocillas, one white, the other black,
race being the chief marker of personal identity. That fact has
been centrally important in how AIDS has been treated in

Ocilla, since all of the AIDS cases thus far reported have been among blacks, and all the decisions about AIDS have been made by whites.

Irwin County is 70 percent white; the town of Ocilla is half white and half black, and the blacks live, literally, on the wrong side of the tracks. The white neighborhood has a handful of fine century-old homes and many more spacious contemporary ranch houses. The black section, with its unpaved streets and falling-down houses, looks like the stage set for *Porgy and Bess*.

Whites in Ocilla take racial separation for granted. They insist that blacks have chosen to go their separate way and that racial tension is a phenomenon imported by outside troublemakers. This is a familiar refrain in the rural South, but history tells another story.

In the aftermath of the Reconstruction, Ocilla was an early stronghold of the Ku Klux Klan, and the KKK still has sympathizers in the town. The Supreme Court's 1954 decision outlawing school segregation is, even now, referred to by old-timers as a dread menace, "The Thing." Fifteen years after *Brown v. Board of Education* was decided, when the clock of "all deliberate speed" had finally run down, Ocilla was finally obliged to accommodate itself to integration. A contingent from the FBI was on hand, in September 1969, to assure that peace was maintained. And a sizeable group of parents removed their children from the public schools, setting up a segregationist academy that stood until 1984; even then, economic exigencies and not a blossoming of racial fellow-feeling forced the private school to shut its doors. During the 1960s, the town's swimming pool was cemented over by local officials unwilling to obey a federal court order and allow blacks and whites to swim together. The weedy and cracked covering remains in place, a symbol of the not-so-distant racial past.

An uneasy accommodation prevails between the races these days. A black man sits on the Ocilla city council, another on the Irwin County school board: they are safe choices, though, men of some years and prudence who are unlikely to stir things up. A few years back, black community leaders from the Ocilla Civic Club persuaded the municipality to build a new municipal swimming pool. This one is in the black neighborhood, and no whites ever swim there.

No one in Ocilla doubts it was white largess, not black power, that got the swimming pool built: for generation upon generation, a handful of white families has held the reins in this almost-feudal town. There is the Paulk family, for instance, whose ancestors were among Ocilla's founders. Today, Ellen Paulk, the public health nurse responsible for teaching adults about AIDS, works in the Irwin County Health Center across the street from the Paulk Funeral Home. Other Paulks work in Ocilla as accountants, insurance agents, and lawyers. When the town celebrated its one-hundred-fiftieth anniversary in 1968, with a wild hog chase and a greased pole climb, Ellen Paulk's daughter was named "Little Miss Sesquicentennial."

And there is the Walters clan, the political princes of the realm. Vernon Walters has been chairman of the Irwin County Board of Education for the past quarter of a century. His brother Emory runs the law firm that represents both the county and the school board and sits on the board of Ocilla Industries. People refer to Emory Walters as Mr. Ocilla—the mayor is a junior partner in Walters' law firm—the man who makes it his business to know, and to influence, whatever is happening. As Edgar Anderson, president of the newly revived, all-black chapter of the NAACP, reports: "Whenever we get together, Emory Walters knows what's happened before I've gotten home from that meeting." The habitually conservative Emory Walters, together with school superintendent Rudene Gentry, determined Ocilla's response to the AIDS epidemic.

Marcella Jackson lives little more than a mile from the Paulks and the Walters, but the social distance is immense. She grew up not in Ocilla but in nearby Coffee County. There, as an eleventh grader pregnant with her first child, she dropped out of school and married the child's father, only to break off the marriage three months later. Soon she met another man and moved to upstate New York with him; several years later, again pregnant, she returned to Coffee County with hopes of making a new start. She enrolled in secretarial school, where she was a top student, met the man who is now her husband, and married him in 1983. That year, the family moved to Ocilla. "I like the town," she says. "It's countrified and everybody knows everybody else." This intimate knowledge, the harsher side of neighborliness, would eventually complicate her life.

Early in 1985, Marcella Jackson gave birth to her third child, a girl she named Jokeena. From the first, Jokeena was sickly, suffering from a wasting disease that baffled the local doctors. She was taken to Augusta, Georgia, for further testing, where she was diagnosed as having SCIDS (Severe Combined Immune Deficiency Syndrome), a rare condition sometimes referred to as the bubble-baby syndrome because children suffering from SCIDS have been kept in sterile plastic bubbles to protect them from infection.

The recommended treatment for Jokeena involved a bone marrow transplant, an expensive operation. A private group in Augusta raised the money to send Marcella Jackson and her daughter to Duke University, along with the child's father who was to be the donor for the transplant. But in the fall of 1985, the doctors at Duke made a stunning discovery: Jokeena's illness was not SCIDS but AIDS. When the entire family was tested for AIDS, it turned out that only Marcella Jackson had been exposed to the virus. Although apparently in perfect health, she had transmitted the deadly disease to her own daughter at birth.

Marcella Jackson professed not to know how she had been exposed to AIDS. "How in the world did I attract this? I'm Miss Goody Two-Shoes," she maintained. "I don't use drugs! I'm not a homosexual!" Her best guess is that the man she had lived with in New York may have been an intravenous-drug user. Yet the girl born out of that relationship was tested along with the rest of the family and found free of the virus.

"I used to dwell on how this happened," says Marcella Jackson, "but now I don't," since even if the advent of AIDS seemed profoundly unfair other concerns were more pressing. Not only was Jokeena fading rapidly but Marcella herself was about to give birth to another child who, as she suddenly realized, might also be infected with the fatal virus. She gave up her job as cashier at a local convenience store and entrusted her two older children to her mother so that she could be with Jokeena. For weeks on end, she shuttled between Ocilla and Augusta, where, night after night, she sat in a straight-backed hospital chair by her daughter's side. It was during this time that she made her visit to the FHA office to explain why she couldn't make the monthly payment on her loan.

Soon afterwards, Marcella Jackson had her first taste of what life can be like for someone infected with AIDS. She had planned to deliver her baby in Augusta but in December 1985, while home in Ocilla, she went into labor early. Rushed by ambulance to the hospital in nearby Fitzgerald, she informed the doctors she was an AIDS carrier. "I thought it was unfair not to tell them," she says.

The doctors in Fitzgerald panicked. They could not deliver the baby because they had no "high-risk facility," they told her, so Marcella Jackson was bundled back into the ambulance. As her husband and her mother followed in the family car, the ambulance set off in search of some medical institution that would have her. Yet when the driver radioed ahead to other nearby hospitals, reporting on her condition, none would admit the expectant mother. Hours later, when the ambulance returned her to Fitzgerald, she was so far advanced in labor that the hospital had no choice but to accept her. As soon as she could, she fled with her newborn son to Augusta, where she knew she could count on more sympathetic medical care. But she wondered about how she could live the semblance of a normal life in Ocilla. "Suppose I get hit by a car. No one's gonna take me to Augusta—that's a long ways off."

Marcella Jackson's newborn son was free from the AIDS infection—the one bit of good news in a string of sorrows rivaling the Book of Job. In November, her father and two of his co-workers were electrocuted by the machinery they were using to harvest the fields. Then in January 1986, Jokeena died, sixteen days shy of her first birthday. Two months later, Marcella Jackson had to cope with the death of her grandfather, who had raised her when she was a child.

By this time, an epidemic of new troubles had set in. Marcella

Jackson's revelation in the FHA office, together with the incident at the hospital in Fitzgerald, made Ocilla aware of the presence of AIDS. The controversy centered on her oldest child, Ndebe, a six-year-old in first grade at Ocilla's elementary school. The issue that school officials raised was whether Ndebe should be kept out of school—not because he carried the AIDS virus, which he didn't, but because his mother did.

It initially fell to Rhonda Walters, Ocilla's visiting teacher and unofficial white ambassador to the black community, to negotiate the delicate terrain of AIDS in the household of Marcella Jackson.

As the visiting teacher, Mrs. Walters, daughter-in-law of Vernon Walters, the chairman of the board of education, tutors sick children and helps to arrange schooling for youngsters who get into trouble. She is an unlikely candidate for the job, a vampishly attractive dilettante in the earnest beehive and polyester world of Ocilla. But Rhonda Walters has plunged into her work with an innocent's curiosity about the underclass and a do-gooder's enthusiasm. In the black community, she is a Mrs. Bountiful who delivers not only education but food and clothing to families on the ropes. "My job is a personal one," she says, "dealing in their homes, dealing with their feelings."

Soon after Marcella Jackson's November 1985 visit to the FHA, Rhonda Walters began hearing the rumors of AIDS. Concerned, she took the stories to her boss, School Superintendent Rudene Gentry, who had been hearing similar tales from a secretary whose sister worked at the FHA. Gentry sent Rhonda Walters out on a fact-finding mission.

"Marcella was as nice as could be," Mrs. Walters remembers. The results of the family's AIDS tests were willingly handed over and confirmed all the speculation: AIDS had reached Ocilla.

On December 9, 1985, at the monthly meeting of the Irwin County Board of Education, Superintendent Rudene Gentry brought board members up to date on the Jackson family. Gentry and the board have sometimes disagreed—in picking a high school principal, for example—but such occasions are rare because Gentry works hard at maintaining amity. In Irwin County and in a handful of other rural Georgia school districts, the superintendent is elected by the voters while the board is appointed by the grand jury, an atypical arrangement that gives the superintendent more political authority, and the board less, than is true elsewhere. The school board in 1985 included one white lawyer, three white farmers, and a retired black school principal. All were men; two had served on the board for a quarter of a century.

Concerning AIDS, there would be no disagreement. After what the minutes describe as a "lengthy discussion" about Ndebe, the young lawyer on the board, Warren Mixon, proposed keeping the six-year-old out of school "until he is tested . . . and the results show that he does not have Aids [sic]." Nobody in the room saw things any differently.

The fact that the boy had already been tested at Duke and showed no trace of the AIDS virus didn't enter into the conversation. Insisting on another round of tests was partly a way of not deciding something, but there was more to it than that. As Superintendent Gentry later said: "How can we trust test results from someplace so far away?" How could a determination made elsewhere be relied on by a community that consistently resisted outsiders' determinations about what was right?

The next day, an official contingent from the Ocilla public schools—Rudene Gentry, Rhonda Walters, and Allen Smith, the elementary school principal—called on Marcella Jackson. She was "open and honest," says Gentry, "which we sincerely appreciated. I asked her, 'What would you want me to do if it was someone else's child?' and she said, 'I'd want my child protected.'" Mrs. Jackson agreed to keep her son home until the school board could learn more about the risks involved—"only for a week or two," Gentry promised.

Gentry would subsequently point to Marcella Jackson's acquiescence as proof that he hadn't bullied her, yet she wasn't exactly a free agent in the negotiation. A black woman in her twenties whose family is barely making ends meet, living in a town with a tradition of deferring to the powers-that-be, will

naturally be loath to take on the superintendent of schools.
"While the school officials didn't say, 'You have to take him
out,'" she remembers, "the impression I got was that I'd better
do it, so I agreed to it." Her misgivings grew as the time Ndebe
was out of school dragged on, and a week or two became a
matter of months.

Rudene Gentry, Ocilla's point man in the controversy over
AIDS, has lived all his life in south Georgia. He prides himself
on being a mainstay of the community, an upright man with a
mission to educate the children of Ocilla and to protect them
against the perils of the world outside.

In 1973, after Gentry had taught and coached for twenty
years in a nearby town, his old high school principal persuaded
him that he was the man to run for the Irwin County superintendent's job. Gentry's competitiveness had been nurtured during his years playing high school basketball on a team that
boasted a seventy-six-game winning streak and several state
championships. He brought to the superintendent's job a faith
in public education, shaped by his Depression-era upbring-
ing as the youngest of six children in a sharecropper's family,
the one who listened nightly at the dinner table to the school
teacher boarding in their home. Gentry's devotion to public
schools had led him to turn down a chance to run the segregationist academy in Ocilla.

Gentry's predecessor, an emigré from Pennsylvania, had quit
in disgrace, with the town awash in tales of an affair with his
secretary and his telling the students of Ocilla that there was no
God. Also, the school district's budget had an unexplained
$300,000 deficit.

The new superintendent set out to balance the budget by
paring expenses and successfully lobbying the community to
raise taxes. Then he moved on to expansion: new school buildings were built, old ones were remodeled, and new staff was
hired to redesign the curriculum. Gentry was confident that
Ocilla's schools would provide at least the educational basics
and, through firm discipline, help to shape the character of

their students. He was well enough regarded by his fellow educators to be named "Superintendent of the Year" in 1980 for the state of Georgia.

When Gentry was first confronted with AIDS, his instinct was to wall off the schools from any possibility of contagion, no matter how remote. In his experience, the risk of infection from diseases such as polio sufficed to keep a child out of school; even a case of lice was reason enough to remove a youngster from the classroom. Yet from the outset, the medical experts he talked to about AIDS unequivocally advised him to allow Ndebe to remain in school.

By the end of 1985, five months after Kokomo, Indiana, had made national news by excluding Ryan White from school, guidance was available on how to handle schoolchildren with AIDS. Although Georgia was hardly an exemplar in responding to AIDS—it had spent no money on AIDS education, and the Georgia Board of Education did not develop an AIDS policy until mid-1987—the state's AIDS Task Force, a commission appointed by the governor, had already spoken. Following the guidelines laid down by the federal Centers for Disease Control in Atlanta, it recommended that children with AIDS stay in the classroom while their condition was evaluated on a case-by-case basis. Implicit in the guidelines is the assumption that a child like Ndebe, who has never been infected by the AIDS virus, presents no threat to anyone.

Gentry got the same advice—keep Ndebe in class—when in late November 1985 he phoned Dr. Lynn Feldman, a pediatrician who is the district health officer in Valdosta. Feldman already knew of the rumors about Marcella Jackson's health from her Ocilla colleague Ellen Paulk, who many months earlier had suspected that Mrs. Jackson's sickly daughter, Jokeena, might be suffering from AIDS. Feldman suggested that Gentry talk with Marcella Jackson.

Gentry had been ready to pull Ndebe out of school when word came that Marcella Jackson had the AIDS virus, even though the youngster himself had tested negative. Dr. Feldman urged him to reconsider. She offered to make a presentation on AIDS to Ocilla's teachers, but Gentry wasn't interested. Instead, he insisted on having Ndebe tested a second time. When the new test results also were negative, Feldman called Gentry. "There is no reason to keep the boy at home," she told the superintendent, but Gentry replied that he had just read an article that said there are no absolutes on AIDS.

"When I heard that," Feldman recalls, "I must admit I was more agitated than I should have been. I told the superintendent, 'You want an absolute, I'll give you one. You can't get AIDS from someone who doesn't have it.'"

But Gentry and the Ocilla school board were engulfed by a fear that would not countenance even the most basic of distinctions: that AIDS had touched Ndebe's household was enough to frighten them silly. Initially, Rhonda Walters had tried to help out Ndebe, bringing crayons, writing pads, books, and a desk for him to work on, and Ndebe's first-grade teacher had mailed some lesson plans. Yet school officials were so panicked by the menace they associated with Ndebe that the boy's lessons went unreviewed by his teacher; and Rudene Gentry, acting under the instructions of the school board, ordered Rhonda Walters to stay away from the Jacksons' home.

It had become clear by the first months of 1986 that the problem of AIDS in Ocilla was not limited to Marcella Jackson, and this revelation raised the pitch of anxiety even higher. Grace Brockington, a neighbor of the Jacksons, had been in the same Augusta hospital as baby Jokeena Jackson, and she too was dying of AIDS. When Grace Brockington died, in January 1986, her family tried to mask the cause of death, but it became common knowledge. Rudene Gentry reacted quickly to this news: in the middle of the school day, Rhonda Walters took Grace Brockington's two children from their classrooms and delivered them to their grandmother. They were tested for AIDS, found not to carry the virus, and they too were kept at home by the superintendent.

Meanwhile, another woman who had lived down the street from Marcella Jackson and Grace Brockington, and who had died some time earlier, was now rumored to have had AIDS. Three people dead of AIDS, in a town of 3,400—three neighbors dead of AIDS, all living on the same block. This freakish coincidence seems the stuff of third-rate melodrama, not real life, but to the people of Ocilla it was all too real. The deaths seemed to describe a mysterious and fast-spreading devastation in their midst, an alien invader with no conceivable intrinsic connection to Ocilla.

In fact, the epidemiology of AIDS in Ocilla is not so mysterious. Explanations based on scientifically familiar routes of viral transmission were available, if anyone had wanted to seek them out. For one thing, a number of Ocilla's black men spend a few months each year harvesting sugarcane in and around Belle Glade, Florida, the community with the highest concentration of AIDS cases in the country. In Belle Glade, as elsewhere, AIDS spreads through sex and intravenous drug use, and some of the migrant workers undoubtedly contracted the virus while in Florida.

Ocilla also has more direct links to drugs. Planes bringing heroin and cocaine into the United States from South America regularly refuel in fields just outside of town, and a sizeable drug traffic has developed. In February 1987, the Georgia Bureau of Investigation showed up in force, arresting nearly three dozen locals involved in the drug trade.

All those jailed by the state agents were blacks; it is in Ocilla's black community that drug use is most visible and most talked about. "When kids see the dope dealer driving his two Cadillacs," says the NAACP chapter president, Edgar Anderson, "they think, 'That's how I want to live!'" But drug use has also left its mark on some white families, and stories are whispered about leading citizens managing the drug deals, as they manage everything else.

Little is said in Ocilla about homosexuality, elsewhere the most common route of AIDS transmission, since a gay man would have to be very discreet to survive there. But Ocilla is the sort of town where married men who secretly prefer the sexual company of other men will slip off on business trips to Atlanta, and the spread of AIDS could only make these men fearful.

Before cases of AIDS began being documented locally, Emory Walters recollects, the popular wisdom was that Ocilla was safe—that the way to avoid AIDS was to "remain seated and keep your mouth shut," a joke whose double meaning links AIDS not only to homosexuality in particular but to disobedience in general. In January 1986, however, homosexuality suddenly seemed not so far away. A black ninth-grade student complained to his counselor about sores in his mouth, and when the sores turned out to be gonorrhea, the boy admitted that he had been having oral sex with several of his male classmates. As the story got around, other students stayed away from the lunchroom where he worked. Superintendent Gentry was not slow to make the connection between one sexually transmitted disease, gonorrhea, and another, AIDS.

But it was heterosexual promiscuity that made people in Ocilla especially anxious. Casual sex in black Ocilla is acknowledged to be commonplace, but sex, like drugs, furtively brings black and whites together. As AIDS spread in the black community, the question was when would it show up on the other side of the tracks.

All of this was known in Ocilla although never talked about. The long-time editor and publisher of the weekly *Ocilla Star*, Bill Bradford, defends Ocilla's reputation by emphasizing that its AIDS cases originated elsewhere. "One woman came back from Miami after spending thirty years there," Bradford says, "and another [Marcella Jackson] contracted AIDS in New York." The people of Ocilla needed to maintain an idealized and purified sense of their own community, because their personal identities were so closely bound to the image of the place in which they lived. To continue to see themselves as good people, it was essential to place the source of AIDS far away.

The fears of contagion surfaced publicly when about twenty parents came to the school board's monthly meeting on January 13, 1986, to talk about Ndebe—a remarkable event, for it had been years since more than a parent or two had appeared for any reason at a board session. Voices were raised that night as, one after another, parents insisted that Ndebe be kept out of school; the most vociferous were among those who had sent their children to the all-white academy. They got their way when the school board voted unanimously that Ndebe would remain home "indefinitely until further information can be obtained concerning the communicable aspects of the disease."

To board member Warren Mixon, there really was no choice. It was irrelevant that excluding Ndebe made no medical sense and that, as lawyer Mixon well knew, Ocilla would lose in court if Marcella Jackson mounted a legal challenge. School officials professed that they felt bad for Mrs. Jackson, but that was irrelevant too. Ocilla—white Ocilla, really—was of one mind on the matter. Had the school board readmitted the boy, Mixon says, "we would have been impeached."

White Ocilla's response to Ndebe was a way of warding off the noxious idea of rights, which had been so forcibly introduced during the civil rights campaigns of the 1960s and 1970s. Bill Bradford at the *Ocilla Star* winces at the notion that Ndebe might have had cause to complain. "Civil rights have a place, but—Lord of Mercy!—other people have rights too!" And Superintendent Gentry adds: "It's time we learned in America that everybody has rights, not just the minorities."

But keeping Ndebe out of school wasn't just an instance of the new racism; it was also a way of insisting on the paramount importance of the community. In most of America, individuality is the guiding vision. In places like Ocilla, though, worlds unto themselves, the community as a whole comes first, and that means protecting everyone against even the remote possibility of dread risk. This is how whites in Ocilla explain themselves— and, with a habitual paternalism, they speak with seeming confidence for blacks as well. "Blacks were even more frightened than whites," says Superintendent Gentry. "After all, it was blacks who were coming down with AIDS." Marcella Jackson saw things differently, however; increasingly, so did black Ocilla.

By late January 1986, Marcella Jackson was feeling that she had been duped by the officials who had told her that, if only she didn't make a fuss, matters would resolve themselves. She had stayed quiet but nothing had happened. Ndebe was still out of school, without even lessons to work on, and no one could say when he might be readmitted. Secretly, for she was scared to stir up trouble, she called a well-known civil rights attorney for help; he telephoned the NAACP in Atlanta, which in turn contacted Edgar Anderson, the president of the Irwin County NAACP.

After spending two decades away, first at college and then

in the Air Force, where he had risen to the rank of captain, Anderson had returned to his hometown of Ocilla in 1984. He had acquired useful training along the way, yet when this quietly dependable man went looking for a decent job he had no luck; there isn't much work for a professional black man in Ocilla. Rudene Gentry, who was to tangle with Anderson, dismisses him as solitary troublemaker, a "little leader" with no followers, but in fact Anderson is admired in the black community. He chaired a committee of the Ocilla Civic Club, the black service organization in town, which was instrumental in reviving the NAACP in Irwin County, and once the NAACP chapter was established, Edgar Anderson became its first president.

When the Atlanta NAACP had alerted Anderson to the fact that Marcella Jackson wanted help in getting her son back in school, he went to see her. Then he talked with the farmers and day laborers, the shopkeepers and funeral directors, who came together both at the Civic Club and NAACP chapter meetings, about taking legal action on Ndebe's behalf. Anderson met with Rudene Gentry, and the superintendent acknowledged that Ndebe was being kept home even though he was not infected with the AIDS virus. This news only strengthened Anderson's conviction that the boy should be in school. But how could he persuade—or, more bravely yet, oblige—the powers-that-be to change their minds?

The fact that black Ocilla was talking about Ndebe made Superintendent Gentry and the school board nervous. Emory Walters, the influential "Mr. Ocilla," had been advising Gentry and the board members behind the scenes. Now he determined to put a lid on the situation. He organized a meeting of the black leadership at a funeral home in black Ocilla. Edgar Anderson was there; so were Bobby Boone, president of the Ocilla Civic Club, and Marcella Jackson. Walters explained that the school board was worried about the safety of its students. Then he put a surprising proposal to Mrs. Jackson. Would she be willing, "in the spirit of cooperation," to keep Ndebe at his grandmother's house, where he had been living since the fall, while the community came to terms with the problem? Although this request got her son no closer to being readmitted to school, she reluctantly agreed.

That wasn't the end of white Ocilla's troubles. When the two Brockington children were pulled out of school in early February, another angry relative had to be dealt with. Ethel Bird, Grace Brockington's sister, had lived in Ocilla until she was sixteen, when she married and, as she says, was "rescued." Now a nurse living in Atlanta, Mrs. Bird returned to Ocilla when her sister was dying to help her mother take care of the children. She was outraged by the town officials' behavior. "It's a farce," she concluded, "I think they're living in the 1800s."

After hearing Marcella Jackson's story, Ethel Bird tried to buttonhole Superintendent Gentry. When he wouldn't talk with her, she became angrier. She went home, having gotten into a "big verbal fight" with school board member Warren Mixon, and advised her mother to take on the school officials. "'Go to court if you have to,' I told her." But her mother demurred. "She reminded me that she had to live in that town," Mrs. Bird recalls.

By mid-February of 1986, the AIDS crisis seemed to have been solved—or at least shelved. Three black children, none harboring the AIDS virus, were nonetheless out of school indefinitely. No one was demanding that Ocilla officials do more to stop the spread of the disease; nor was a step so giant as a lawsuit very likely. Ocilla had not learned anything about AIDS; instead, its leaders had focused on keeping things quiet, honoring irrationality in the process. Then, on February 15, a front-page story in the *Atlanta Constitution* brought Ocilla's period of grace to a rude close: the town would have to defend its conduct to strangers.

To hear the leaders of white Ocilla tell it, David Beasley, the *Atlanta Constitution* reporter who broke the Ocilla AIDS story, is the embodiment of evil. "He made up ninety percent of what he wrote," Rudene Gentry expostulates, delivering a judgment that, though baseless, is repeatedly voiced, "and he got Marcella Jackson all riled up." Bill Bradford at the *Ocilla Star,* who had filled Beasley in during his initial visit, later refused to talk with him, and others in the town responded the same way. "By the time he wrote his man-in-the-street piece, a month later, the only people he could get quotes from were the town drunks," Bradford says. Some expressed their antipathy toward Beasley more directly. When he returned to Ocilla after writing his first article, the tires on the young reporter's car were slashed.

Beasley had been sitting in his small dark office in Macon when the call came from his editor in Atlanta. As usual, he was all alone in this Siberia of a post, an unprepossessing figure almost hidden behind disorderly heaps of files, writing stories about south Georgia and dreaming of a better job. There had been a small item in the *Ocilla Star* about a child with AIDS in school, the editor told him, that should be checked out.

The young reporter called Superintendent Rudene Gentry, who curtly informed him "That's old news," then slammed down the phone. Beasley got in his car and headed south to Ocilla. By now, Marcella Jackson was ready to talk, though not yet prepared to be identified in print. What Beasley learned from her, he says, "shocked and flabbergasted" him.

"Homework Mailed To A Child Whose Mother Is A Carrier," read the headline of a story that contrasted the fears of Ocilla with prevailing medical opinion. The piece quotes Allen Smith, principal of Irwin County Elementary School: "Would I want to put my wife in a room with that child to teach him? No. I wouldn't send her into a room with smallpox either." But reporter Beasley gives Marcella Jackson the last word. "We're up against ignorance and hatred, and we're up against just not knowing."

That story set other reporters on the trail. Suddenly the TV stations from Atlanta were calling Rudene Gentry, and journalists from around the country were checking the story. Was it—could it be—true that a boy who did not carry the AIDS virus was being kept at home without any instruction? The Justice Department's Community Relations Service got interested too, and a black investigator, Bob Ensley, was sent to scout the possibility of discrimination.

Something plainly had to be done. On February 21, two and a half months after Ndebe had been taken out of school, Superintendent Gentry called an old friend in the governor's office for help. He was put in touch with Dr. Keith Sikes, the chief epidemiologist in the Georgia Public Health Division and the man who oversees the state's AIDS program. Sikes volunteered to come to Ocilla the very next day. Gentry settled on March 6, two weeks in the future.

During the troubled days preceding the scheduled visit from Sikes, it began to seem that Ndebe's case could only be resolved in court. Edgar Anderson, made bold by all the media attention, pledged that the NAACP would support a lawsuit. And on March 3, Marcella Jackson went with her son to the Irwin County Elementary School and asked that he be allowed to return. She knew she would be turned away, and she was, but now she could prove to a judge that her child was not wanted. For his part, Emory Walters tried persuading Georgia Attorney General Michael Bowers to take up Ocilla's cause as a test case on AIDS. Walters has a fine reputation as a trial lawyer—he once bested F. Lee Bailey in court—but on this issue he didn't know the law. Bowers bluntly told him that Ocilla would be crucified in court.

White Ocilla's leaders weren't exactly eager to welcome Sikes and his team. They came from Atlanta, which hardly counted as Georgia, and surely couldn't be trusted with the town's secrets. But the visit also offered the promise of possible reconciliation to those in Ocilla who had come to the reluctant realization that they would lose if they persisted in outright opposition. Perhaps the visitors could suggest a settlement that would somehow satisfy Marcella Jackson and the NAACP while not outraging parents who had spoken out against Ndebe's admission.

Keith Sikes is the very antithesis of a high-powered public health official. The one-time veterinarian, nearing the end of his career, had made his way up the bureaucratic ladder by doing a decent job without giving offense. Not on AIDS, not on much of anything, has he been inclined to exert his authority, a fact that drives some of his subordinates around the bend.

If you are looking for a natural-born conciliator, though, Keith Sikes is your man. He was, providentially, a south

Georgian and so, presumably, more acceptable to Ocilla. For several months he had been kept up to date on Ocilla's school situation in conversations with Lynn Feldman, the district's health officer, but had not forced himself on the town, choosing instead to wait for an invitation. Sikes came to Ocilla knowing what he wanted to accomplish—get the three children back in school—and knowing also how little room he had for maneuver. "I was there to serve them," Sikes makes plain. "They let me know they had their autonomy."

Sikes and his colleagues—Adele Franks, an epidemiologist on loan to the state agency from the CDC, and Elfreda Stanley, a black nurse-epidemiologist—gave Ocilla's elite (and, in a separate meeting, the teachers in the Irwin County schools) a crash course in AIDS. Carefully, they explained why the three children who had been kept out of school posed no threat to their classmates. School officials urged a widespread regime of AIDS testing, but Sikes and Franks argued against this, emphasizing instead the importance of educating Ocilla about AIDS.

The discussions remained generally civil, as the school board members struggled to keep their feelings in check. Emory Walters didn't trouble to hide his anger or his disbelief at what the scientists were saying; the others, Sikes remembers, "looked to be involved in serious soul-searching."

What the white Ocilla leaders wanted was assurance. "We have no guarantees from any source that the boy [Ndebe] definitely cannot transmit the disease, or that he is not a carrier," Superintendent Gentry complained, in a story in the *Ocilla Star* that appeared the day of Sikes's presentation. When Gentry and Sikes happened upon two students, one of whom had cut himself on a rock and then accidentally smeared some of the blood on his friend, the superintendent saw all his fears vindicated. "Dr. Sikes, that's a daily occurrence in a school. What if the boy who cut himself had AIDS?"

Sikes urged the school board to readmit the three children and to develop an AIDS education program. But he said little, either to the school board or, in a separate report, to his boss, Public Health Director James Alley, about the larger implications of what Elfreda Stanley had unearthed during some disturbing discussions in black Ocilla. In addition to the reported cases of AIDS, Stanley discovered anecdotal evidence of several cases of AIDS-related complex (ARC); and the rumors of "widespread drug use and sexual promiscuity," mentioned by the state team in its report, meant that more AIDS cases were likely. As the report noted: "Ocilla may be at high risk of a continuing epidemic of AIDS and ARC."

More disturbing yet, the causes of the spread of AIDS in Ocilla—the Belle Glade connection, sexual promiscuity, and drugs—were not confined to Ocilla. They applied to life throughout much of south Georgia and suggested that the incidence of AIDS in the region might have been grossly underreported.

Ocilla, panicking about children who did not have AIDS, needed to refocus its energies, to guide the behavior of its adult citizens in the face of mounting numbers of residents who did have AIDS. And the state of Georgia needed to be a much better data-gatherer and educator. That is what Keith Sikes might well have concluded, but Sikes is not inclined to sound an alarm. The epidemiologist's report minimized the issue by confining it to the schoolchildren of one small town.

Keith Sikes's visit turned out to be the catalyst for Ndebe's return to school, but under very special terms. It is fitting in a town prone to frequent biblical references that the resolution was perversely Solomonic: the boy would be allowed back— but only if he submitted to monthly AIDS testing and only if he stayed away from his home, continuing to live with his grandmother.

The idea was to make other parents feel more secure, school officials explained, but it seemed cynical to Marcella Jackson, who was advised that she could secretly visit her son on weekends. This was a face-saving measure for the school board, and one that inflicted real pain on her family, but she didn't have much choice. A court battle could take many months and, although the fledgling NAACP chapter had volunteered its assistance, would severely strain the delicate fabric of relations between black and white Ocilla.

At the school board's March 11 meeting, the decision was announced: two days later, Ndebe and the Brockington youngsters, who had remained with their grandmother after the death of their mother, would return to school. Bob Ensley, the Justice Department's Community Relations Service staffer, lauded the outcome as "very positive." Almost as soon as Ensley had arrived in Ocilla, in early March, he had abandoned the inquiry into possible discrimination that had brought him there— the claim was baseless, he concluded, without even talking to Marcella Jackson. Days later, the investigator who had become the invisible federal presence left town.

On Thursday, March 13, reporters from all over Georgia and from the wire services were swarming over a town so inbred that a single stranger walking down the main street attracts notice. This was Georgia's first controversy over AIDS in the schools, and the reporters were having a field day. They invaded the county health center, bombarding genteel Ellen Paulk with questions. "It got to the point where I was forced to be rude," she shyly admits.

School officials, who damned the media as the cause of their problems, were downright hostile. When an Atlanta TV crew, which had brought its "Mobile Live-Eye Van" to the scene, asked Principal Allen Smith to use the school's telephone hookup, the principal not only refused but urged the school's neighbors to do likewise. Superintendent Rudene Gentry emerged from his office to accuse David Beasley from the *Atlanta Constitution* of lying about Ndebe's being made to live with his grandmother— even though this precise stipulation had appeared in the school board's minutes and in the *Ocilla Star* on the same day.

It was as if the school superintendent, like others in the town who invented a fairy-tale history for curious outsiders, was try- ing simultaneously to maintain two kinds of truth about Ocilla. One kind could safely be told to townspeople in the local news- paper, which aimed, in the words of its editor, Bill Bradford, at "portraying Ocilla as a community of love and progress," and which had tried to "ease things through" on AIDS. The other kind was a spiffed-up version of reality, denuded of possible embarrassments, to be retailed elsewhere.

If the reporters anticipated a confrontation, they were dis- appointed. Ndebe slipped undetected into the school building and returned to the first-grade class he had last seen in November. While his teacher had done a lot of soul-searching about whether to stay on, and her husband, the high school principal, came close to making her quit, she was at her desk that morning. Only one parent kept his child home that day, and he claimed that the reason was a dental appointment. One of the fathers who, back in January, had been loud in his demands that the school board keep Ndebe out of school, maintained a vigil in his pickup truck, which he parked across the street from the school; the only thing he accomplished that entire day was watching and waiting.

"I can't believe you all did this," another disgruntled father told Emory Walters, as he reluctantly brought his child to school, but no organized opposition arose. It was not long before life in Ocilla resumed its usual tranquil rhythms, even as the judgment of the school officials that divided a family remained intact, accepted by Ocilla officials as a fair price to insure that tranquility.

Ocilla has reinvented its recent history, not only for outsiders but—since memories are short—for itself as well, turning the episode into a parable that vindicates the community's way of life. Ndebe was home for only a few weeks, it is said; he was never denied a tutor; he was never forced to live with his grandmother. "Our community handled AIDS as a God-fearing community," says Emory Walters, "with intelligence, courage and sophistication."

As Ocilla tries to bury its past, something else seems to have been buried too. Here, as in other communities that had to change their behavior toward people with AIDS without going through the harder process of changing their minds, the instinctive response to the troublesome topic is reticent and defensive. White Ocilla is convinced it was right, but knows that others disagree—knows, too, that on this issue it cannot live entirely by its own rules. In a deep sense, nothing about AIDS has been resolved in Ocilla, nothing realized, nothing reconciled. Everything is held in, pinched and constricted. Consequently,

156

the truth is not broadcast—as it is in Swansea, for instance, where all, including the tempests, is open to inspection—but is buried like the fragments some archaeologist must later patiently paste together. Tales are created, "characterized by a deep-seated reluctance to face up to the truth and [an aggressive orientation] toward hiding the truth."[2]

In the years since Ndebe returned to school and the reporters went away, the reality of AIDS has become much more familiar in Ocilla. Townspeople remain unhappy about what AIDS has done to their community's reputation—they are tired, says school board member Alphonso Owens, of being told "Oh, you're from the town that has AIDS"—but in modest ways they have tried to do something about the situation. Anonymous tests for AIDS are now available in a neighboring town, along with counseling. Although the hope is to inform infected people about their condition, there is understandable skepticism about just how secret the test results will be.

Lynn Feldman, the district health officer, has been organizing AIDS education sessions in schools and hospitals throughout south Georgia. While a unit on AIDS has been incorporated into the high school curriculum, it is of uncertain value since parents, who were allowed to edit the materials, emphasized chastity and removed all references to condoms.

These efforts are unlikely to be enough. In this poor town in a poor state, where jobs are few and futures uncertain, sex will continue to be easy, and adolescents, white and black, will continue to turn to drugs—which spells more AIDS cases. Ocilla is one part of small-town America that now faces big-city problems without big-city know-how.

School Superintendent Gentry has continued to root out Ocilla's AIDS cases with a religious zeal. By 1988, the number was in double digits—startling in a town of 3,400, and wholly out of line with official state figures, which identify only twenty-five AIDS cases in a twenty-four-county swath of south Georgia. Thus far, all the AIDS victims have been black.

With each new rumor, Gentry is on the scene, making sure that any school-aged children in the family are tested repeatedly. Now, however, these children remain in school until the test results are in. Testing has become a ritual in Ocilla; like storytelling, it is a way to mask what is really happening. The superintendent defends what amounts to a compulsory AIDS testing regime as "good for the family, good for the kids, and good for the community," and the Georgia Board of Education apparently agrees. In July 1987, rejecting the CDC recommendations, the state board authorized school districts to carry out widespread and repeated testing of students, teachers, and other employees suspected of having AIDS.

Where Ocilla and the state—indeed, Ocilla and much of the rest of the country—part company, though, is in their response to children with AIDS. Georgia's state officials would keep them in school, and a 1987 statewide poll shows that, by a plurality of forty-nine to thirty-five percent, Georgians support that policy. Ocilla school officials state flatly that when children with AIDS do appear—not *if*, they acknowledge, but *when*—they will keep them out. The kinds of controversies that have developed elsewhere in the country over children with AIDS have focused in Ocilla on youngsters who do not even have the virus. And despite visitations from Atlanta—even from Washington, in the guise of the Justice Department's Community Relations Service—outside agencies have not imposed a new Reconstruction. Ocilla endured the embarrassment of unkind attention, and youngsters related to people with AIDS now remain in school. But with the officials and the media long gone, Ocilla has otherwise been able to honor its irrationalities.

Ocilla is thus unique in the annals of AIDS. Perhaps there was more ignorance and bigotry in Ocilla than in other towns that, at about the same time, learned to live with the reality of AIDS in schools. What happened in Ocilla was also due to a powerful distrust of science—a sense that, as school attorney Emory Walters puts it, the scientists have chosen sides, that they are "defensive of people with AIDS."

Most importantly, the people of Ocilla made such extreme evaluations about risk because of the perverse meaning they attached to the idea of community. This was no popular democracy at work, but a town where the rights of individuals, particularly black individuals, didn't count for much. The very idea that race had anything to do with the way Marcella Jackson was treated is dismissed as part of reporter David Beasley's mischief making. Edgar Anderson, who talked about bringing a lawsuit, is also given the back-of-the-hand treatment. "That little NAACP leader was simply trying to butter his own bread," says Rudene Gentry.

Yet it was the whites in Ocilla who defined and defended the community, who could say so readily that the majority must come first. And that, inevitably, meant keeping Ndebe out of school—out of sight, even, at his grandmother's. Vernon Walters and Rudene Gentry might have persuaded the town to do things differently if they themselves had a different outlook, but their very standing among Ocilla's leading citizens meant that their beliefs coincided naturally with those of their neighbors; someone with the values of Swansea's Jack McCarthy could not have survived here. It is impressive that Marcella Jackson could even conceive of protesting what was happening to her in Ocilla, and easy to understand why Grace Brockington's mother could not.

Ocilla could scarcely have acted otherwise while remaining Ocilla: that is the shadow side of a closed community. But the deeper irony is that the Manichean view of the world, the determination to describe oneself as good and to wall oneself off from the evil others, that characterizes Ocilla's response to AIDS, also threatens to destroy the community. As the epidemic courses through Ocilla, the ties of common enemy and common travail will unravel, with neighbor set against neighbor, compassion replaced by the techniques of control.

For Grace Brockington's children, and for Ndebe Jackson, the AIDS crisis in Ocilla is a fact of daily life. The Brockington youngsters still live with their grandmother and are tested for AIDS every three months. "I told my mother, you don't have to let them," Ethel Bird says, "but she goes along with it." The children have suffered from the experience, says Mrs. Bird. "They hate being singled out. My niece used to be friendly with a white girl in town, until her parents forbade their daughter to spend time with the daughter of someone who died of AIDS."

It is Marcella Jackson who, in the minds of the townspeople of Ocilla, embodies the controversy over AIDS. For many months after her son Ndebe returned to school, she was shunned as an untouchable. She went looking for work, but no one would hire her, and she is sure she knows why. The cashier in the local grocery store dropped her change into her hand, coin by coin, from a height of eight or ten inches. Yet as one year faded into the next, people began coming around to her house. "They started treating me as if nothing happened," Mrs. Jackson says. She and her husband, who stayed out of the picture during the troubles and who is also out of work, have had to survive on his $177 monthly unemployment check. The reality, which Marcella has come to accept, is that they cannot make a life for themselves in Ocilla.

Marcella Jackson is a survivor who has kept herself together by burying her feelings, a woman who is afraid to cry, for "If I ever got started that would be it. I could never stop." Her worst days of fear are behind her, and she no longer dreams of crosses burning on her front lawn. What keeps her going is the conviction that "everything happens for a reason. I'm just waiting to find what the reason is." It is hard, though, for her not to feel bitter about her wrecked life. "God and I aren't so close any more."

Ndebe continues to live with his grandmother and, until school let out in June 1986, attended classes in Ocilla without incident. During that summer, though, his grandmother moved to Fitzgerald, and Ndebe was enrolled in the Ben Hill County schools.

Ndebe's sister has adjusted to living with her grandmother since it is almost the only life she has known, but it has been a hard life for the boy. Although he sees his mother almost every day, he does not really understand why he cannot come home, and the separation has marked him. In 1987, Ndebe, who used to do well in school, began doing poorly; he sometimes picked fights; and he took things that didn't belong to him. Marcella Jackson feels guilty for the harm he has suffered and worries that he is "moving in the wrong direction." She wants her son home. But she doesn't want to exhume the passions of the past.

In August 1987, Marcella Jackson sadly watched TV reports

of an arsonist's fire that destroyed the home of the Ray family in Arcadia, Florida; against fierce opposition, the Rays had insisted that their HIV-infected sons attend public school. "I thought to myself, that's what would have happened to me, if I had pushed."

Rudene Gentry isn't sure what would transpire if Mrs. Jackson tried to enroll her son in the Irwin County schools once again. "After all the fuss Marcella made, I would have to be convinced that she's doing this for the good of the child, not the publicity." The idea that something as simple as maternal love might motivate Marcella Jackson seems not to have crossed the superintendent's mind.

"CLEAR AND PRESENT DANGER": FLETCHERS CROSSING

My life closed twice before its close;
It yet remains to see
If immortality unveil
A third event to me.
                    Emily Dickinson

From the moment fifteen-year-old Marcus Robinson stepped off the plane in the early spring of 1985, he was out of place in the slow-moving Southern town of Fletchers Crossing.* Robinson was very black and very tall, almost six feet, and at 120 pounds he looked painfully thin. His skin was pockmarked with acne; his teeth had not been well cared for.

What was most remarkable, at least for Fletchers Crossing, was how Marcus carried himself. He was dressed to kill. He wore an earring and had long, manicured fingernails, sometimes coated with red polish; he curled his eyelashes; when he walked, he seemed almost to flutter. Marcus didn't talk about being gay. Indeed, when asked directly, he would often strongly

---

*The sensitive materials in this chapter are partly drawn from sealed juvenile court records. Access was allowed on the condition that real names of characters and locales not be used. In addition, to preserve the privacy of Marcus Robinson, certain details have been altered, and even events now part of the public record are not identified as such.

deny it. But in a tradition-bound community where homosexuality was barely discussed and less tolerated, what Marcus said
didn't matter. His appearance spoke for him.

Marcus Robinson had been sent to Fletchers Crossing from
Philadelphia, shipped off like a package by a woman known to
him most of his life as his mother. He was to live with his elderly
aunt and uncle because he had been running wild in city streets.
Perhaps spending some time with Aunt Bess, known in the
family as the praying aunt in acknowledgment of her devout-
ness, would straighten him out.

But no one had consulted Marcus about this plan. From almost the instant he arrived, he wanted to escape from Fletchers
Crossing. He began to misbehave—minor league stuff, really,
but noticeable—in hope that he would be sent back to Philadelphia. Marcus had miscalculated badly; what he attracted was
the attention of the authorities. He was removed from the home
of his aunt and uncle, who simply gave up on him, and made a
ward of the state. Partly because of his behavior, partly because
of his apparent gayness, he was placed in a mental hospital for a
month's observation. There, he was tested for AIDS—"just in
case," the records say. The test results showed that Marcus
Robinson, although to all appearances in good physical health,
carried the deadly virus.

Now the public officials in Fletchers Crossing were obliged to
deal with a problem that was truly novel: this was the first time
any community is known to have assumed responsibility for a
boy infected with the AIDS virus through homosexual contact.
And because Marcus was a ward of the state, responsibility ex-
tended not only to determining whether he would be permitted
to stay in school but also to managing the intimate circumstances of his life.

The Centers for Disease Control reports that, as of September, 1988, 1,445 youngsters under the age of nineteen—965
under the age of five—had contracted AIDS. The numbers
have more than doubled in a year. Other experts estimate the
true incidence at 3,000 and project 20,000 cases by 1991. Some
developed the disease through transfusions of tainted blood or

the blood clotting factor that hemophiliacs depend on. Most are the offspring of mothers who transmitted the disease *in utero*.

When moralizers blame people with AIDS for their condition, they exempt children: in the calculus of blameworthiness, children are innocent victims. But a gay teenager with AIDS becomes a double source of fear and loathing, because of both his sexual preference and his disease. He also presents a whole new universe of legitimate concerns. As a homosexual, he typically finds himself outside of ordinary high school social life, and casual sex is the easiest way to make contact. The possibility that a sexually rambunctious teenager—an adolescent, with all the impulsiveness of the young—will transmit the disease adds a very real dimension of risk not comprehended by the CDC's guidelines to school officials for handling AIDS.

In June 1987, a fourteen-year-old boy with the AIDS virus was briefly quarantined by state health officials in a Pensacola, Florida, mental ward. The teenager, a runaway, had been sexually active and was drawn into a child pornography ring. That same month, Surgeon General C. Everett Koop told a congressional committee that teenagers might well become the next group to be caught up in the AIDS epidemic. "Teenagers often consider themselves immortal," Koop said. They are prone to dismiss the warnings of adults, to experiment with sex and drugs. Although only 291 teenagers were recorded as having AIDS as of September 1988, that figure is deceptively low: the long latency period of AIDS means that many of the 15,000 known cases in their twenties became infected as teenagers.

In Fletchers Crossing, none of this was familiar to state and local officials, social workers, probation officers, and educators who charted the next steps in Marcus Robinson's life. They were very much on their own. This story is partly—but only partly—about bureaucrats who gave up on a tough case, whose only interest was ridding themselves of their burden by putting him in jail, in a locked mental hospital ward, or on a bus bound for Philadelphia. It is also about public officials who treated their responsibilities to a runaway adolescent as a calling. Above all, it is an account of a boy learning to manage a spoiled identity[1]—a

boy whose personal history gives the lie to the adage that there
are no second acts in American lives.

The relatively progressive history of the southern state in
which Fletchers Crossing is situated helps to explain why
Marcus Robinson was not, in fact, put on a bus, banishing the
problem along with the child. Though the state has not developed a sophisticated AIDS program—it relies entirely on federal funds for its limited efforts at AIDS education—it is a
regional leader in providing other social services. And while
its leading politicians include some of the nation's most vol-
uble proponents of quarantining those with the AIDS virus, the
governor's office—and hence the state's administrative machinery—has been in moderate hands for most of the past
quarter-century.

Several cities in the state can make a plausible claim to cos-
mopolitanism, and several have enjoyed the boom times that
have come to the New South. But Fletchers Crossing, a politically conservative community in the heart of the Bible Belt,
is not among them. Although the drowsy city of 30,000, situated in Oakley County, is not without its antebellum charm,
it also has more than its share of unemployment and boarded-
up downtown stores. Blacks remain concentrated in Fletchers
Crossing, but many whites have moved to surrounding suburban developments, with their shopping malls and ranch-style
homes. This familiar racial pattern is reflected in the county-
wide public school system. Fletchers Crossing High is three-
quarters black, while the three Oakley County high schools are
almost entirely white.

Manufacturers of clothing and auto parts, as well as tobacco
farms, are major employers in Oakley County, but the biggest
source of income is several nearby military bases. Even though
residents sometimes imagine themselves to be social innocents
lost in time, the presence of large numbers of servicemen means
that the community is not insulated from the contemporary social problems of the outside world, including AIDS. Four of

the seven AIDS cases reported in Oakley County were among whites.

Because the woman who raised him couldn't figure out what else to do, Marcus Robinson landed in this faraway and parochial place. Until then, his Philadelphia neighborhood had been all he knew. He had done well in elementary school—with an IQ of 117, he had natural talent—and he had never been in trouble with the law. The woman who raised him felt more comfortable treating him like her little girl—she taught him knitting, crocheting, and cooking—and when he was growing up, most of his friends were girls. But as he approached puberty, Marcus started hanging around with the boys on the block. His schoolwork began slipping as he stayed out later and later. "I never saw fifth period," he recalls.

"I got beatings for staying out," says Marcus, but that didn't keep him home. "Mom had no control over me," he acknowledges. A spiteful neighbor informed Marcus that the woman he called "Mom" wasn't his real mother, that his real mother had died from a drug overdose and Mom was really his aunt. "I got nosey and found the death certificate. I said to her: 'You ain't my mother. You can't tell me what to do.'" Marcus was ten years old at the time.

When Marcus was thirteen, his aunt petitioned the court to have him declared an uncontrollable child. "We sat together in court, my mom and I, the judge reading the case," Marcus remembers. "My mom started crying, I did too. I was hurting. 'We're going to have to take him away from you,' the judge said. After the hearing was over, I was waiting alone in a room for them to take me when I saw the open door and ran home." Two years and many incidents later, there was no reprieve: Marcus was on his way South.

Back in fifth grade, Marcus first had sex with a boy. "I was shocked then," he remembers. "I went on like nothing had ever happened. . . . My mom had told me that homosexuals are bad people, and so I thought this means I'm bad."

With the onset of puberty, Marcus began having "fun times" regularly with the boys on the block. For a little while, he had an eighteen-year-old boyfriend named Jeff. "With Jeff, it wasn't wrong, just not all right." Then there were lots of others, men he would pick up at a neighborhood park. "I'd stay out all night, start walking around, get into something with some one, come home. I never thought much about it. That's what I was there for, I thought."

Some of this Marcus set down in his diary, which was found by his aunt. "The sex is one reason I was sent away from Philadelphia," Marcus says. "Philadelphia was just too fast."

Marcus Robinson was used to the freedom of the streets, but what he found in Fletchers Crossing was a tradition-minded, God-fearing family. The three daughters in the household had been brought up to say "yes, ma'am." His aunt took him to her Baptist church—she prayed over him regularly, she later told the social workers—but religion didn't take.

"We disagreed about everything," says Marcus. He was yearning to return to Philadelphia and, when his aunt announced she would not take him back, he took off. In June 1985, Marcus appeared in juvenile court for the first time, on charges of being a runaway. The judge declared him legally "undisciplined." If Marcus's "Mom" in Philadelphia had actually been his real mother, he could indeed have been sent back. The judge learned, however, that she was not even his legal guardian and so had no obligation to care for him.

The news that he wasn't being returned to Philadelphia was devastating to the teenager. He tried to kill himself by taking an overdose of sleeping pills. When that failed, he plotted his next escape and, three months later, was back in court, again as a runaway. This time, he was locked up for seventy-two hours in the detention center that serves as a holding tank for juveniles. Once again, his relatives up North would have nothing to do with him.

Marcus Robinson was confronted during the months to come with revelation piled on revelation—about his family's lack of concern, about the enmity he evoked in others, eventually about his own mortality. Sometimes he acted badly, sometimes outrageously. How else might a teenager be expected to respond? Sometimes he had help from those around him. More often he had only their frowning judgments.

For the rest of his stay in Fletchers Crossing, Marcus was ringed by grownups with varying claims to professional status and varying bureaucratic authority, whose judgments determined the character of his life. There was Jerry Moran, his mental health worker and the one person to whom he opened up. There was also his doctor, Jonah Atlas, who styled himself a hip liberal and who matter-of-factly told Marcus he was going to die. And there were the two officials who battled over his fate: Jim Parsons, the caseworker with the county social services agency, and Ray Aventi, the court counselor.

Parsons, a marine veteran, had served on the Fletchers Crossing police force before getting his social work degree and starting to work with juveniles in trouble. He puts in long days worrying about his boys, keeping tabs on the most minute details of their lives, checking with school officials for truancy, combing the streets in search of youngsters violating parole by staying out too late. Blacks fascinate Jim Parsons; his hobby is reading black history and black sociology. Homosexuals make him uneasy, start him telling off-color jokes.

The paperwork and pussyfooting that go with the bureaucratic life frustrate Parsons. "If you're not going to do the job," he says, "you should get out of the way and leave room for someone who will." What he gives is tough love. What he wants in return, most of all, is obedience. "If the rules are broken, there has to be some punishment," says Parsons. "Otherwise, the kids figure they can do whatever they want." For him, the line between the police work he used to do and his current job as a social worker is exceedingly fine. His approach sometimes succeeds with the typical juvenile in trouble, the car thief or the boy with too-ready fists; for someone like Marcus, though, it makes less sense.

Ray Aventi, the court counselor who also saw Marcus Robinson regularly, is a gentler sort. He has chaired Oakley County's Children and Youth Council for nine years—a plaque acknowledging his service hangs on the wall of his office—and he sees himself as an advocate for the children whose lives he monitors. In Aventi's book, rules decidedly come in second to what is best for teenagers in trouble. This attitude put him directly at odds with Parsons, whom he describes as a friend, when the two struggled to design a plan of action that made sense for both Marcus and the community. Their problems were compounded by the need to maintain absolute secrecy: if word ever leaked out, it was feared, Fletchers Crossing would blow up.

When Marcus promised to stay put, the runaway petition was dismissed in September 1985. But during the succeeding months, he was charged with a series of petty crimes. In November, he was accused of stealing a check for $15.36 and of "carrying a deadly weapon, to wit, a case cutter"—a tool for opening boxes. On New Year's Eve 1985, he pleaded guilty and was placed on a year's probation. If he was off the streets at 8:00 o'clock weekdays, 9:00 o'clock weekends, and otherwise obeyed the rules, the court declared, the slate would be wiped clean. Yet only three weeks later, he was in trouble again. He broke into a 1982 Oldsmobile Cutlass and stole a fake pearl necklace, valued at $20, which he mailed to a girlfriend in Philadelphia.

This time, Marcus was classified a delinquent and made a ward of the court. In February 1986, he was placed in an "attention home," a halfway house for juveniles. Two weeks later, the woman who ran the home complained that Marcus had threatened her and tied up one of the girls living at the home. That same day, he ran away. This is the only item on his record that even hints at violence, and, according to Parsons, Marcus's misbehavior may have amounted to nothing more than horsing around. What was going on in Marcus's mind is revealed in a suicide note he wrote, which specified to the minute—8:39 P.M.—the time of his death. Though nothing came of the suicide threat, the plea for attention was unmistakable.

Back to the detention center went Marcus Robinson, this time under lock and key. Four days later, the director informed Juvenile Judge Robert Smithers, new to the case but destined to play a pivotal part in it, that Marcus was "well-behaved but quiet and withdrawn." One week later, the director reported that Marcus had loosened up, "enjoys playing games and participat-

ing in activities with the other students." Nonetheless, Judge
Smithers had Marcus committed for thirty days to a nearby private psychiatric hospital. The reason, on the record, was to get
a more detailed appraisal of the boy's "emotional problems."
Yet a discussion in court also concerned Marcus's "homosexual
type characteristics," and what was seen as his exotic behavior
may well have prompted the unusual placement.

After what Marcus had been through, the psychiatric hospital where he spent March of 1986 seemed a good place to be.
His proper behavior got him out of the locked facility, earning
the privileges—the chance to smoke, to take meals in the cafeteria instead of the ward—that come with following the rules.
"For each level [of freedom in the institution] I had to write
a little essay, telling them something that I learned, like, 'I
learned leadership.' I would use an example of one of the
people I'd helped to get *their* levels by making sure they didn't
mess up." The one thing he hated was the group counseling sessions. "I ain't gonna talk," he'd say. "I don't have any problems."

The hospital records portray Marcus as a "rather slender,
somewhat effeminate boy," who was "nicely dressed" and "spoke
readily in a rather sophisticated way." His psychological evaluation showed him to be "unusually self-deprecating, vulnerable
and feeling defenseless. This can signify an anxious plea for
help . . . he feels misunderstood."

While hospitalized, Marcus Robinson vehemently denied
ever having had any sexual relations, homosexual or heterosexual. But the hospital psychiatrist decided to "check him for aids
[sic] just in case there has been some homosexual experience."
When the test results show that Marcus carried the AIDS virus,
he became—instantly—a pariah. The psychiatric facility wanted
him out immediately. On March 27, with no other placement
available in Oakley County, Marcus was dumped into a Fletchers
Crossing boarding house, occupied mostly by derelicts, which
agreed to accept him only because one of the other residents
had AIDS.

At the boarding house, reports accused Marcus of curfew
violations, and charges were made, but never pressed, that he
tried to steal a billfold. The man who ran the boarding house

"kept hitting on me," Marcus remembers. In June 1986, clinically depressed, he was sent to the psychiatric ward of the Oakley County Hospital for observation.

Marcus was informed that he had the AIDS virus as soon as the test results were available, yet for many months he had no clear sense of the implications of his condition. He would plead to his psychologist, Jerry Moran, whom he began seeing in April: "Please tell me exactly what is going on." Yet how does one get across in simple English the complex idea of having a virus that may, but need not, assume deadly form, a virus that someone can spread to others even while remaining perfectly healthy himself? How does one explain such a thing to a young man who, despite his personal history, is still inclined to deny that he has ever had sex and who, like other teenagers, still imagines he will live forever?

These difficult questions were answered in the most simplistic of ways by Marcus's doctor, Jonah Atlas. In December 1986, at the request of the officials working with Marcus, Atlas called him into his office. "You are going to die," he said.

This was plainly an overstatement, since it is not yet known whether everyone carrying the AIDS virus will contract the disease. It may partly reflect Atlas's general lack of knowledge about AIDS. Although the oncologist regarded himself as the local expert, and although he spent several hours each week taking his message about the perils of AIDS to schools and companies, this young emigré from New England was laden with misinformation. In a videotape he prepared, Atlas declared that, in Oakley County, the only real risk of AIDS transmission came from sex. Intravenous drugs were a cause of AIDS only in New York City, he claimed—despite abundant data to the contrary. But Dr. Atlas's message of doom was plainly what the anxious caseworkers and bureaucrats in Fletchers Crossing wanted Marcus Robinson to hear. They feared that he was spreading the disease to others and they hoped to scare him celibate.

No reliable information is available on just how much sexual contact Marcus was having, for at different times he told different stories. During his sessions with psychologist Jerry Moran, he initially declared that he found the very idea of homosexuality repugnant and resented Moran for even raising the subject. Yet, as the relationship between the boy and the counselor deepened, Marcus opened up. He claimed to have had sex with a dozen older men known to him only by their first names—all out-of-towners whom he said he had met on the streets of Fletchers Crossing.

During his June stay in the Oakley County Hospital, Marcus told a different story: he had had sex with two teenagers and an adult, he said. Over and over that spring, Moran urged Marcus to stop having sex. The boy would promise to abstain only to confess later to some new encounter. Finally, after his release from the county hospital in July, Marcus announced he was done with sex. Moran believed that his message had gotten across. Jim Parsons was unconvinced.

In July 1986, Marcus Robinson was placed in the home of Grace and Arthur Lamont. Mrs. Lamont, a native of the Caribbean who came to this country as a young woman, is an institution in Fletchers Crossing. Now in her sixties, this indomitable black woman has taken in the hardest cases—a six-year-old child who is blind, retarded, and wheelchair-bound; an eighteen-year-old who is just a judge's whim away from prison—and given them a home. She is "Mamma," Mrs. Lamont proudly says, to more than twenty boys and several girls who still come back to see her during holidays. Uneducated, deeply religious, a commanding presence in her own home, Mrs. Lamont brooks no nonsense from her charges. If they don't behave, back they go into the lockup or the streets.

Because her modest home had failed a safety inspection, Mrs. Lamont was no longer permitted to care for foster children, but she could still board youngsters who had gotten into trouble with the law. With no one else willing to accept Marcus, Parsons turned to her. When Mrs. Lamont learned that the boy had been infected with the AIDS virus, she was reluctant to have him in her household. "Why are you giving me your trash?" she asked Parsons angrily, and agreed to take the boy only after she was assured that he didn't actually have AIDS.

That summer and fall, Marcus Robinson mostly did what he

was told by "Mamma" Lamont, who tried, in her words, to "straighten him out." She admired his talents. "That boy can type anything. He's good at making up poems, stories; he can crochet and knit too. He has the smarts." She spoiled Marcus, she recalled, giving him money to buy the clothing he craved. And Marcus would walk around town to pay the household bills, coming home with the receipts.

Marcus went to school, as he had done regularly since arriving in Fletchers Crossing, and did well. An earlier academic report had noted that his grades were mostly "A"s and "B"s, and concluded: "Marcus is an above-average student. He is a hard worker. His behavior in class is very good." But sometimes Marcus would cut his last two periods, study hall and Spanish—common enough practice at Fletchers Crossing High, where warm afternoons found almost as many teenagers hanging out as sitting in class. And sometimes he would stay out past the 9:00 P.M. curfew that was a condition of his probation. He would talk for hours on end with his best friend, a classmate nicknamed Fruit Loops, or with a woman in her early twenties, a young mother who lived in a nearby housing project and who became almost a mother to him. Or he would while away time at the fast food places and the game room at the mall.

All this typical teenage behavior proved a trial to Mrs. Lamont, who could not begin to deal with a boy as complex and as different as Marcus Robinson. Marcus chafed under her regime. He kept his room in squalor. Mrs. Lamont had locks installed on her bedroom door because she believed he was stealing money from the house—a charge he denies.

Marcus's effeminate behavior scandalized Mrs. Lamont. "I cut his hair when it started getting girlish. He started hanging around the kitchen, but I told him, 'There ain't no way two women are going to do the cooking in this house.'" One of the "boys," a twenty-year-old who had lived with Mrs. Lamont while Marcus was there, added that he "knew how to fix Marcus—with a baseball bat."

While going through Marcus's personal possessions, Mrs. Lamont came upon the scribbled draft of a love letter, addressed to another boy in Fletchers Crossing and dated June 1986. It is as sweetly evocative and, in the context, as suggestive of impending tragedy as anything a modern Romeo would write.

"So I saw you down on Main Street," the letter begins. "I called a friend and told him how you looked—how cute you are to me, wearing white pants with a gray two-tone shirt. I think you look fantastic. . . . I know you smoke herb, drink beer and champagne. It was love at first sight, and I hope and think so. . . . My heart almost stopped when you waved and said hi. I want you and I love you."

The letter, delivered to Jim Parsons by a furious Grace Lamont, apparently was never sent. Marcus later described it as part of his fantasy life; when confronted, the boy to whom it was addressed denied knowing anything about it. But the notion that a teenage boy who carried the AIDS virus was trying to woo another teenager—was even imagining what it would be like to woo another teenager—symbolized everything that Parsons feared. He turned the letter over to the court counselor Ray Aventi and it became part of Marcus's file.

One day in October, Marcus came home with his undershorts bloody. A few weeks earlier, he had had surgery for rectal abcesses, and bleeding is common after such an operation. But despite that fact, and despite the fact that anal sex would be unbearably painful so soon after surgery, Mrs. Lamont was sure the boy was having sex. She communicated her suspicions to Parsons and wondered aloud how long she would be willing to keep Marcus under her roof. For months, Parsons had been angered by Marcus's casual attitude toward the rules of his continuing probation. He had no place to put the teenager if Mrs. Lamont turned him out. And he fretted that Marcus might contaminate the population—whether with gayness or with AIDS wasn't entirely plain. The tale of the bloody shorts offered one more reason for Parsons to try ridding himself of his problem.

Parsons wanted court counselor Ray Aventi to inform the court that Marcus Robinson had violated the terms of his probation, in hope that the boy would be sent to a state training school, a jail for juveniles. But Aventi refused. The probation violations amounted to nothing more than an occasional late

night out, no reason to send Marcus away. "At training school,"
Aventi said, "they are not prepared to deal with a boy who is gay
and who has been exposed to a disease like AIDS; he'd have
to be isolated there. I did not file the petition." In late November 1986, acting on his own, Parsons filed a motion in Oakley
County Juvenile Court urging that Marcus be sent to training
school.

Oakley's juvenile court chambers do not resemble a courtroom. In what used to be the City Council's meeting room, participants cluster in comfortable armchairs around a T-shaped
table; the judge sits, not above the proceedings, but at the head
of the table. This arrangement matches the character of the
hearings, which are intended not only to do justice but also to
watch out for the adolescent's best interests. It was in these
chambers that Marcus Robinson's case, number 85-R-66, was
heard by Robert Smithers, the judge whose order sending
Marcus to the psychiatric facility in February had led to the discovery that the boy had the AIDS virus.

Judge Smithers has headed the Oakley County juvenile court
since 1982. He comes from an old and distinguished family,
and while he doesn't insist on all the formalities, he leaves no
question about who is in charge. Smithers has a reputation for
acting cautiously: he "calculates each word before he talks,"
Parsons says. And Smithers believes in following the rules, not
bending them to the exigencies of the situation. "The judge
wasn't intimidated by any of the folks, state or local, who got
involved in the proceedings," noted Jerry Moran from the local
mental health department. In a politically charged case, this
may well have been his greatest virtue.

Smithers ordered Parsons and Aventi to embark on a nationwide search for an agency that might be willing to care for the
teenager. What they learned from their inquiries was discourag-
ing: child service agencies wouldn't take on someone infected
with the AIDS virus, and AIDS groups had no experience with
teenagers. Nor was Pennsylvania, Marcus's original home, willing to assume legal responsibility for the teenager.

At this point in the proceedings, the fear that Marcus would spread his lethal disease by having sex became a dominant theme. Parsons argued that Marcus had to be locked up—somewhere—because, as he told Judge Smithers, the teenager was "a clear and present danger to the juvenile population in this community." But Smithers was not ready to be pushed into rash action. Instead, he ordered the Oakley County Mental Health Department director, Martin Sargent, to head a team that would include all representatives of all the social service agencies, state as well as local, with any responsibility for Marcus Robinson's case. The team would construct a collective evaluation and make a recommendation.

In a state where local control is the byword, and bureaucrats from the capital are often regarded as officious meddlers, conscripting the state agencies was a bold move. The judge's order was greeted in Fletchers Crossing with a mixture of relief and unhappiness. Local officials had exhausted their options and nearly exhausted their funds; the ruling conceivably meant that state agencies would now shoulder the burden of the case. But the intrusion of outsiders would inevitably change the character of the proceedings.

"Do you know," Jim Parsons said, rolling his eyes clear up to the ceiling, "one of those people actually asked me what *kind* of gay sex Marcus was having—as if that made a difference!" Since even those with AIDS can practice safe sex, the answer to this question actually does make a difference, if one is trying to decide whether Marcus Robinson poses a threat to anyone. But the question itself bespoke a degree of familiarity with, and acceptance of, homosexuality that was foreign to most of the local contingent.

At a series of court sessions extending over several months, sixteen officials, representing almost as many agencies, talked about how to handle Marcus Robinson. It seemed that the entire state and county social services bureaucracy had gathered to decide the destiny of one boy. Marcus was present throughout the hearings, sitting with Grace Lamont in the spectators' section—"Any moment, I was sure they would send me off to training school," he remembers—while a few feet away the experts were setting the terms and conditions of his life.

In a December 4 report to the court, meant to pull together

all the evidence in the case, County Mental Health Director
Sargent argued for quarantine: "[Marcus Robinson] currently
demonstrates a lack of appropriate social judgment and irresponsible sexual behavior and behavioral problems. His presence in the community represents an immediate danger to
other juveniles and a more appropriate placement should be
made immediately."

These were strong words, intended to force action, but they
were based on surmise not fact. The psychiatric evaluation, on
which the mental health director's statement was supposedly
based, noted that Marcus had recovered remarkably well from
his bout of depression. While Grace Lamont still complained
that the teenager was "disrespectful"—he had, in fact, gotten
into a shoving match with her husband on one occasion—she
was not eager to have him removed from her home. She was
still fond of the boy, she said. Perhaps it was a brief visit in December by Marcus's aunt from Philadelphia that softened her
feelings. "That woman drew away from Marcus like he was poison when she learned that he had AIDS," Mrs. Lamont recalled. Jerry Moran, the therapist who had been seeing Marcus
regularly since April, concluded in a separate report that he is
"coping well." As for the explosive matter of sex, Moran accepted Marcus's word that "he has abstained" for half a year,
and was no longer picking up men on the streets of Fletchers
Crossing.

The subtleties of Marcus's development, the hints of a new
maturity in the face of death, escaped the notice of officials
whose minds were made up by this time. They were responding
not to Marcus the person but to Marcus the case. Each expert
conclusion entered into his burgeoning file was read as evidence for the next conclusion, until the file took on more reality
than the boy himself.

At the mid-December court session that considered Dr.
Sargent's report, local officials offered a series of alternatives,
none workable. Jim Parsons again urged sending Marcus off to
training school. But "He'd be killed there," said Ray Aventi,
who countered by proposing the "structured therapeutic en-
vironment" of a state psychiatric facility. This rather more be-

nign proposal wouldn't work either, though, since Marcus was not mentally ill.

A plainly exasperated Parsons then offered a solution Swiftian in its simplicity: "Why don't we put him on a bus and ship him where he came from?"

"In this state, we do not put children on buses," responded Joan Browning, head of the Family Services Unit of the State Department of Social Services. Judge Smithers just smiled, and that was the end of that idea.

During the hearings, Browning regularly dueled with Parsons, for whom she had no respect. "He doesn't know what he's doing," she said, the professional's ultimate insult. "He's punitive, completely negative in his outlook, always stirring up fusses. He has more than a trace of racism and more than a trace of homophobia. I wouldn't want him near *my* adolescent son." Parsons's visible hostility toward Marcus made Browning angry. "Of course the boy is no angel. But he's a lot less of a behavior problem than most of the kids the juvenile system handles. And when you consider what he has gone through. . . ."

It was Browning, along with the court counselor Ray Aventi, who during the next two months kept the proceedings focused squarely on Marcus Robinson. Browning has the kind of pleasant, no-nonsense style that gets things done in the South. She has worked in the state's Social Services Department for over twenty years and has held her present position since 1978. She sees herself as the professional's professional. "I am not subject to pressures to do anything that I don't think ought to be done. That is my job," she says matter-of-factly.

Browning wasn't naive about the politics of the case. After all, high-ranking local officials, not without influence in the capital, were demanding quarantine, and the object of their concern was not a ready candidate for widespread public sympathy. Yet Browning knew that Judge Smithers was not going to act out of desperation. It was plain from how he was conducting the proceedings that he wouldn't settle for anything other than what he considered appropriate. Browning was secure in her job, for she knew that her boss "wouldn't be pressured into doing anything in a hurry." And her boss knew her very well too: "That's why he asked me to go to court for the department. It makes a difference to have been around for a long time." It was Joan Browning whose intervention ultimately changed the complexion of the Marcus Robinson case.

Meanwhile, matters seemed at a standstill. At the conclusion of the January 7, 1987, hearing, with no solution imminent, Judge Smithers happened to ask Jim Parsons whether anyone at Fletchers Crossing High knew that Marcus had been exposed to the AIDS virus. "No they didn't," said Parsons, "because public health told us early on that school officials had no reason to know."

The judge thought differently, and that afternoon Parsons talked with Principal Larry Prince. The very next day, Marcus Robinson was out of school.

As the negotiating about his future went on around him, Marcus had remained a generally good student. During the fall of 1986, he had missed several weeks of classes when he was hospitalized for rectal surgery. But he was "catching up and making the effort to stay up," said Marcus's algebra teacher in a December report. He was "weak in some areas of grammar but writes fairly well and seems to enjoy writing," said his English teacher. Nor was there any hint that Marcus was a behavior problem.

That fall, ahead of almost every other county in the state, the Oakley County Board of Education had gone on record with an AIDS policy statement. Dr. Atlas, the local oncologist who had made AIDS his specialty, felt that it was important for the schools to confront AIDS calmly, rather than deal with the issue in the midst of the crisis an actual case would provoke.

Atlas knew about Marcus's condition; he had already operated on the boy and, in December, would pronounce his premature death sentence. But maintaining the secrecy that medical ethics prescribes, the doctor said nothing about his patient. Together with a pediatrician who was a school board member, he drafted a policy statement modeled after the Centers for Disease Control guidelines. In November, the guidelines were approved without controversy. Yet the first time the school system was faced with a real AIDS case, the procedures established by the guidelines were sidestepped.

The timing of Marcus's "dropping out" was purely coincidental, Principal Larry Prince insisted. Prince began teaching in the Oakley County schools in the 1950s, when they were legally segregated; he is an adroit bureaucratic politician who is now the desegregated system's top-ranking black professional. The way Prince tells it, Marcus had been cutting classes regularly. On the afternoon of January 8, he had been brought to the office of the assistant principal, Wilson Walker, who handles the discipline problems, by a teacher who saw the boy hanging around the corridors. When given a choice of returning to class or quitting school, Marcus signed his dropout papers and walked out the door. As Walker, another longtime black administrator, wrote in a memo to Parsons: "I informed [Marcus Robinson] that if he was not going to class, that he should withdraw from school. He then went to guidance and filled out withdrawal papers."

"Minutes earlier," says Prince, "I had taken the call from Parsons about Marcus's condition. I just happened to be walking down the hall when I saw my assistant. He was talking to the boy about his leaving school. 'You make sure that he *wants* to drop out, that we aren't forcing him out,' I said. 'Otherwise it sure looks bad for us.' Anyone with AIDS has a legal right to be in school; I didn't want a discrimination suit."

But others in Fletchers Crossing contradict the principal's version of events. Both Jim Parsons and Ray Aventi, who have been dealing with Prince and Walker for years, believe that the educators used Marcus's absences as an excuse to get rid of him. Fear of AIDS and fear of controversy were the real reasons, they say. "Those class cuts are just an 'out' in the rules," says Aventi. "They're going to cover themselves." The actual chronology of events gives cause for such skepticism. According to Parson's case records, Marcus Robinson was not called into the assistant principal's office the same day as Parson's conversation. The encounter took place a day later, time enough for the two administrators to plan their strategy.

The lives of bureaucrats are filled with missions unaccomplished, hopes thwarted. Every once in a while, though, they accomplish wonders—or at least set wonders in motion. That is

what happened in the case of Marcus Robinson. The cumber-
some social services machinery, prodded by the court, found a
placement that worked, and so made a new life possible. It
acted with the secrecy, amazingly maintained, that in this instance may have been vital to success.

In February 1987, however, no one was talking about miracles.
The hearings had dragged on for months with no resolution in
sight, and Marcus retreated deeper into his shell. Although his
being pressured to drop out of school upset him, Marcus hadn't
argued with the school officials because he knew that he would
shortly be leaving Fletchers Crossing. But increasingly he felt
shut out of everything that was being done in his name.

One placement looked promising: Caring for Kids, a univer-
sity-affiliated agency based in Lorraine, a city several hundred
miles away, which had considerable experience in placing hard-
to-settle youngsters. Marcus had visited with the agency staff
one January weekend, then spent some time with his prospec-
tive foster family. He met the friends of the family, shopped at
the flea market, rode around the town—even went to church.
The weekend made him ecstatic. "They're a real family," he told
Parsons, who had driven him to Lorraine. "They do things together." As soon as he was back in Fletchers Crossing, Marcus
wrote the agency a letter: "I can't wait to come back," he
declared.

In Lorraine, though, things were by no means settled. As the
winter rolled on with no decision about Marcus, Terry Breen,
the staff psychologist at Caring for Kids who had volunteered
to work with him, was growing impatient. The young professional from Colorado understood troubled teenagers well, for
he had been a resident counselor in a group-care home. When
the possibility of taking Marcus had initially been broached in
late December, the agency staff had told lots of AIDS jokes, gal-
lows humor for uneasy professionals. But Breen was not fazed
by Marcus's history or his disease. "If we're dealing with youngsters that others won't take," he said, "we should at least try,"
and his colleagues went along.

Yet there still remained people to convince—most importantly, a foster parent—as well as mountains of paperwork to

get through and mountains of resistance to overcome. Lorraine had few likely foster homes; Carole Walker's just happened to be the right place. As Marcus had said when he visited earlier, the Walkers were a real family. Carole, a preschool teacher in her late forties, and her grown daughter, who trained salespeople for a department store chain, lived in a well-kept two-story frame house, all plants and family photos, in a solidly working-class black neighborhood of Lorraine. Carole's son lived down the block with his own family, her mother and sister lived nearby, and everybody on the block regularly dropped in to visit the unofficial mayor of Lorraine.

Staff Psychologist Terry Breen was worried about how Carole Walker would respond to taking in a boy with AIDS. The disease itself wasn't her primary concern, for she had already done her homework. Marcus's past behavior was another matter. As she told Breen, "I'm not nervous about that part. . . . But if he's going to stay with me he will have to be part of the family and follow the rules."

From the first visit, the two hit it off. Marcus began by telling her bits and pieces from his life, then filling in the details. Mrs. Walker had endless questions to ask; she was not inclined to judge, but she wanted to understand. She saw him not as a case but as a person; and he badly needed an adult who would give him attention and affection. "I wanted the challenge," Carole Walker says. "I knew I could win. And I love children. I hope someone would give my children a second chance if they needed it."

After Marcus's initial visit, Mrs. Walker told her family what she was going to do. The conversations weren't easy. "'He has *what?*' my son said, more amazed than asking a question. Then he walked around and walked around some more. Finally, maybe forty-five minutes later, he shook his head and said, 'Mom, you must know what you're doing.'"

Breen lined up a local AIDS support group for Marcus, thus satisfying one concern of Judge Smithers. The critical next step was persuading the board of directors of Caring for Kids to accept responsibility for the teenager. Marcus Robinson was, far and away, the most controversial case in the history of the organization. When the facts were put to the board, they worried about the possibility of bad publicity, which could blow the program out of the water, and about the risk of legal liability. Some board members quoted Scripture to express their antipathy to Marcus's gayness. Others focused on the fact that he was an out-of-stater. "He's introducing AIDS to Lorraine," one participant at the meeting said—a statement that, though inaccurate, reflected widespread local beliefs. So heated were feelings on the board that one member quit when his colleagues voted to take the case. But the majority became excited by the challenge of doing something no one else in the entire country seemed willing to do. The remaining sticking point was admission to the high school, a matter of vital importance to the judge. School officials were reluctant to enroll Marcus, finally agreeing to talk about the matter in a meeting set for mid-March.

All Marcus knew was that there was no news. That led him to slip deeper into a depression. On February 26, 1987, the coldest February 26 on record for Fletchers Crossing, Marcus dressed himself in short shorts and sandals and went parading in the neighborhood. An hour later he came home exhausted. That night, he was admitted to Oakley County General Hospital, where he was diagnosed as an AIDS-related complex (ARC) case. Dr. Atlas feared that Marcus had pneumocystis pneumonia, a common opportunistic infection of AIDS patients, but the tests proved negative.

Marcus's desperation walk changed the equation. With Dr. Atlas unwilling to release the boy from the hospital until a better home could be found for him than the Lamonts, Judge Smithers approved the move to Lorraine even without a firm commitment from the school administrators there. On March 15, Jim Parsons loaded Marcus in his car and, wondering aloud who would reimburse him for the gas and the McDonalds stop, drove him to Lorraine.

"The first time I met Marcus," said Terry Breen, "he reminded me of a pup that had been beaten too much. He was superthin. He spoke in a whisper—you had to put your ear right alongside his mouth to hear him. He answered questions in um-hums and un-unhs. As I watched him with Carole, he started opening up, getting back his confidence. Now you can't stop him from talking. The more Marcus told her, the more Carole said 'I still like you, that's OK,' the more the real Marcus came out, teasing and cracking jokes, sitting up straight and stating his opinions." "That first Saturday morning," Marcus recalls, "I started opening up. I began laughing: 'You're all so crazy, so silly.' I'm still being silly."

Marcus has come home—really, he has found a home. During the summer, the Walkers took a trip to Florida that Marcus couldn't stop talking about. "We saw everything," he says, "St. Augustine and Disneyworld and Jacksonville. Ma"—Marcus calls Carole Walker Ma—"said we could have a quarter any time we were bored, but the only time I got bored is when I had to go to bed." The family has gone fishing too. "Marcus didn't know how to bait a hook but he caught a fish," Mrs. Walker says. And every night, the two of them would walk three miles around the track at the nearby high school.

Carole Walker accepts Marcus's gayness—by now, she knows more about the furtive pleasures of adolescent gay life than most adults—but she urged him to "tone down your act" and he agreed. The nail polish and the earring are history. For hours on end, Marcus talks to Carole, just as he used to talk to the young mother and Fruit Loops in Fletchers Crossing. "You are a part of my family," Carole often tells Marcus, "and there are things that I need you to do as part of the family." That makes him feel wanted. And nothing is held back in their conversations. They embody the thorough sifting of events and feelings, pleasures relived and pains explored, that psychologists can only wish their clients would engage in with those they love. Marcus has learned that he can speak his mind without being punished for all the things that Grace Lamont, Jim Parsons, and his aunt in Philadelphia regard as sinful.

Even sex, the most delicate issue for Marcus to manage in his day-to-day life, can be talked about. "It's not so hard anymore, not to have sex, but I still think a lot about it," he says. "I told Ma about this boy, what he looks like. I could talk to him, but he's going to want to do more than talk—and then I have to make up lies." It is as if, facing death, Marcus has become an innocent again, since it is only by forgetting the many things he knows about the world that he can survive.

Since Marcus has been living in Lorraine, he has not been involved in a single episode that even the most overreaching social worker would regard as a sign of trouble. On the contrary, the Marcus who has emerged is a boy who wants to give—to give back, he says—something of value. Such caregiving instincts were evident in Marcus's behavior at the psychiatric institution in Fletchers Crossing. But there, helping others had an immediate payoff in earning privileges; the change in Lorraine seems more profound and more permanent. Marcus Robinson, safe in a new and loving world, safe too from the pull of his personal history, has in a sense been reborn.

One day, Carole Walker cut herself with a kitchen knife. "An open wound is the one thing we have to be careful with," she reminded Marcus. "I know," the boy replied. "I'll be very careful. I wouldn't want what I have to happen to anyone, especially to you."

Marcus sees the world as an unfair place filled with pain, too few people willing to help others. This is hardly remarkable, in light of the life he has lived. But what is remarkable is that he wants to do something to change all that—particularly when the issue is AIDS. When a man named Frank, who had befriended him in the AIDS support group, was hospitalized with pneumocystis pneumonia, Marcus visited him regularly. "Other people may be scared of AIDS but I'm not. I've got the disease. I can bring something to people who are alone and dying, even if it's just reading a book out loud."

What remained to be negotiated in Lorraine was Marcus Robinson's return to school. The teenager was eager to be back in class, to get on with his life, but it almost proved his undoing. In September 1987, page one headlines in the *Lorraine Gazette* announced that an unnamed high school student with AIDS-related complex was attending Lorraine High. At that moment, it seemed as if an adolescent whose very identity was bound up in his anonymity, and the flight from his past that anonymity represented, might be forced to go public.

The city of Lorraine, in sharp contrast to Fletchers Crossing, represents the New South. The prosperous community of 75,000 includes a sizeable liberal contingent, artisans and professionals drawn by the beauty of the surrounding countryside, as well as a gay community of some size attracted by Lorraine's reputation for tolerance.

But there is no confusing Lorraine with San Francisco: Lorraine remains a Southern city with a solid core of conservative gentry, where a fundamentalist preacher has had the power to dictate the substance of sex education in the public schools. It is also a city where AIDS remains a novelty that has not lost its power to shock. While fourteen AIDS cases had been reported in Lorraine by mid-1987, each case was considered sufficiently newsworthy for the *Gazette* to contact the local hospital, collect the facts, and go to print. When a prominent anesthesiologist died of AIDS during the summer of 1987, the newspaper headlined the fact, despite the man's expressed wish for secrecy. "This was someone who was dealing so closely with the population," says executive editor Pete Johansen—a comment that suggests, erroneously, that patients were therefore at risk— "and people had the right to know." The resulting controversy resembled the stir caused by the national media's handling of Liberace's death, with letterwriters variously decrying the paper's sensationalism and praising its report on "something we need to hear." Two months later, the *Gazette* ran a matter-of-fact account of the life of a gay man with AIDS, and several readers, including one local doctor, angrily demanded to know why the paper was "glorifying homosexuality."

In late March, Caring for Kids psychologist Terry Breen and Marcus Robinson met with John Simonson and Norris Turnbull, the principal and assistant principal at Lorraine High School. Like their counterparts in Fletchers Crossing, the Lorraine educators found a rule that enabled them to keep Marcus out of school, at least temporarily, while ducking the AIDS issue. In Fletchers Crossing, the invoked rule concerned cutting classes; in Lorraine, an attendance rule was the ostensible reason for not admitting him. Marcus had already missed too many days of school, the principals declared.

Deeper fears—about AIDS and race and gayness—underlay the reliance on bureaucratese. When he first heard about Marcus, Simonson remembers saying to himself, "Why me, O Lord?" The principal's daughter was enrolled at the high school, and he momentarily feared for her safety. But she reassured her father somewhat: "I'm not going to catch AIDS," she said, "because I'm not going to do sex or drugs." When the panel of Lorraine medical and educational experts who reviewed Marcus's case early in March pronounced him fit for school, Simonson began to reckon with the possibility that Lorraine might become the first community in the state knowingly to enroll a youngster with the AIDS virus.

What Simonson offered, however, was something less than immediate admission. He first suggested home instruction for a few hours a week, but Breen rejected this as insufficient. Then Simonson proposed slipping the teenager into the "alternative high school," where most of Lorraine's problem children are enrolled. But the head of that school took one look at Marcus, who had come decked out to the meeting, and confided to Breen: "We've had kids like Marcus before—effeminate kids. To be honest with you, he wouldn't last two weeks there." For his part, Breen was anxious for what he called a normal placement, which would allow Marcus to be treated like any other student.

All this made Marcus feel bad—"like I did something wrong," he says, then adds, half-jokingly, "If I'd worn jeans there wouldn't have been any problem." Breen suspected that if he pushed the school officials to the wall, they might give in. Indeed, when the school district privately contacted the state Attorney General's office about Marcus, the word was that, legally, he was entitled to enroll. Yet if he pushed, Breen realized, he might only make Simonson angry; what Marcus needed was friends in high places, not school officials counting on him to fail.

The race factor made the principals particularly resistant to Marcus's cause. A decade and a half earlier, Lorraine High had been legally required to integrate. It was a tense and sometimes violent period. Enrollment dropped by more than half as many white families moved outside city limits. The high school, formerly all white and traditionally regarded as one of the best in the state, became the butt of racist jokes: Congo High, some whites called it. The school, now half black, had slowly regained something of its former status. Neither Simonson, who is white, nor, especially, assistant principal Turnbull, who is black, wanted to do anything that might reopen the racial wounds. "It's a fragile community," says Simonson; and Turnbull, highly sensitive to the reputation earned by blacks, asserts: "We don't need any more trouble from black students." By coincidence, Turnbull's best friend is Larry Prince, the man who had pushed Marcus Robinson out of Fletchers Crossing High School, and Prince had already filled Turnbull's head with horror stories about his former pupil.

Simonson had another worry: since the Lorraine curriculum was different from Fletchers Crossing's, and since Marcus had already missed months of school, beginning classes so late in the year might spell academic suicide. It would make better sense all around, the principal argued, to postpone enrollment until the beginning of the new academic year. Then, Marcus wouldn't stick out; he would be just one among 400 students entering the tenth-through-twelfth-grade school for the first time.

That is where matters were left in the spring. Caring for Kids tried to persuade the administrators of the local Job Training Partnership Act's summer program to arrange a summer job for Marcus, but Elizabeth Day, the program's director, was having none of it. "You've brought in ten teenagers with AIDS from New York," Day said, turning a single case into a plague upon the town. And Day made no secret of her feelings about homosexuals. "I feel sorry for you because you have to work with him," she told Terry Breen. "And I feel terribly sorry for that poor family he's living with. But I don't feel at all sorry for him. He got exactly what he deserves." During the summer of 1987, Marcus stayed home, being tutored in English and algebra by Carole Walker's grown son and daughter, and by Frank, Marcus's friend from the AIDS support group.

It was his third day on the job, Lorraine School Superintendent Sam Hannon ruefully recalls, when the associate superintendent, Tony Boughton, broke the news: a student with ARC was planning to enroll at Lorraine High. Hannon, a Ph.D. from the state university who had worked for several years as a curriculum specialist in the state's education department, had just moved from a neighboring school district. The conservatism of that district, its unwillingness to make educational changes or to raise school taxes, had frustrated him. Lorraine, he believed, had the professional talent and the willingness to spend the money needed to make it one of the best school districts in the state.

Hannon describes himself as a committed professional—"not a good ole boy who got where he was because he knew someone"—and as a good listener, a "people person." The man whose bookshelf prominently features Dale Carnegie's *How to Win Friends and Influence People* had done a considerable amount of hard persuading in his old job: there, several years earlier, a three-year-old girl with herpes enrolled in a class for the profoundly retarded.

Parents of the girl's classmates, frightened that their children would contract the easily spread disease, organized a boycott to press their demand that she be removed from class. After long negotiations, a compromise was arranged: a teacher's aide was assigned full time to monitor the girl's naturally impulsive behavior; during the brief periods when the aide could not be present, the girl was kept in a playpen. Slowly, the other parents put aside their fears and allowed their children to return.

The herpes controversy was Hannon's introduction to the media, and it wasn't pleasant. TV crews tried to get into the preschool classroom, and some reporters played up the plight of a small child confined in a pen, ignoring the rest of the story.

That news slant, says Hannon, made it more difficult to bring everyone together.

AIDS was an even harder question, Hannon thought, "one of the more emotional issues of our times." Associate Superintendent Boughton was anxious to keep Marcus Robinson out. "This will cause all our children to withdraw," he insisted. But Superintendent Hannon wasn't ready to make a decision. Until learning about Marcus, he had given no more than a *Newsweek* reader's fleeting attention to the topic. He talked with local AIDS specialists about the transmission of the disease, and what he was told reassured him that AIDS was not easily spread. However, what Hannon found out from Principal Simonson about Marcus's personal history deeply troubled him.

Here was no Edenic pastoral tale featuring an instantly lovable thirteen-year-old like Mark Hoyle, in Swansea, Massachusetts, a boy whose deepest passion was baseball. Marcus Robinson was a sexually active teenager, entirely capable, to judge from the record, of spreading a deadly disease to unknowing gay classmates.

Several days later, Hannon met with Terry Breen. Marcus had settled into Lorraine and was intent on making a "fresh start," Breen told him. "As long as the boy behaves responsibly and wants a new lease on life," the superintendent replied, "I'm not going to stand in his way. But with the first evidence that he isn't acting up to standards and out he goes."

Simonson spelled out to Marcus precisely what those expectations were. Not only was unsafe sex forbidden; anything that might look like sex, safe or unsafe—anything that might lead to sex—was unacceptable. There was to be no flirting with boys, no dating. Indeed, the principal said—straining the limits of his authority—it would be best not to hang around with the gay crowd, for among teenagers the line between "I like you" and "let's get it on" is exceedingly fine. Simonson was confident that he could keep tabs on Marcus, outside as well as inside school. The dean of boys at Lorraine High, the designated disciplinarian whose door carred a sign reading "The Office of the Affairs of Male Students," also organized the town's recreation program, which gave him instant access to the adolescent grapevine.

"You've got to be superhuman," Carole Walker told Marcus when she heard what he was expected to do.

The adolescence of Marcus Robinson has been dominated by the dictates of powerful public authorities. It is as if he were living out Henry James's *A Small Boy and Others,* with an endless stream of bureaucrats substituted for an endless procession of relatives and tutors. Big agencies are supposed to go by the book—not in Marcus's case, though. Whether schools, juvenile courts, or social service bureaus have been doing the ministering, it has not been the institution's rules but the character of the person behind the institutional mask that has mattered most.

Both Larry Prince at Fletchers Crossing High and Sam Hannon, the Lorraine school superintendent, are veterans in the politics of running schools. Both understand how important it is to maintain order, to keep passions under control. But the two men place very different values on the needs and rights of the students they are charged with educating: that much is apparent in the radically different ways each of them approached Marcus Robinson.

Confronted with the news that Marcus carried the AIDS virus, Prince saw his task as waste disposal—getting rid of a student who now looked to be nothing but trouble. Prince was much too smart a bureaucrat ever to say this publicly, or to vent his feelings like Elizabeth Day, the woman who ran the summer jobs program in Lorraine and regarded the gay teenager as an evil person who "got exactly what he deserve[d]." Yet Prince knew exactly how to manipulate the school's attendance rules to get his way; and he knew too the importance of concealing what he had done from the school board, which had adopted quite a different AIDS policy.

Superintendent Hannon, faced with Marcus Robinson six months after Prince, did what professionally trained managers are supposed to do: he summed up best-case and worst-case scenarios. Hannon reckoned with the possibility that sizeable numbers of parents would take their children out of school, at least for awhile, if the facts of the case became generally known. Then he made a decision that was moral as well as pragmatic. He took a "calculated risk" to give the teenager a second chance.

Comparable differences in official attitudes are evident in the attempts to find Marcus a home—or to banish him. Social service agencies that deal with children in trouble are supposed to pursue what is in the youngsters' best interests, emphasizing rehabilitation over discipline. But in deciding the right placement for Marcus Robinson, the punitive approach warred with the therapeutic as the street level bureaucrats, Jim Parsons and Ray Aventi, argued their differing philosophies before the juvenile court. In Philadelphia several years earlier, the juvenile court had been so lackadaisical that Marcus had simply slipped through its net and "escaped" home. In Fletchers Crossing, though, Judge Smithers paid close attention, using the considerable authority of his office to insist on a handcrafted remedy. Smithers chose to rely not on the local agencies, with their parochial perspective, but on a high-level state official, Joan Browning, who combined a professional's commitment with the passion of a modern-day Jane Addams.

All these figures of authority lived within a world of rules; no one of them had absolute power over Marcus's fate. Were it otherwise, Jim Parsons would personally have put Marcus on a bus bound north, and Larry Prince wouldn't have been so insistent that all the school-leaving paperwork be on file. But Marcus wound up where he did—in a home, and in a school—because of the personal convictions of the individuals in charge, not the rules of the bureaus they represented.

These mandarins of childhood are typically regarded as a poor substitute for natural love. And the childminders themselves are often denigrated as time-servers or worse. The chronicle of Marcus Robinson suggests that these familiar views need some rethinking.

Life in the best of homes is certainly much richer than anything the state can hope to provide on its own. But the state can be a judicious matchmaker between caregivers and children. Carole Walker is a foster mother paid $1,000 a month from the

public treasury to give Marcus the priceless love he did not receive from relatives; she was located by officials who had it in
mind to rescue this one boy.

The attention paid by a judge, a juvenile court officer, and a
superintendent to this difficult case seems extraordinary. Even
Jim Parsons, despite his apparent animus, was more the exasperated parent than the time-serving bureaucrat. Perhaps it is
happenstance, but more likely it speaks to the character of
many of the people who make children's fates their professional
responsibility: whatever the explanation, the fact is that Marcus
Robinson has survived under the ministrations of these bureaus and these bureaucrats. More than this: he has been able
to start over again.

As summer 1987 neared its end, Superintendent Hannon
had made his decision. Now he had to persuade the school
board, which knew nothing of what had transpired the previous spring, to back him up. In executive session at the regular
August board meeting, Hannon laid out the facts of the case to
a startled congregation. Some board members recalled the fight
over integration. They feared that, if the news leaked, parents
would withdraw their children; they even talked about the possibility of violence. But unanimously, the five-member school
board authorized its new chief to take the lead. "This was still
the honeymoon," Hannon explains. "If I'd said 'He should stay
out,' they would have been happy to go along too."

The superintendent launched a quick AIDS education plan.
At the beginning of the term, AIDS was on the agenda at all the
neighborhood PTA meetings and in two-hour assemblies for
students. In the week before school, a session on AIDS was held
for all the high school teachers, followed by a special meeting at
which the teachers who would have Marcus in their classes were
told his name and his condition. "Those teachers are entitled to
know," Hannon insisted, overriding Terry Breen's arguments
about the need to preserve privacy by keeping the teenager's
identity a secret. At that second teachers' meeting, the superintendent emphasized the importance of confidentiality. "The

district could lose state funds," he said, "and a child's life could be ruined. You'll be tempted to tell your friends, but you can't even tell your spouse."

The meetings seemed to go off without a hitch, and students started the year with nothing more serious on their minds than the fortunes of the Marauders, the high school football team. Then, sitting in his office after the second day of classes had ended, Superintendent Hannon received a phone call from the *Gazette*. "We have an unsigned letter," said executive editor Johansen; one of Marcus's teachers, though pledged to secrecy, had gone surreptitiously to the press. "Do you care to comment?"

There had been some debate in the *Gazette* newsroom about whether to do anything with the anonymous letter about an AIDS case in Lorraine High. While some staffers urged openness, others were more worried about the damage disclosure could cause. But Johansen finally decided the letter was news. "If I hadn't run the story," he says, "what would I have said to a parent who called?"

When questioned by the *Gazette* editor, Superintendent Hannon felt he had to confirm the allegation. To deny it—to tell a lie—might well create bigger problems for the school system. Hannon would try tracking down the miscreant teacher, whose letter the superintendent regarded as grounds for dismissal, but that was for another time. Now he arranged to talk with a *Gazette* reporter who, Hannon promised, would be given "all the facts."

It was 4:00 P.M., too late for a teachers' meeting—that would come after school the next day. But while the reporter was on her way to his office, the superintendent contacted every board member and started planning a general community meeting to be held two nights later. He also phoned Carole Walker and Marcus to warn them of what was coming.

The recent events in Arcadia, Florida, weighed on Hannon's mind. Just the week before in that central Florida farm town, the enrollment of three brothers, ages eight to ten, all hemophiliacs who carried the AIDS virus, had prompted warnings of violence and a massive pupil boycott. Ultimately, it led to the torching of the family's home, an event that drove them away even as it made Arcadia a symbol for know-nothingism in the national imagination. Hannon prayed that there wouldn't be another Arcadia in Lorraine. What actually happened was far better, less conflict-ridden, than anyone could have hoped for.

The *Gazette*'s page one story which ran the next day was a model of journalistic probity. It stressed the scientific consensus that AIDS could not be spread casually and noted the meticulous review the Lorraine case had received from the expert panel. Perhaps the furor over the story about the doctor who had died from AIDS had chastened the paper; perhaps, as executive editor Johansen says, the *Gazette* had become more "sophisticated" in its AIDS coverage as it gained experience. In this instance, the paper opted for hypercaution. It gave no hint of a fact that could evoke concern—no suggestion, for instance, that casual contact was not the only conceivable way AIDS could be spread among sexually active high school students.

Hannon appeared on all the local TV stations the night the news story appeared. He was joined by the county's respected Health Department director, William McPhee, and by Tom Stillman, the county's AIDS specialist, whose credibility was heightened by the fact that his own children attended Lorraine High School. All delivered the same reassuring message.

The superintendent made much of one fact: the student in question did not have AIDS, but AIDS-related complex, ARC. That emphasis was deliberate. Since ARC was less familiar than AIDS, Hannon thought, it would sound less scary, and the threat posed by a student who "only" had ARC wouldn't seem so great; indeed, the superintendent said, the student's condition would be closely watched, and the enrollment question would be revisited if the disease progressed to AIDS. This was good public relations but bad, or at least misleading, science. In fact, anyone carrying the virus can spread it, and those with fullblown AIDS are least likely to do so.

Attendance at the high school did not drop following the *Gazette* story and the TV news shows. Only a handful of parents called the high school with questions about AIDS, and when a reporter asked high school students for their reaction, the teenagers, who had just had an exhaustive AIDS education session, professed to be unworried. "No one seems bothered," said one sophomore. "I just don't feel like I'm in danger. I'm just not going to get around people's blood."

Barely fifty people showed up at the community meeting held the day after the *Gazette* article appeared, and a number of them announced that they were there to lend their support to the superintendent. For the most part, the questions parents asked were easily fielded. The only charged moment came when one parent insisted that he had a "right to know the name of the student with the AIDS virus."

"We are keeping no secrets . . . we are keeping the name confidential," Dr. Stillman responded, and no one in the audience pressed the issue. On Sunday, five days after the story broke, the *Gazette* published an editorial praising all concerned: parents for not "overreacting," school officials for their "sensible approach," and the community for its "compassion."

Lorraine accepted the news with a matter-of-factness that needs some explanation. The community likes to think of itself as enlightened, and townspeople talked about not wanting to be another Arcadia. Moreover, in a community rightly proud of its considerable medical talent, the unequivocal support the schools received from two such admired doctors as Stillman and McPhee was vital, and the unmuddled statements delivered by the doctors were reassuring. The particular framing of the issue as a question of ARC, not AIDS, may also have stilled concerns.

Relevant too is the fact that this case involved a high school student rather than a younger child. Parents in Lorraine seemed to believe, against all odds, that their teenagers were mature enough to keep out of the path of inadvertent harm but too innocent to court harm. Remarkably, not a single parent spoke out about the risk of AIDS transmission from drugs or sex. In New York City that same week, TV stations carried a public service announcement from the city's AIDS-prevention campaign that showed a teenage boy writhing in agony and covered with lesions. The hellish image played on feelings of shame, transgression, and punishment as the voice-over warned sternly of

what happens when you "ask for AIDS." In Lorraine, apparently, no such thoughts ever entered the consciousness of the
community. If Marcus Robinson's identity and sexual history
had been known, things might have been very different. And it
is this possibility—the teenager's mask might slip, or be pulled
off—that keeps school officials on edge.

The morning the "AIDS in Lorraine High" story appeared in
the *Gazette,* Marcus Robinson was in school—afraid, he says,
that "hundreds of parents might find out who I was and come
after me," but there anyway. He was walking down the corridor
toward the main entrance when a bevy of cameramen appeared. Quickly, he slipped behind a door.

Those first days in school were hard for Marcus. In the halls,
other students would point at him and whisper, "I'll bet that's
the one. He'll be dead soon." And some students warned the
county health worker who had delivered the AIDS lectures that
"If anyone finds out who the person is, they'll kill him." Yet
soon enough, the whispering died down. Students didn't stop
being curious about who might have ARC, but their suspicions
became more broadly diffused; during one tragicomic moment, the finger of implication was pointed at a fifteen-year-old
white girl.

Within a week, classmates were coming up and introducing themselves to Marcus. A girl in his chemistry class, named
Margie, developed a crush on him and maneuvered to secure
the lab seat next to his. They have become friends, and Margie
tells Marcus all the stories of her life. Marcus can tell only some
of his stories, though.

At Lorraine High, Marcus Robinson is an honors student,
with all "A"s and "B"s on his report card. Several of his teachers
were initially uneasy about someone whom chemistry teacher
Nora Cunningham described as a "sissy little kid." But as the
year rolled on, such trepidations slipped away. "He is so helpful
to the other students. There is one girl who misses a lot, and he
has helped her to catch up," says Estrella Sánchez, his Spanish
teacher. Words like "helpful" and "pleasant" and "polite" show

up on all Marcus's evaluations. And Nora Cunningham has changed her mind about him. "The day of that news story, with the TV all around, it must have taken a mountain of courage to walk through those doors and act normal. He's the bravest person I know."

There is a sadness beneath the surface, Marcus's teachers say, that stops him from being the free spirit that marks his natural self. But how else could things be, with the possibility of death and the deeply felt need to conceal his feelings always present? Being normal is his constant preoccupation, and this means "passing"—not as white, as some light-skinned blacks once used to do, but as healthy. The smallest moments—not drinking from the water fountain, turning down a bite of a classmate's candy bar (or not being able to offer a bite of one's own)—are freighted with significance. They are, at once, a source of danger to others and a threat to his own secret. "I think about it almost every day," says Marcus. "I don't want anybody to get AIDS." Nor does he want anyone to learn that he has the virus. "I'm glad people don't know. This way, they treat you as a normal person."

Marcus Robinson may die tomorrow or, with the help of AZT, the drug he is taking, he could live for decades. He manages his life day by day, doing his homework with perfect penmanship, talking things through with his "Ma," watching too much TV, eating endless amounts of pizza. But he also harbors dreams about the future. "I want to be in the yearbook ten times," he says. "I want to make an impression on the world before I die."

CHAPTER SEVEN

The Bite:
Atascadero, California

At 11:25 A.M. on the morning of September 8, 1986, the nineteen kindergartners in Classroom Six at the Santa Rosa Road Elementary School in Atascadero, California, were settling down for story time. It was the fifth day of the new term. Lori Parker, the young kindergarten teacher, and her aide, Pat Broker, were moving around the room. They coaxed the children into putting away their Unifix cubes and Cuisenaire rods and sitting, mouse quiet, in a semicircle to hear what was happening in *The Napping House.*

Two of the youngsters, Ryan Thomas and a classmate, were whispering and giggling to each other—or so the most widely accepted version of the story goes. Ryan, a wide-eyed munchkin of a child, was a blur of energy. His usual playmate, Justin Smyres, sat a few feet away, feeling abandoned. Justin is big for his age, more than a head taller than Ryan, often insecure about his ability to make friends and able to get his way by the sheer force of his size.

Angry at being left out, Justin elbowed Ryan in the head then grabbed Ryan's hair and yanked him down, forcing Ryan's face into his lap. Ryan struggled vainly to get up. Then he bit Justin, who yelped, drawing Pat Broker's attention, and Justin turned Ryan loose.

Such incidents happen thousands of times each year in schoolrooms across America. They are perfectly commonplace—except when the boy who bites happens to have AIDS. That bite, and the Atascadero school district's quick suspension of mercy, became the AIDS story for the fall of 1986.

Eight previous months of meticulous planning—hours and hours of meetings aimed at finding a rational solution to the highly charged question of whether a young child with AIDS should be allowed in school—went by the board. It was as if Atascadero's worst nightmare had come true. A carefully crafted arrangement, which enabled Ryan to enroll in a small class of kindergartners whose parents had agreed to the placement, was abandoned overnight. The whole controversy was taken out of the community and dumped in the lap of a federal court judge.

No case of AIDS being transmitted through a bite has been documented, and all the credible medical evidence says that the odds against this happening are extremely high. But that evidence is known only to specialists who read the medical journals. To most parents, the bite of a child with AIDS is an awesomely fearful event which, even if unintended, seems to pile risk upon risk. To allow an AIDS-stricken child who bites into the same school as one's own youngster can appear to stretch compassion beyond its breaking point.

The Spaniards must have had a sense of humor. Why else curse a community in the coastal hills halfway between Los Angeles and San Francisco with the name Atascadero, which means mudhole? "It's a great place to raise children," townspeople say defensively. "And besides, housing is cheaper here than in San Luis Obispo." But that's the only comparison that operates to Atascadero's advantage.

San Luis, as the neighboring town is generally called, is middle class, Atascadero more working class. Atascadero and the north county gather the water in reservoirs, only to have it shipped off to San Luis. San Luis has the handsome new shopping malls, and its weekly Thursday night street party rated a flattering mention in the *New York Times*. Downtown Atascadero features Dot's Knit 'n' Knots, and the Swish 'n' Swirl laundromat. Cal Poly, a state college of some renown, is in San Luis Obispo. Atascadero has a state hospital for the criminally insane, the town's biggest employer.

Atascadero's best days all lie in the past. It was founded three-quarters of a century ago as a "Valley of Peace" by a visionary named E. C. Lewis, who moved out from St. Louis where he had created the University City neighborhood. Lewis had even bigger dreams for Atascadero. But his ambitious plans for the People's United States Bank and a local oil boom, for factories that would turn out steam-engine cars, artificial corks, dolls, and dried fruit all collapsed. Lewis ultimately wound up $10 million in debt and in jail for mail fraud. What survives of his big dreams is a monumental brick town hall. Almost everything else has been torn down or left to molder, while mini-malls sprout on the fringes of town.

During the past few years, Atascadero has grown quickly and haphazardly. When the state highway was widened, it bisected the community, turning it into what one resident described as "seven exits off a freeway." Some 20,000 people live in Atascadero, twice the population of a decade ago, many in garden apartments and characterless tract-style homes slapped up to meet the demand.

Newcomers are typically refugees from southern California who come to escape the problems of the city. Many of them retired couples, they fled from multiracial urban life in favor of a town that is nearly all white, hoping to leave behind drugs and street people, pornography and homosexuals and all the rest. Such innocence is only a dream, though, for marijuana fields—and the other temptations of the outside world—are close by. In 1986, after a drug bust at the high school, the school board got so worried about drug dealing that it authorized a baby-faced cop to go underground. Two years earlier, state investigators were everywhere, looking into stories that a porn ring centered in nearby Bakersfield was mutilating young children in snuff films and burying their bodies. Nothing ever came of the investigation—except scared parents.

Aside from a concern to keep spending down, which has made the local homeowners' association a potent political force, residents are not much interested in participating in Atascadero's civic life. Indeed, not until 1979, more than half a century after the notion was first talked about, did Atascadero become a town by voting for incorporation, and a sizeable minority of the citizenry would be just as happy if the county still ran things.

Traditionally, the same civic apathy applied to the public schools. In size, the Atascadero Unified School District is the biggest in California, almost as big as Rhode Island. But size did not translate into quality; parents cared more about boosting the Future Farmers of America, or about getting *Catcher in the Rye* and *Of Mice and Men* off the library shelves, than about academics. They put very little money into the educational program, and the neglect showed. Teachers set low expectations for their students, of whom only a handful went off to college. Equipment in the science labs and vocational classrooms was ancient. In athletics, the Atascadero Greyhounds were always the doormat. "Why can't we be as good as San Luis Obispo?" teachers would lament.

Academic standards have been raised considerably since 1977, when Anthony Avina became superintendent. Students now perform in the top twenty-five percent, statewide, on academic achievement tests. Even the athletic teams are in better repute—the Greyhounds regularly win the league football championship—and the district has found state money to spruce up its schools. "The old philosophy was 'Help kids feel good about themselves,'" Avina says, "I changed that. Now the philosophy is 'Kids will be happy if they're busy.'"

But many of the old ways endure. Emil LaSalle, a rancher elected to the board in 1983, won his seat on a pledge to reintroduce the Future Farmers of America into the school curriculum. A sizeable group feels that too much emphasis is currently being placed on academics, that the schools are becoming too college-prep oriented. And Atascadero's schools have had no sex education, because fundamentalist ministers, who carry considerable weight in the town, insist that teaching about sex promotes promiscuity and homosexuality.

Although San Luis Obispo County, which includes both Atascadero and San Luis Obispo, had already recorded seventeen AIDS cases by late 1985, AIDS itself was just the subject of scabrous jokes before the tumult over four-year-old Ryan Thomas. Soon enough, the townspeople got an education in AIDS; and until the bite, that education served them decently well.

In November 1985, Tony Avina had received a startling piece of news from Allan Gathright, a *San Jose Mercury News* reporter: the following September, a four-year-old child with AIDS would be enrolling in kindergarten. The minute that the reporter, who had been tipped off by a county health worker, left Avina's office, the superintendent dashed off a memo alerting his key staff people.

Tony Avina writes lots of memos. He is temperamentally cautious, a firm believer in what he calls "process," the kind of man who habitually tests the political winds. Avina speaks proudly about beefing up remedial instruction, convincing the high school's business department to enter the computer age, and loosening the purse strings of a district notorious for its fiscal conservatism; about strengthening the vocational offerings and getting English teachers to push their students harder.

A native Californian, Avina came to Atascadero after a series of jobs in southern California. He was on an administrative fast track that slowed down because his family refused to move on, to follow him to the city superintendency that was logically his next job. But as the high turnover rate among superintendents attests, the fast track can also be slippery. School superintendents have to respond to the wishes of school board members, the people who hire and fire them. In theory, boards set the policy that administrators carry out. But the line between policy and management is exceedingly fine; superintendents in many school districts complain that board members meddle in day-to-day affairs, and board members complain that superintendents become czars.

Until 1983, when several new members were elected to the Atascadero board, Avina "ran the school district as his own show," recalls Carl Brown, a New England transplant who teaches English at Cal Poly–San Luis Obispo and is one of the reform-minded board members. But with Brown, as well as Roy King, self-styled "retired zoologist loudmouth potmaker and intellectual," and Emil LaSalle, farmer and prideful curmudgeon, joining the seven-member board, Avina had to tread warily.

Avina was initially inclined to keep Ryan Thomas out of school. "He didn't start with the liberal high ground," notes George Rowland, the San Luis Obispo County Public Health Director, who became the school district's medical authority on AIDS. For his part, Avina points out that "this is an issue that could have blown Atascadero apart." A few months earlier, when Roy King urged the superintendent to "look at AIDS" and how it might become a problem for the school system, Avina replied: "I wouldn't touch it with a ten foot pole." "Back then," Avina recalls, "nobody wanted to talk about AIDS. It was too closely linked to homosexuality."

Robin and Judy Thomas, Ryan's parents, who first approached Avina shortly after the reporter's visit, wanted a quick decision about their son. In a letter to the superintendent, Dr. Joseph Church, the Los Angeles pediatric AIDS specialist who had diagnosed Ryan's condition, wrote: "I strongly urge that [Ryan] be allowed to attend regular school." But Avina saw things from a different vantage point. He had a conservative community to worry about—a community that, as board member Roy King noted, "may not be culturally ready to accept the fact that a gay disease, 'God's punishment,' is here." "I knew there would be outrage," says Avina, and to contain the outrage he appointed an AIDS advisory committee.

The committee was expected to acquaint itself with the latest medical evidence on AIDS in developing a school systemwide policy. It was February 1986, just half a year after AIDS had become an issue in Kokomo and Queens, and few people in the bucolic community of Atascadero knew much about the scientific findings on AIDS. Even more important, Avina believed, the process of talking things through was meant "to ventilate, to make people feel okay with the final decision."

This was the only way Atascadero could come to terms with AIDS, the superintendent thought. "We need plenty of public input," he told the Thomases. But medical expert Rowland concluded that Avina had acted "as much out of cowardice as anything else . . . he wanted to jump in front of the bandwagon." And to Robin and Judy Thomas, forming a committee looked like a classic bureaucrat's ploy for stalling.

It was a "y'all come committee," as Avina described it, and dozens of people did show up for meeting after meeting. There was the superintendent, making an appearance not to offer his opinion but to tell people his ambition: that "everyone is going to win." There was Roy King, who turned himself into an AIDS expert. "I made damn sure people knew that there are gays in the schools right now . . . I wanted the gay community protected."

Many of the parents who came were aghast at the idea of Ryan's attending school. "We're not big fanatics," declared Kathy Wentzel, mother of an elementary school child. "We don't say 'We're scared of AIDS, period.' We've done a lot of studying ourselves. And the doctors in our town believe an AIDS child should not be in school." Robin Thomas was there, too, carrying his son Ryan on his shoulders, a visible reminder that they were not debating an abstract issue but deciding how a boy with a fatal virus in his bloodstream would live out his life.

Avina recalls the meetings as "establishing a climate of respect for one another's opinions." But AIDS touches on so many deep-rooted feelings of dread that passions can drive out managed courtesies, and in Atascadero things sometimes got visceral. "One of the mothers stuck her kid in my face and screamed, 'Why do you want to kill my child?,'" Robin Thomas remembers. The Thomases received obscene calls and hate mail, and they weren't the only ones to be harassed. Kathy Wentzel answered her phone one day and heard a man demand, in a muffled voice, that "you bitches stay out of the Thomas situation or else."

Gradually, though, both sides gave ground. The Thomases

agreed to certain precautions, like a separate locked toilet for Ryan, which while medically unnecessary did ease some people's fears. Many parents were reassured by George Rowland, who had shaped San Luis Obispo County's AIDS policy and was on hand to explain how AIDS is transmitted. Those who stuck to what Rowland described as a "line 'em up and shoot 'em philosophy" muttered about pulling their children out of school, but they never commanded much popular support.

Rowland embraced the message that leading AIDS researcher Dr. Merle Sande had delivered to his fellow doctors in a just-published *New England Journal of Medicine* editorial: it was indeed "time to take a more influential and active role in quelling this hysteria over the casual transmission of AIDS."[1] The quiet-spoken public health official was able to neutralize many of the fears that Atascaderans brought with them to the meetings. Some of their questions had been asked before, in Kokomo and in Swansea. But this case posed a new dimension: Ryan Thomas was nearly ten years younger than Ryan White or Mark Hoyle; for children so young, the Centers for Disease Control guidelines urged caution. And to those who saw Ryan Thomas at the placement committee sessions, often asleep in his father's arms, he seemed immature even for his age. Parents wondered whether he could be counted on to understand the gravity of his disease and to act responsibly. "How about blisters popping on the monkey bars?" they asked. "What about sweat or saliva in the sandbox?" And at every meeting, parents worried about biting.

"I didn't give them guarantees—there are no guarantees—but I did let them know how extremely unlikely it was that anyone could catch AIDS in school," says Rowland. "Would you send your child to school with Ryan?" Rowland was asked. "Absolutely," he replied. Over a period of months, Rowland persuaded a popular local pediatrician, Dr. James Tedford, to endorse Ryan's enrollment, and Tedford's conversion helped to change the minds of others.

The committee sought the help of the California State Department of Education. But the state's education and health departments were preoccupied with fussing over who had

206 ATASCADERO, CALIFORNIA

responsibility for AIDS and schools. "The district felt isolated," says Avina. "It was as if the state were saying, 'Let's step back and watch what happens.'" The guidelines the committee finally drafted were more restrictive than the policy recommended by the CDC. They applied not only to children with AIDS but also to their siblings—which plainly violated California law—a provision prompted by lingering fear that AIDS could be transmitted casually. The guidelines also created a placement committee, whose concerns any AIDS-afflicted child wanting to attend school would have to satisfy. And, uniquely among school districts, they gave parents a veto over whether their children would remain in the same classroom as a youngster with AIDS.

At a school board meeting held in the modernistic high school media center on April 13, 1986, nearly one hundred parents debated the new rules. Though the rules mentioned no specific cases, Ryan Thomas was on everyone's mind. Almost all the parents who spoke out that night wanted the boy kept at home. "You"—the school district—"are subjecting my children to the possibility of slow ultimate death," David Marazza insisted, and the liability-minded father demanded that Atascadero take out a $10 million surety bond for each of his children. Avina tried playing peacemaker—"Nobody's wrong, everybody's right: this is too complex an issue," he said—but the vociferousness of the opposition scared the school board into putting off its decision. Two weeks later, though, with the opposition "all exploded out," in board member Roy King's words, the board gave the policy its unanimous assent.

During the mid-May kindergarten "roundup" at the Santa Rosa Road School, which Ryan would be attending if the placement committee approved, nineteen parents signed permission slips saying that it was fine to place Ryan in the same class as their children.

"I'm proud to announce that this is an academic kindergarten," Principal Chuck Wilbur said at the roundup, and that emphasis on rigor has made the Santa Rosa Road School the most highly regarded in Atascadero. Real estate ads make a point of noting when a home is located in "the SRR attendance zone." Although the school has enough low-income pupils to qualify for federal aid, its achievement scores are the highest in the district, and its "back to basics" education philosophy appeals to many parents. "Santa Rosa Road was the best school in the district for AIDS to happen in," says Superintendent Avina. "The chemistry is great between parents and teachers."

When Principal Wilbur, an emigré from Los Angeles, realized that Ryan would likely be enrolling in Santa Rosa Road, he began assiduously to deliver an education on AIDS to everyone associated with the school. Presentations were directed at teachers and janitors. ("How do you deal with vomit?" one janitor asked a hospital administrator who talked about AIDS precautions. "Always double-bag it," came the reply.) The school's PTA put on two meetings, inviting doctors to explain the facts about AIDS, and while the PTA's parent leaders had strong views of their own, they were constrained to remain neutral. "I was supposed to stay opinion-free [as a PTA co-president] and leave the politics to the school board," says Gerrie Dahlen, "but I had a hard time with my personal feelings. As a mother, I would care too much for my child to put him through this torment. I'd be trying to enrich his life. It'd be different if he were an eighth grader . . . but a kindergartner is another story."

Students also were instructed on AIDS; afterwards, when the sixth-grade teacher took a poll, the majority voted that Ryan belonged in school. Yet on the playground that spring, the free-floating anxieties of the young found voice. There was talk about "the homosexuals in Africa," surely a garbled translation of their parents' dinner conversation, and the ultimate invective became "I hope you get AIDS."

Just before school was to begin in September 1986, the placement committee that was to recommend whether Ryan Thomas would attend kindergarten met for two hours with the family. It was hard going.

Almost no one in the room except the Thomases was enthusiastic about Ryan's starting school. In an assessment of Ryan's readiness for kindergarten, conducted during the summer by

Kris McDermott, a retired school principal, Ryan had not performed well. The boy was "very young in what he can do," McDermott reported to the committee. "He has very few skills." Leslie Sherwin, a parent on the committee, told the Thomases that Ryan might be best off in a "Mommy and Me" class, while Greg Howe, co-president of the Santa Rosa PTA, renewed his concerns about biting. Christene Owre, a school nurse, was troubled about how Ryan would deal with stress. "It's not just Ryan that's at risk of getting sick, it's other children," pediatrician Jim Tedford reminded the group. And Roger Grass, a lawyer who represented the Atascadero schools, noted that four-year-olds were not legally required to attend school. "Use your best judgment," Grass urged the other members of the committee.

The committee ultimately gave its reluctant approval to Ryan's attending kindergarten. Although committee members would have preferred that the youngster spend a year in preschool, the Thomases had already pursued that possibility, only to be told that their son was too old. The idea that Ryan stay home for a year of maturing was not an unusual suggestion—each of Superintendent Avina's own children had done so—but the Thomases rejected it out of hand. They disputed McDermott's evaluation of their son's abilities. What he needed most, they felt, was the companionship of other children.

The first day of school had already been held, with Ryan at home, when the school board convened to make its final determination. This was no discussion about rules but the real thing, and seventy parents came, almost all of them bent on keeping Ryan out. "Sure, I feel sorry for the kid," said Zonk Thompson, a construction worker. "But I don't feel sorry enough to subject my little daughter to AIDS." Dr. Duane Thompson, a local dentist, warned the board: "Are you prepared to deal with the complete dichotomy that is going to result—parents against parents, children against children?"

The school board unanimously sided with its placement committee. As the committee's chairwoman, school psychologist Michelle Andre, told the board, "There is no medical reason that Ryan Thomas cannot attend school." Although two families did remove their children from Santa Rosa Road, the controversy seemed to be at an end. Avina congratulated the community for its "humaneness"—an earned pat on the back, since Atascadero had accomplished what Swansea had done. It had taken many months longer, the going had been rougher, and the final decision had been more grudging, but the community had agreed to accept a child with AIDS—four-year-old Ryan Thomas, far more problematic than polite and thoughtful teenager Mark Hoyle—into its schools.

Yet even as Robin Thomas celebrated that night with a bottle of champagne, he worried about what the next chapter would look like. "What's going to happen tomorrow or next week?"

During the months preceding the opening of school, a four-by-eight-foot sign stood in front of the Thomases' bungalow: "Stop AIDS Discrimination," the sign read, "Help Get Ryan in School," a visible symbol of the battle being waged. Ryan's battle had really begun when he was born, two months premature and weighing just four pounds. The infant had to be flown several hundred miles north to Oakland for blood transfusions to keep him alive; but as the family learned early in 1985, the blood had carried the AIDS virus. "I didn't know anything about AIDS," says Ryan's father Robin, "except that it was a homosexual-type disease and that everyone died who had it."

During the first few years of his life, Ryan was constantly in and out of the hospital with painful ear infections and bouts of pneumonia. In the spring of 1985, just after the AIDS diagnosis, Ryan's temperature zoomed to 105. The whole family brought the boy to Children's Hospital in Los Angeles; after a few days Judy and Robin Thomas left their two older sons, Richard and Robert, with Judy's sister. The couple returned to the hospital, and for the next two weeks one parent was always at Ryan's side while the other catnapped in the family's van.

Ryan Thomas made it through the bout with pneumocystis pneumonia and began receiving the twice-monthly two-hour transfusions of gamma globulin that are standard treatment for young AIDS patients. "It hurts a lot," says Ryan, who knows that he has what he calls "my AIDS"—he believes that he is the only person in the world with the disease. When Ryan sees a story about AIDS on television, his father says, he thinks it is about him.

For some months after the diagnosis, no one outside the family knew about Ryan's illness. Dr. Church, who diagnosed Ryan's condition, had advised that approach. "If you tell people," he said, "they'll shy away." But the silence became too hard to maintain. Ryan was sharing his baby bottle and his toys with the children he played with, and the Thomases felt the playmates' parents deserved to know. "Finally, I just couldn't keep lying to people, saying that Ryan had a blood disorder," Robin Thomas recalls. "I told everyone—it's too bad if they can't accept it."

The Thomases were determined that their son should lead a normal life, and that meant going to school. They knew it wouldn't be easy. "People who were friends for fifteen years stopped talking to us right after we told them about Ryan," Robin Thomas recalls. Robin says he was fired by the home-insulation firm he worked for, after his boss informed him that "city officials" had complained that he was "making too much noise" about his son's right to attend school. And when the Thomases brought their problems to the *Atascadero News*, the local weekly, they got little support. "I'm not an aggressive journalist," says editor Lon Allen, explaining his generally understated coverage of the controversy. Allen had another reason for reticence: he had taught at Atascadero High before taking over the newspaper in 1972 and knew that this story would only mean headaches for his good friend Tony Avina.

The setbacks convinced the Thomases that they had to go it alone. They are well known in Atascadero, where both had attended school, but they are not much liked. They were "renters," townspeople pointed out— transients with few stakes in the community. When neighbors gossiped, they spread rumors that the Thomases were irresponsible parents, heavy drug users. Such tales embittered Robin and Judy, who saw their children as the centerpiece of their lives, and confirmed the family in its feeling of isolation.

Although employees at the local Denny's restaurant raised over $1,100 for Ryan during the 1985 Christmas season, the Thomases felt cut off, able to trust only their family and the reporters, including Allan Gathright from the *Mercury-News,* who attached themselves to their cause. "The Thomases had so much of a 'make my day' attitude," says Jennifer Bacon, whose daughter was in Ryan's kindergarten class, "that sometimes they couldn't see the people who wanted to help them." They identified with the Whites in Kokomo, cheering when Ryan White won his court case in April 1986 and encouraged when Charles Vaughan, Jr., one of the Whites' lawyers, volunteered to assist them in Atascadero.

Fighting for a cause is nothing new for Robin Thomas. As an Atascadero High School student in the early 1970s, recently arrived from Los Angeles, he showed up with shoulder-length hair. School officials ordered him to get it cut. Robin refused— "I wanted the right to decide for myself," he says, recalling the incident—and was suspended. It was the principle, not the coiffure, that mattered. To prove his point, Robin went to his graduation, wife and infant son Richard by his side, sporting a crew cut. Getting Ryan into school came to feel like the same kind of issue.

During the winter and spring of 1986, the Thomases' distrust was fueled by what they regarded as the animosity of their neighbors and the conniving of the school system. "When are you going to get off your duffs and do something?" an angry Robin Thomas demanded of the school board early in 1986, before the advisory committee had even held its first meeting. "We were overcautious about a lot of things," says Principal Chuck Wilbur, and that didn't sit well with Robin. "They put us through hell," he said. The two older Thomas boys, Richard and Robert, were getting into fights with other kids who biked past the house shouting "AIDS monster" when they glimpsed Ryan.

The Thomases were understandably impatient—maybe too impatient—for their child. Everything that went wrong became part of a conspiracy against them. They felt uneasy about Avina, unconvinced that the superintendent cared about their son's welfare. They were angry when the placement committee held

212   ATASCADERO, CALIFORNIA

off meeting until the last possible moment in September, angry too at what they considered the insults of the parents who had spoken out against Ryan's admission. "Don't take it personally," those parents kept saying, but to the Thomases it was *all* personal.

The TV cameras, which had appeared at the May roundup, were back to capture the first few days in Classroom Six of the Santa Rosa Road Elementary School. This time they recorded Judy Thomas making sandwiches for her son and Ryan walking into his new classroom holding his brother Robert's hand. One camerawoman, desperate for something to shoot, filmed Ryan interviewing his older brother about his first day in school. Ryan took the fuss in stride. "He just thinks he's handsome," his father explained.

"Ryan blended well with everyone," said his teacher, Lori Parker. Although this was Parker's first year as a full-time teacher, it marked her return to the town where she had grown up and the grade school she had attended. The previous spring, when she was doing her practice teaching in Atascadero, she had told Principal Chuck Wilbur that she wouldn't have any trouble teaching a child with AIDS, since she had learned about such children in college. "But the night after I took the job, I woke up a wreck. I asked myself, 'What have I got myself into?'"

Once the term began, though, things seemed to be fine. All the precautions were in place, with pencils and crayons for individual students and a teacher's aide to escort Ryan to his own locked bathroom stall. "The kids treat Ryan like a prince," Parker said, and other teachers helped out too. "'Keep up the good work,' they'd say, and 'Come into my classroom and escape from the media.'"

Some parents were upset about what they regarded as the Thomases' publicity-mongering. "They linger on TV," said PTA co-president Gerrie Dahlen. "They're using Ryan to get the recognition they never had before." And Judy Thomas confessed to a moment of sadness at Ryan's leaving home. "I'm missing one very important part of my life right now," she said, since the boy she called her "little shadow" was not by her side.

But Robin Thomas was exultant. It was worth all the fighting, he declared, "just to see Ryan today with the other kids."

Then came the bite.

To the parents of the children involved, the episode wasn't a big deal. Ryan had only defended himself. "I bit him because I couldn't get up," he told his parents, who learned about the incident from a note safety-pinned to his pants. Besides, his bite hadn't even broken the skin; Justin Smyres had been wearing jeans. "Maybe some illiterate people believe you can get AIDS from a bite," said Mike Smyres, Justin's father, who blamed his own son for going after Ryan in a fit of jealousy, "but I know there's only two ways you can get AIDS, and that's through blood or sex—period."

Superintendent Avina took the bite far more seriously. Lon Allen, editor of the *News,* received a call from Avina that night, and the superintendent was distraught. "Ryan bit a child today; it just makes me sick." The superintendent quickly reached a decision: Ryan had to go.

"It's as if he decided that he had been right all along in wanting to keep Ryan out of school, and now he was going to make sure Ryan stayed out," says school board member Carl Brown. "It was a gross overreaction," complains Kay Wells, whose daughter was in Ryan's class, and who wrote to Avina complaining of a "witch-hunt." "They were crucifying the little guy," Wells says, "punishing him for defending himself, while the boy who had started the fight wasn't being punished."

That night, a contingent of top-level administrators, including Avina, Avina's top aide Paul Anderson, and Principal Chuck Wilbur, visited the Smyers house to inspect the bite personally. All those high-powered eyes saw what the teacher's aide had reported—no broken skin, just a little redness. Nonetheless, Ryan was immediately suspended from school, and the placement committee was reconvened.

Ryan's story, which until then had attracted mostly local attention, instantly went national. "Reporters were coming out of the woodwork," Robin Thomas recalls. "There were calls from as far away as New York and Toronto. Sometimes it seemed like we were watching a movie."

Now it was The Bite, an incident abstracted from its particular facts. The particulars—a boy defending himself with a bite that hadn't pierced the skin—did not distress those most directly affected, the parents in Classroom Six. But such reassuring details went forgotten in later simplifications, and in the escalation of events Atascadero became polarized.

On September 15, the school board voted unanimously to insist on a psychological determination of whether Ryan was likely to act out again. Reluctantly, Robin Thomas went along. The report by the board-appointed psychologist described Ryan as "lovable . . . an attractive" child who "does not appear to be angry or prone to excessive impulsivity," but went on to note that, under extraordinary pressure, Ryan might possibly lash out. This evaluation could be said to describe any child, but it unnerved the placement committee, which wondered whether a single bite foreshadowed a pattern of biting. If so, that would be grounds for excluding anyone, not just Ryan.

Committee members were equally frightened by a letter from two German doctors, published that week in the British medical journal *Lancet* and widely publicized in the popular press, which purported to describe the first instance of a child transmitting AIDS by biting. Public Health Director Rowland wasn't convinced by the letter—"speculation, not a scientific study," he labeled it—for he knew the research findings on AIDS and saliva. These studies indicated that the virus had been isolated in the saliva of several AIDS patients but not in most other similar specimens. Moreover, the amounts were minute, so saliva was an extremely unlikely route of transmission—as one San Francisco researcher said, it would take several gallons of AIDS-infected saliva, poured directly into the bloodstream, to expose an individual to AIDS.[2]

Rowland estimated the probability of AIDS being transmitted by biting at one in one hundred thousand, and, on the basis of the psychological report on Ryan, estimated the odds that they boy would bite again, this time breaking the skin, at one in ten. Rowland's calculations made for odds of a million to one against Ryan Thomas spreading his disease through a bite. Research on biting, unknown to Rowland, confirmed the extreme unlikelihood of spreading AIDS this way. But even if the public health officer had had those studies at his fingertips,

the vampirish horror of a bite weighed more heavily on Atascaderans' minds than medical probabilities.

Rowland proposed that the risk of transmission through biting be explained to the parents of Ryan's classmates—who,
after all, had volunteered to enroll their children in Classroom
Six—and that the choice be left up to them. But the placement
committee rejected that idea, and urged instead that Ryan
be barred from school until the following fall. "While people
talked about rights," said committee chair Michelle Andre, "we
focused on the needs of everyone."

Five days later, on October 6, the school board took up the
matter in a public meeting. By this time, ACLU lawyers were
representing the Thomases, and they had requested a two week
postponement before the board made its decision. "We wanted
to stay out of court," says the Southern California ACLU's legal
director, Paul Hoffman. "We thought we could put together a
powerful argument that would convince the board to let Ryan
back in."

But Superintendent Avina, caught up in the antagonisms of
the hour, sensed a trap. He dismissed the ACLU's suggestion as
nothing more than a way for the ACLU to buy time so that it
could prepare its lawsuit. "The request was made too late," he
insisted, despite the fact that it had been delivered as soon
as Hoffman had received word of the placement committee's
recommendation.

Robin Thomas saw things differently. "It's just a bunch of political garbage that's getting in the way now," he said.

Though most of the parents of children in Classroom Six
backed Ryan's right to stay in school, they hadn't been able to
organize; Avina, citing the need for confidentiality, had refused
to release their names and phone numbers. A few of them
wrote individually to the placement committee on Ryan's behalf, and at the school board meeting a nurse who had worked
with AIDS patients argued that the boy should remain in class.
But that night, almost all the voices the school board heard
were of parents convinced that Ryan didn't belong in school.

A local dentist pleaded with the board to keep the youngster
home. "I have a daughter with childhood diabetes. You don't
know what it's like to have a sick child. . . . If there's any way

that you can avoid this trauma—do it." One particularly angry father made a stir when he railed about "green monkeys . . . and green kids" who transmitted AIDS; he immediately apologized to the Thomases for his "slip of speech." Then, behind closed doors, the Thomases were invited to present their case. It was a tense encounter. "We had other business to deal with that night," Avina recalls, "including an expulsion case, and I kept urging the board to move things along." The ACLU's Mickey Wheatley remembers it differently: "Avina was giggling and whispering."

Every school board member except one voted to keep Ryan home—but only until January 1987, when enrollment would again be up for review. The lone dissenting vote on the school board came from Emil LaSalle, who feared a possible lawsuit.

Carl Brown recalls thinking that the decision made no scientific sense, because "all the literature convinced me that there was no risk of AIDS being transmitted from a bite." It made good political sense, though. Come January 1987, after things had calmed down, Brown thought he could convince the board to readmit Ryan. But that October night, with tempers so high and the superintendent so strongly committed to Ryan's expulsion, there was no place for dispassion. Roy King agreed that a compromise was the right approach. "It's very important that we all work together on this," he said. "It's too small a community for us to be continually separating ourselves."

But this strategy didn't sit well with either the superintendent or the Thomases. Avina wanted to keep Ryan out of school— "so badly," says Brown, "that when he was at the edge of things he lost his judgment. He'd pull anything out of the bag to win." Kay Wells recalls that Avina appeared at a parents' meeting to argue against Ryan's readmission. "At an earlier meeting, he was telling us 'You're courageous, the board is courageous.' Now he's saying, 'I can't give you guarantees that your children can't get AIDS from him.'" In a closed meeting, Avina relayed to board members the claims of anonymous callers that Ryan had a history of biting. And he went so far as to urge, unsuccessfully, that the board hire a private investigator to dig up facts proving that Ryan was not fit for school.

Paul Anderson, Avina's assistant, started surreptitiously ob-
serving Ryan's behavior in tutoring sessions held in the district's
administration office. "During one session, I told Ryan, 'You're
not acting like a five-year-old,'" Robin remembers. "They took
that down to use against us." Ryan had been transformed from
a kindergartner to an exhibit in a lawsuit.

Robin Thomas rejected the board's attempt at compromise.
"The wait is not going to answer any questions," he said imme-
diately after the school board meeting. In a matter of days, the
ACLU filed suit against the Atascadero schools in federal dis-
trict court, demanding the immediate reinstatement of Ryan
Thomas.

When the ACLU learned that they had drawn Alicemarie
Stotler as the judge in *Thomas v. Atascadero Unified School District,*
the lawyers were nervous. Stotler had a reputation for fairness
and thoroughness, and that was a hopeful sign. But she was
a Reagan appointee who had been an Orange County district
attorney, and those aren't exactly the credentials of a civil
libertarian.

The ACLU's job was compounded by the legal difficulty of
the Thomases' case. It is one thing to believe that Atascadero
had panicked into overreacting, something altogether different
to persuade a federal court judge that a boy with AIDS was
entitled to the protections of the 1973 federal Rehabilitation
Act—a question never before decided in federal court. Moreover, the school district could plausibly rely on the CDC guidelines, which suggested a more "restrictive" setting for children
who "display behavior such as biting." That's why Atascadero's
lawyer, Roger Grass, had boasted to the placement committee
that the Thomases "didn't have a prayer."

Shortly before the hearing, Paul Hoffman at the ACLU received a call from School Legal Service, a Bakersfield firm that
handles the legal business of numerous southern California
school districts including Atascadero. "We've got news that will
make the ACLU want to back off the Thomas case right away."

The "news" came from the report of a nurse to whom Judy

Thomas had confided in July. Ryan had bitten another child, the nurse reported. He had also shaved off his eyebrows and tried setting a plant on fire with a lighter. Hoffman checked out the story with the Thomases and emerged unimpressed. It turned out that, a year earlier, Ryan had been bitten hard by a little girl. She claimed that Ryan bit her back, but she had no teeth marks. The other incidents were equally inconsequential. At age two, after watching his father shave, Ryan had taken a razor to his eyebrows. The same year, he learned to use a lighter when his grandmother taught him to light her cigarettes. When Judy found him practicing on a rubber plant, a talking-to from an Atascadero fireman ended the pyrotechnics. These were "ordinary childhood problems," as Judy Thomas said, nothing to make—or dismiss—a federal case over.

The Thomases were feeling restive when they came to federal court, for the huge Third-Reichian Deco courtroom in downtown Los Angeles where their case was argued is intimidating, and they were uncomfortable with the legalese being tossed around.

Frank Fekete, the School Legal Service lawyer who argued Atascadero's case, stressed how "reasonable" the school district had been, how it had bent over backwards to do what was best for both the family and the community. Fekete also talked about the supposedly shocking revelations, eyebrow-shaving and the like, contained in the nurse's report. "We have a child here who has set fires, cut electrical cords," he declared. This was no ordinary pupil, Fekete added, citing the guidelines of the American Academy of Pediatrics, but one who posed a "greater risk." The Thomases were holding back, he contended, keeping Ryan's problems a secret.

That claim stirred ACLU lawyer Paul Hoffman to passionate retort. Arms waving, voice rising, the attorney demolished the claim that Ryan was a disturbed youngster. He mocked the notion that Atascadero had been reasonable: on the contrary, he insisted, "The district simply won't listen, [not even to] their own public health officer." No other Atascadero child had been put through such hoops just to be admitted to school, Hoffman reminded the court—all because of a risk no greater than "a jet engine falling from the sky."

Comparing AIDS to a jet engine's descent from the heavens was a flashy way of making an argument that, by the fall of 1986, was indeed substantiated by research on how AIDS was transmitted. All research showed the same thing: AIDS was spread only by blood or sperm. Six separate studies of 234 relatives (but not sexual partners) of persons with AIDS had been conducted, and not a single instance of household transmission of the virus had been found. A several-year study of hemophiliac children living in a French boarding school, youngsters particularly likely to bleed and inclined to roughhouse with one another, reached the same conclusion.[3]

One report that Hoffman relied on directly addressed transmission through biting. Thirty health care workers had been bitten and scratched by a brain-damaged hemophiliac with AIDS. Despite the fact that some of the lesions were severe enough to produce scars, not one of the workers carried the AIDS virus.[4]

There was, to be sure, the *Lancet* letter of September 20, concerning the alleged transmission of AIDS from an infected sibling to his older brother through a bite. That report had understandably frightened the Atascadero placement committee, but it was not good science. Hoffman solicited a declaration from Dr. Edward Gomperts, director of the hemophilia Comprehensive Care Center at Los Angeles' Children's Hospital, who pointed out that the mother who reported the bite was not sure she had seen teeth imprints. Moreover, she had no recollection of bleeding or a break in the skin, the only remotely plausible way, said Gomperts, that a bite could spread the disease.

All this evidence, ACLU attorney Hoffman argued, rendered out of date the CDC's fifteen-month-old guidelines, with their cautions about children who display biting behavior. Such cautions were also directed to children who bite regularly, children pediatricians describe as biters, and Ryan did not fit that description. (On this point, the CDC's Dr. Martha Rogers, who helped draft the guidelines, agrees. "If we thought AIDS could be transmitted in a minor bite," Rogers says, "we wouldn't have put [preschoolers] in school at all because kids that age sometimes do bite.")

Atascadero's decision had no scientific basis, Hoffman concluded. It was just "irrational fear and politics. . . . The decision makers could not withstand the community pressure. . . . They have been running scared from the beginning. . . . [Atascadero] can't come to grips with the fact that there's fear on one hand and the reality of the lack of risk on the other."

Judge Stotler asked few questions during the hour-long argument and, immediately after, read a brief prepared opinion. The school board found itself in a "difficult position," the judge acknowledged, but "there is no evidence that Ryan Thomas poses a significant risk of harm to his kindergarten classmates or teachers." Ryan could return to school immediately.

The fact that the ACLU did win speaks volumes about the caliber of its litigating. ACLU's Los Angeles office considered itself the best-equipped firm in the country to take on the Ryan Thomas lawsuit, and with good reason. ACLU staff attorneys had just drafted a friend-of-the-court brief in a U. S. Supreme Court case on a closely related legal issue: whether tuberculosis is a handicap (an issue ultimately decided in the plaintiff's favor). And nine months earlier, the ACLU had won a state court ruling ordering another California school district to admit a student with the AIDS virus.

By contrast, no one at School Legal Service, representing Atascadero, knew very much about AIDS, and this inexperience showed in the thinness of their case. "They let us sound authoritative," Paul Hoffman recalls, "and that's a fatal mistake."

Only a handful of people, most of them reporters, were present for the landmark ruling. Standing on the courthouse steps minutes later, Robin and Judy Thomas hugged each other as the TV cameras recorded the moment.

School Superintendent Avina expressed his relief that the court decision had settled "a potentially explosive situation." "This was a win-win case for us," he said. "We had a policy that was reviewed by our lawyers. If the court changes that policy, that's OK; if it finds the policy acceptable, that's OK too." The judgment had taken matters out of the hands of the administration and the school board, absolving them of responsibility. If anything went wrong, the court could be blamed.

"Let's get back to business," said board member Roy King.

"We don't want to replay *Brown v. Board of Education*." There was a feeling that it would take some striking piece of evidence, "a *Lancet*-type thing," to overturn the ruling. Besides, said King, "it's only a matter of ten weeks [before Ryan would have come up to review under the board-approved plan] . . . and court costs are high." No appeal was filed.

That was the end of the legal story—but not the end of Ryan Thomas's troubles. All along, the Thomases had said they were fighting not for their son's readmission but for the right to decide what was best for him. The day after Thanksgiving vacation, Ryan returned to school. He was nervous, Judy Thomas told reporters, and at the end of the school day, the boy who had earlier relished attention was too shy to talk.

The youngster who, during the first days of school, was described by Lori Parker as the class darling, was now insisting that he "hated" school; he wanted his mother or one of his brothers constantly in class with him. "He felt like he was under so much pressure, like everybody was watching him and waiting for him to do something wrong," said Robin Thomas.

On December 4, 1986, Judy Thomas took her "little shadow" out of school. She blamed the school district for willing Ryan to fail. She also blamed herself. "We've been so uptight. Ryan has probably picked up on that."

Happily, young children change their minds. After staying home for a week, Ryan decided to try school one more time when his parents assured him he would be free to call it quits again if life in Classroom Six proved too stressful. The boy has since remained in school, though on some days he refuses to attend, and he has stayed healthy, too. Judy Thomas was hoping that Ryan could at last be "just like the other kids." Meanwhile, though, parents of some of the other youngsters in Classroom Six were reporting that their children were being ostracized, that the stigma of AIDS had spread to them. These parents had agreed that their children would share their kindergarten year with Ryan. Now they wondered whether the group would be kept together, and isolated, for all the years of school.

As Ryan enrolled in first grade in September 1987, camera crews from the local TV station were again present. Otherwise, though, both the family and the town have stayed out of the limelight. "There are times I didn't know if we could make it," recalls Robin Thomas. But then he adds, with a show of bravery: "I'd do it again, though. They're not going to tell me where Ryan can and can't go."

The Thomases remain very much on the fringe of life in Atascadero. Like Jeanne White in Kokomo, they are accused of using their child's fatal disease as a way of making themselves rich. Even Jennifer Bacon and Kay Wells, parents who sympathized with their plight, have sometimes been puzzled by their behavior. "You can't just make a freak show out of a kid, dragging him from reporter to reporter," says Bacon. And Wells notes that "Robin can give the impression that he's more interested in having won the case than in his son. And he hasn't always done the most expedient or politic thing." But Wells sees the other side of this story too. "I couldn't handle myself at all times with aplomb. When you see the tears, you get a feel for the struggle those people have gone through."

The hostility in the community has occasionally bubbled to the surface. In February 1987, four men drove into the driveway to the Thomases' front yard and tried to entice Ryan into their car with promises of candy and a trip to Disneyland. Police refused to investigate what Robin Thomas believes was an attempted kidnapping.

That episode made the family anxious to move away from Atascadero, to start over as the Whites did when they left Kokomo. The Thomases had hoped that their son's story, like Ryan White's, would be made into a TV movie. If that happened, they planned on using the money to move to Los Angeles—anonymous, laissez faire Los Angeles. But the TV movie did not materialize, and the possibility of a new beginning has receded into the realm of daydreams.

When the story of young Ryan Thomas is just a dim recollection, when outsiders no longer associate Atascadero with the fateful bite, this town—very much like Kokomo—is likely once again to think about AIDS, not as an epidemic that for the foreseeable future can only grow worse, but as a freak occurrence. "After the court rules, the situation isn't going to go away," ACLU attorney Hoffman had warned during the court hearing, but to Superintendent Tony Avina, the decision really meant that the Atascadero Unified School District could return to the business of worrying about the education of its other 4,499 students.

It is in towns like Atascadero, where passions seldom run high, that you might anticipate a relatively conflict-free resolution of the AIDS crisis. Here, after all, were decently educated people who watch the evening news and read the national newsweeklies, and who in 1986 could grasp as well as any layman the fact that AIDS is not easily spread. Here townspeople had been given a chance to voice their concerns and to draft a policy that the school system adopted. By the fall of 1986, when Ryan was admitted to school, a peaceful resolution seemed at hand.

The bite, of course, undid everything—the bite and Superintendent Avina's reaction. If Ryan Thomas had been a thirteen-year-old who could control his emotions and his behavior, not an impulsive kindergartner who bit another child at a moment of stress, the process of decision-making constructed by the superintendent would have worked. But parents' fears were reawakened by the bite. Here was a child, they said aloud, who posed a special menace, and here was a family of transients, they said sotto voce, that was more interested in publicity than in the needs of their dying son.

Tony Avina's reaction to the bite only reinforced those fears. A more meticulous administrator confronted with the same news would have avoided a rush to judgment. He would have learned quickly about the differences between an incidental bite and habitual biting, and about the tenuous relationship between biting and AIDS—even as Sam Hannon in Lorraine had set out to learn about AIDS and homosexual behavior. A good leader would have used that knowledge, as Jack McCarthy did in Swansea, to keep the peace—to invite a full deliberation that could bring all the facts to light. There were certainly people in

Atascadero who deserved to be listened to, and who urged such a course: Dr. George Rowland, the local AIDS expert, whose judgment the school had previously relied on, and the parents of Classroom Six, who knew the situation best.

But on the subject of AIDS, Avina had never really led, had never been either the voice of expertise or the voice of compassion. Instead, as Rowland had noted, Avina had sought out the bandwagon of community sentiment, then jumped aboard. Ryan Thomas's single bite made the issue one of damage control, and all Avina's subsequent moves were intended to remove his problem, not address what had become a more complicated factual and moral issue.

With Avina playing the role of adversary, and with the Thomases, seemingly confirmed in their attitude of distrust, looking to the ACLU for help, there was no longer any room for settlement. Indeed, there was no longer much to talk about. The "compromise" the school board offered—keeping Ryan out of school until his case could be reviewed three months later—held little appeal for the Thomases. They had compromised earlier when they agreed to a separate toilet, and compromised again when they agreed to a psychological evaluation following the bite. But those gestures, they felt, had only been turned against them. Besides, the Thomases were not confident that in Janauary the school authorities would change their minds and allow Ryan back in school; the superintendent's conduct during the private session gave them little cause for reassurance on that score.

This is why *Thomas v. Atascadero Unified School District* became, not a discussion among parents and school professionals, but a case that each side desperately wanted to win—a case that was resolved in a strange venue, a federal district court in Los Angeles, and in a language, the rhetoric of precedents and rights, far removed from the talk of Atascadero.

The judicial decision delivered a civics lesson, to anyone who chose to listen. It was a reminder to Atascaderans that they were not free to decide things entirely as they pleased, that the concept of rights—codified in the federal Rehabilitation Act, ultimately deriving from the underlying constitutional right of any person in this society to fair treatment—defined the outer bounds of their discretion. Judge Stotler's reasoned judgment echoed an observation that Alexis de Tocqueville had made about America a century and a half earlier—when civil discourse breaks down, the concept of rights, interpreted by a judge, ultimately defines the terms of membership in a community. It is the rights embedded in a national covenant that make it so hard for communities to banish the feared and disliked, whether they are Nazis in Skokie, Illinois, or blacks in Forsythe County, Georgia, or street people or homosexuals or children with AIDS.

Such lessons are better learned in public conversations that allow ideas and values some room for play. Public talk can become a way of sorting out the reality of people's fears and the tolerability of risks, as well as a way of understanding the wounds that building walls can inflict on those who construct the barriers. But without a leader to point out those values, the conversations in Atascadero in the weeks after the bite were fed by fear. In such circumstances, it is better that the idea of rights acquire meaning in a distant courthouse than not at all, as happened in Ocilla, Georgia.

A price is paid in relying on a court and a stranger to settle a community's problems: those opposed to the decision are left no way to sift through their anger. When Atascadero decided not to appeal Ryan's court-ordered admission, a vocal parents' group felt they had been sold out. For a while, they made AIDS their cause. They looked for a strategy to change California's AIDS policy but wound up only with a villain: homosexuals.

"I have much compassion for Ryan, who was an innocent victim," wrote Cindy Doll in a letter than ran in the *Atascadero News*, "but no compassion whatsoever for the disease itself. . . . [The court decision] merely paves the way for homosexuals to be declared a 'minority group' by virtue of the fact that they are being discriminated against. The next 'blessing' that would be bestowing upon you and your children is that you will have Atascadero (and others) forced into hiring minority group homosexuals to teach in your public schools. . . . Don't be so naive to believe that the ACLU is not planning for this succession of events."

This theme of a gay plot to set the AIDS agenda was repeated by an Atascadero contingent that ventured more directly into politics. The group did not endorse political extremist Lyndon LaRouche's state ballot initiative on AIDS—which contemplated quarantining people with the AIDS virus—because, as Santa Rosa Road parent Kathy Wentzel said, "This meant taking on powerful homosexuals." However, Wentzel and several others flew to Sacramento to meet with their state assemblyman, Republican Eric Seastrand. They urged Seastrand to introduce a bill requiring that school districts be notified whenever a child with AIDS was enrolled—California's privacy laws protect the confidentiality of that information—and advanced the same proposal at the statewide PTA convention. But their idea went nowhere. It was homosexuals, they surmised, who were undermining such measures.

These frustrated Atascaderans saw themselves as rebuked by the court and shut out of the political discourse. Now they were reaching for a scapegoat: the "powerful" homosexuals. It was irrelevant that this attribution of power had little basis in fact, that California's AIDS policy was primarily being shaped, not by influential homosexuals, but by a conservative Republican governor with little inclination to court gay voters. What counted was the perception of these citizens of Atascadero that their lives were being manipulated by malevolent outside forces. Homosexuals were assigned a role like that given such historically despised groups as the Jews. The message of the judicial ruling in *Thomas v. Atascadero Unified School District*—that, in the end, the school board and the superintendent had acted without evidence, had succumbed to the fears of the community—went ignored, as Atascadero's leaders were quick to redescribe history. "If it wasn't for the bite, this town would be lauded for the way it handled the issue," says Tony Avina. But what the superintendent cannot see is the impact of his own behavior on the unfolding of the Ryan Thomas story, his politically charged reaction to the biting incident and the strong feelings his reaction invited.

"There was no crisis," declared an editorial in the *Atascadero News,* the local weekly that determinedly puts a pleasant face on things. Among Atascaderans themselves, the general sentiment is that nothing much had happened, that the pace of community growth remained a far bigger issue than AIDS would ever be, that the Ryan Thomas story had been blown out of all proportion, sensationalized by that familiar enemy, the reporters who grabbed what they wanted and ran.

In Atascadero, the reluctance to teach schoolchildren about the dangers of AIDS persists. AIDS is regarded as part of sex education, which remains a touchy subject the superintendent is unwilling to pursue. "They still think it's Happy Valley," says County Medical Director George Rowland. "They still believe it can't happen here."

Triptych: Chicago

Why did it happen in this and not in some other way? Because it happened so! Chance created the situation; genius utilized it. But what
is chance? What is genius?

Leo Tolstoy, *War and Peace*

The pleasant-looking men and women who gathered outside
Chicago's Pilsen Academy in March 1987 looked like Jehovah's
Witnesses in their go-to-meeting clothes. But the message they
brought was not the Word. "The blood of your own children
will be on your hands," they shouted, "if you allow this child
with AIDS in your school."

These words would scare anyone. They were particularly
chilling to the people living in the Pilsen neighborhood of Chicago. The old-line Chicano community knew very little about
AIDS. But from years of fighting, the people of Pilsen did know
the Board of Education, which had ordered that this child be
enrolled, and what they knew made them uneasy. Was this unnamed youngster with the deadly disease just the latest and
worst thing that downtown was dumping on Pilsen's doorstep?

The debate in Pilsen went on for weeks in the school and
on the streets, in homes and neighborhood organizations. A
fortnight later, it was the nice-looking strangers, unmasked as

camp followers of political extremist Lyndon LaRouche, who were driven off. The *doñas* of Pilsen listened to their own people, the Chicano doctors and the Chicano members of the Board of Education, as well as to a Jewish principal who over the years had earned their grudging trust. And the people of Pilsen took their cue from the *doñas*.

This was not the first time a child with AIDS had enrolled in Chicago area schools, nor would it be the last. Two months earlier, in January 1987, the affluent suburb of Wilmette had allowed an elementary school child with AIDS to remain in school. Although unprecedented in the state of Illinois, so flawlessly did Wilmette carry it off that, from the outside, the event looked stage-managed. Only those who really knew the story appreciated how much, for all the meticulous preparation, it was good fortune, together with parents willing to learn the facts and a family that was its own best advertisement, that carried the day.

But Wilmette's experience, as the media recounted it, became a symbol of compassion—a piece of history that the people involved in the Pilsen confrontation could look to. And Pilsen's story, in turn, helped shape events two months later, in May 1987, when another potentially explosive situation arose: a foster father enrolled his AIDS-striken young son in the Nettelhorst Elementary School, located in Chicago's predominantly gay neighborhood.

WILMETTE

The Chicago suburb of Wilmette, situated on Lake Michigan some fifteen miles north of the city, looks like an upscale version of a Norman Rockwell painting. The brick-paved streets in the older Wilmette neighborhoods, shaded by venerable elms, are lined with rambling colonials and Midwest Victorians. Sailboats and cabin cruisers stand at attention in the harbor. Farm houses are still to be seen, although the farms themselves are no more than a nostalgic memory, their land turned over to tracts of brick ranch houses. The outfields of the softball diamonds and the fairways of the golf courses stay a brilliant green, even in the middle of summer. The tallest structures in town are the steeples of the churches, mock-Gothic cathedrals and simple shingled houses of worship that poke through the elms.

The townspeople of Wilmette also seem to have walked straight off a Rockwell canvas. Everyone in town makes at least a comfortable living, and almost everyone is white. Though the population of 30,000 is divided roughly equally among Protestants, Catholics, and Jews, most of the people who live in the pleasant community have taken on the protective coloration of the WASP. Even the children look like ads for Laura Ashley and Brooks Brothers, and a local joke has it that, when the high school was deciding on its colors, gray flannel was the top choice.

There is old money in town, and new money too; houses in the Indian Hill Estates go for half a million dollars and up. But unlike Kenilworth, its neighbor to the north, Wilmette does not put on airs, and its politics is decidedly more liberal than in the other so-called power suburbs north of Chicago. Perhaps the reason is the influence of Evanston, the town that separates Wilmette from Chicago proper, which is home to both a major university, Northwestern, and a sizeable black population; perhaps it is also the ethnic and religious diversity of the community.

The true pride of Wilmette is its public schools. There are four elementary schools and one junior high in town (the high school is managed by a separate board), all lavishly supported with tax dollars and carefully watched over by parents. It is a rarity for a family from Wilmette to send its children to private schools, though most of the families could afford to do so. In Chicago, many parents—including many non-Catholics—scrimp to send their youngsters to parochial schools, out of a belief that they will learn more there. In Wilmette, approximately one-third Catholic, one of the two parochial schools was forced to close for lack of enrollment.

Enrollment has been declining in Wilmette's public schools too, as escalating house prices have put the town out of reach for many young families. Since 1970, the number of students has dropped from 4,900 to 2,400, and fewer than one adult in five now has a child in the Wilmette schools. These demographic facts have forced the school district to make hard choices: How should it configure its grade structure? Which schools should it close? Such questions can evoke the passions of parents, even in seemingly placid Wilmette. It is not merely a matter of how long a bike ride Johnny has every day but the more important matter of identity, for individual schools in Wilmette take on the character of their neighborhoods.[1] The Jews, the German Catholics, the old-line families, and the nouveaux riches—each group has its own school.

The school superintendent and the seven-member school board who decide these questions—who decided to keep a child with AIDS in school—are habitually attentive to the shifting political currents of Wilmette. Superintendent William Gussner, who came to Wilmette in 1983, thrives in tight spots. In his previous job, as assistant superintendent of a prosperous bedroom community outside St. Louis, he helped develop, and then sell to hostile white neighboring towns, a city-suburb racial integration plan. Gussner prides himself on paying meticulous attention to details. What he describes as his "personalized" style of running the schools, an out-and-about style, means that not much escapes his attention.

Though the citizens of Wilmette would shrink from the notion that a political machine runs the schools, the way school board members are picked would have been the envy of Mayor Daley. A caucus of some eighty people, representing local organizations such as garden clubs, the Junior League, and the PTAs, screens the candidates and puts together its slate. The election is merely a formality, since no one has beaten the slate in recent memory. Wilmette has adopted a sanitized version of ward politics, with the slate studiously balanced to take account of the geographic and ethnic divisions in the community—although, as one might expect, no one discusses this.

Bill and Fran McCardle* had moved into one of Wilmette's old colonials in 1983, when Bill's company transferred him to

---

*The family members' names and some family details have been changed to preserve confidentiality.

Chicago. The McCardles hadn't gotten involved much in school affairs; they were not "PTA types," recalls Paul Nilsen, principal of the Central School, which the two youngest of the six McCardle children attended. When they learned, in April 1986, that their son Jamie had AIDS, the McCardles didn't tell anyone, not even their own children. But many months later, after the whole family had worked its way through the denial and then the worst of the pain, they decided that keeping the secret was tearing the family apart. They would enjoy a peaceful Christmas holiday, Bill and Fran agreed, then talk to the principal of Jamie's school.

As a family, the McCardles had known more than their share of hard times. Bill's first wife, Mary, died of cancer in 1982, just four months after the disease was diagnosed; his mother, who came to take care of the children, also died suddenly. Then things seem to turn around. Bill met Fran, a teacher in the inner city schools and later a social worker, a woman with the kind of instinctive warmth that could gradually win the affection of the grieving children of another mother. Together they rebuilt the family and had another child of their own.

Jamie had been adopted in May 1982, just months before Mary's cancer was diagnosed. They boy's natural parents were both intravenous-drug users who had abandoned him when he was six weeks old, and Jamie had lived in foster homes until he was nearly two. "When he came to us, he was totally withdrawn—not a normal child, emotionally," Bill recalls. When he was enrolled in school, Jamie was placed in a class for children with emotional difficulties. Though plagued by a string of minor health problems, the boy had gradually emerged from his shell. "We have had the joy of watching him develop," says Bill. And then, in April 1986, came the news from the adoption agency: Jamie's mother had full-blown AIDS. The boy, when tested, was found to have the virus.

Suddenly, Jamie's long bouts of illnesses made sense. And suddenly, says Fran, "our world cracked."

Initially, mother and father responded differently. To Fran, it was important to talk through what the news meant, to make sense of the death sentence Jamie had been handed, to explain it to Jamie and his brothers and sisters, and to tell people who would come to know their son. But Bill was deep into denial—deep, also, into what he calls his lawyer routine. For months, he was hell-bent to insist on his rights, to fight for his son's privacy and his own.

As soon as the diagnosis was in, Bill started reading everything on AIDS he could get his hands on. He learned about what Ryan White had gone through in Kokomo, and he didn't want that to happen to Jamie. Bill worried that his children would be ostracized and that bricks would come flying through his living room window. When the McCardles had talked with their pediatrician about the possibility that Jamie had AIDS, the doctor had bluntly told them that he wanted nothing to do with the boy. If that was the doctor's reaction, what would the schools say?

Slowly, though, the story began to leak out. Fran worried about how other mothers would react when they learned that their children were playing with a boy who had AIDS, and she told several of her neighbors. The other McCardle children each told a close friend or two. One day just before Christmas vacation, Jamie whispered to his teacher, Jane Gold,* that his mother had told him a secret. "She said that when I was in my mom's stomach, my mom passed a disease on to me before I was born. But if I eat the right food, I'll probably live to be OK." A worried Jane Gold phoned Fran McCardle, who said: "Let me work on this over vacation; then I'll explain what's going on."

Fran and Bill had gone to the Howard Brown Memorial Clinic, a gay-run health center in Chicago, and had gotten good advice and needed comfort. The initiative was Fran's but the experience had had an especially deep impact on Bill. He used to be scornful of homosexuals, but now he became deeply admiring of how they supported the sick and dying among them—and deeply angered at how the Reagan administration was playing on the nation's fear of homosexuality. By December, Bill says, "I realized, finally, that I had a child who was going to

*Gold's name has been changed to preserve confidentiality.

die. I should be dealing with that reality in our family, not only for Jamie but for the other children and for myself."

On the morning of January 6, 1987, not knowing what to expect, the McCardles called on Principal Paul Nilsen at Central Elementary School. "Part of me was ready to say, 'Here's our lawyer,'" Fran remembers, but that wasn't necessary. "I'm glad you've come here," the principal told them. "This is where your son belongs."

From talking with Jane Gold and another teacher whom Jamie had confided in, Paul Nilsen knew that something was up. But Nilsen has been putting parents at their ease since he became principal of Central in 1971. Nothing about Central Elementary School's program is especially imaginative; like the other Wilmette schools, Central is, as School Board President Don Stephan characterized it, "on the cutting edge—but a bit behind the blade." What makes Nilsen so special is the respect and behind-the-scenes support he offers his teachers, the care he devotes to the concerns of the parents, and the teddy-bearish warmth in which he envelops the students, who greet him by name as he walks through the halls. "If AIDS had to happen someplace in our schools," says Superintendent Gussner, "it's good that it was at Central."

The day after the McCardles went to see Paul Nilsen, Bill Gussner and Don Stephan met for their weekly breakfast. "Just one more thing," the superintendent told the board president, after the third cup of coffee. "Make it quick," said Stephan, who was running late for an appointment in the city. "There's a boy with AIDS at Central," Gussner said. Stephan sat back down.

Nilsen had gone to Gussner immediately after his meeting with the McCardles, and together they began mapping out strategy. Now Stephan made his contribution. Although AIDS was not something he knew much about, the board president's profession gave him a head start in thinking about how Wilmette should proceed. Stephan is an executive with Hill & Knowlton, one of the biggest public relations firms in the business, and a specialist in handling corporate crises. AIDS had the potential of being Wilmette's Bhopal.

The decisions came thick and fast. Secrecy was essential if

Wilmette was to be prepared by the time the story broke, which could happen at any time, considering the number of people the McCardles had already told. The idea was for Gussner and Nilsen to keep up their daily rounds while surreptitiously slipping in the AIDS work that had to be done. Other key administrators and the members of the board would be brought into the picture at regular meetings over the following week.

Eventually, a hot line was set up, and everyone who had a stake in the enterprise was given a packet of articles and a Q-and-A that explained why children with AIDS did not endanger their classmates. The list of those informed included all the people who worked in the schools; other town officials (who had to be assured that Wilmette planned no cover-up); the local pediatricians; the staff at St. Xavier parochial school; the clergy; the media; and, most importantly, the parents.

Principal Paul Nilsen's almost instinctive reaction to reach out to the family was echoed by his fellow administrators and members of the school board. "We're a pretty competitive bunch," says Board President Stephan, speaking of his colleagues, "all around the same age, in our late thirties and early forties. We work well together, there aren't many real fights, but sometimes we try to do too much by committee." It is a conscientious group, whose meetings have been known to run past midnight.

In deciding what course Wilmette should follow, the school board found little to debate; the only disagreements were over the details of how to get the message out. "The decision was essentially self-dictating," says Stephan, because of the medical and legal advice that Wilmette had received. A year earlier, the school administrators had quietly adopted the AIDS guidelines of the Centers for Disease Control, while asking their lawyers to draft a policy statement covering infectious diseases in general. Board members prided themselves on checking their emotions at the door, making a decision based on medical and legal evidence. The last thing they wanted was for Wilmette to be seen as another Kokomo, which in their minds connoted irrationality.

Gussner and Stephan decided early that the school would be identified. That would localize the concern and minimize the chance of panic. No one wanted a repetition of the Queens,

New York, experience in which official silence meant that the
afflicted youngster could be in any school. But to maintain confidentiality, the Wilmette school authorities released no other
details to the public: not the name of the child or his grade
level, not how he had been exposed to the AIDS virus, not even
his sex. Whenever Nilsen or Gussner referred to the youngster,
it was always "he or she." Indeed, Gussner was so insistent on
keeping the secret that Stephan had to order him to divulge it
to the board president.

It was not until January 20, two weeks and a day after the
McCardles had met with Nilsen, that Wilmette went public.
That morning, 2,000 copies of the packet of AIDS materials
were mailed to parents. The superintendent and the board
president made the rounds of all the schools, accompanied by
Dr. Ellen Chadwick, the area's top pediatric AIDS specialist
who happened to be one of the referring doctors working on
the case, and Fred Lifton, the district's longtime attorney.

There was an audible gasp from the teachers at Central,
Stephan remembers, when they were told, first thing in the
morning, that one of their students had AIDS. At the other
Wilmette schools, the reaction ranged from "That's their problem" to "Why does this child have to be in school?" to "We trust
you." At Central that day, the children learned from their teachers that one of their classmates had a disease called AIDS. "We
didn't want a big assembly," says Nilsen. "The classroom teachers
are really counselors to their kids."

At 4:30 that afternoon, Stephan and Gussner repaired to the
superintendent's office. Gussner had been attending a superintendents' meeting in Florida. He had flown back that morning
and sped from O'Hare airport to Wilmette in the midst of a
blizzard; he was wiped out. As soon as they walked into the
office, the superintendent and the board president were met by
Rick Rosenthal, a Chicago TV reporter whose child, it so happened, had gone to Central the previous year. According to
Wilmette's timetable, the media were not supposed to come into
the picture for another day; by then, the packet would have
been in the parents' hands. "Gentlemen, you have a problem,"
said Rosenthal. "We do now," Stephan replied.

Don Stephan knew that the way the media handled the AIDS story was crucially important, but, in Chicago, the slant they would take was unpredictable. Although the *Tribune* can be staid to a fault, the *Sun-Times* had become more inclined to seek out the sensational under its buccaneer owner Rupert Murdoch. And the local TV stations were not above a bit of sensationalizing themselves, if it meant a boost in ratings.

Wilmette was the lead story on each of the TV stations that Tuesday night, and page-one news in both Chicago papers the next morning. What the reporters wanted was the identity of the child, but that, they were told, was legally privileged information. When a TV crew went out to Central School to gather parent reaction, it happened upon a parent who had adopted three handicapped children. From the school district's point of view, the interview couldn't have gone better. "Life is full of risks," the parent told the interviewer. The newspapers described what the *Tribune* reporter called the careful balancing act the Wilmette schools were engaging in as they weighed the needs of a sick child against the concerns of the community.

Within forty-eight hours, as the first meetings with parents were being held in Central's auditorium, the journalists had their angle: Wilmette was the community that cared, the town that had bucked the panic that had ripped other places apart. It helped that key media figures knew Wilmette firsthand: two of the TV reporters lived there, as did the reporter covering the story for the *Sun-Times* and the managing editor of the *Tribune*. It helped, too, that Don Stephan knew how to talk to reporters and that Bill Gussner had regularly faced tough questioning while promoting integration in Missouri.

The facts were also more or less in line with the media's version of events. In the days following the announcement, parents weren't pulling their children out of Central Elementary School, and civility continued to reign. One of the local weeklies, *Wilmette Life,* noted the "business as usual" atmosphere at Central, just one day after the story hit the news. The teachers' union president was quoted as saying that the teachers at Central "were dealing with the children's concerns rather than their own."

There were, to be sure, parents who told reporters they believed that the child should be kept home, parents who didn't want their own children exposed to what one mother called "the modern-day plague." But these comments were effectively neutralized by the words of fathers and mothers who endorsed what the schools were doing, and who cautioned that "this is the time for this community to remain cool."

On January 23, three days after Wilmette had gone public with its decision, the Sun-Times rhapsodized about the "admirable example" the town had set. The editors praised the schools for finding the facts and getting the facts out; they lauded the community for its "thoughfulness and calm." So much were the media won to Wilmette's cause that when one unhappy parent leaked Jamie's name a few days later, no one would repeat it.

The parents' meetings were not in fact always so calm or the parents themselves invariably so rational. Among the 400 mothers and fathers who packed Central Elementary School for the sessions held the afternoon and evening of January 22 were some who insisted that the adopted procedure, taking questions on 3 x 5 cards, effectively sanitized the discussion; charges of censorship were in the air. Other parents were unconvinced that the decision to keep a child with AIDS in school made sense. Fran McCardle was sitting in the audience, a silent observer absorbing the impact of the fears.

"I'm very concerned, very nervous, and very frightened," said Dr. Alieh Arjmand, an obstetrician from India with a practice in Chicago. Arjmand buttonholed everyone she could find, parents and administrators and reporters, telling them that she wanted to transfer her two children out of Central. Dr. John Phair, a Northwestern Medical School professor and nationally known AIDS expert who spoke at the parents' meetings, a man who looks every bit the part of the all-wise doctor, recalls another uncomfortable moment: an angry buzzing spread through the audience when, following the advice of Fred Lifton, the cautious school attorney, Dr. Phair told the assemblage that the way in which the child had contracted AIDS was irrelevant.

"How do we know there isn't a molester on the loose?" one

parent demanded, and others murmured the same concern. Fears about a molester were eventually put to rest when Phair, known to many in the audience because he lives in neighboring Winnetka, prevailed on Lifton to allow him to reassure parents that the child had not been sexually abused. And most of the parents' questions were far more mundane. Ph.D.s cited references to medical journals when they asked about the scientific evidence; lawyers stuck to their last, inquiring about legal liability. The team of experts picked by Gussner deftly fielded even the most technical issues, and the audience seemed generally satisfied.

At the end of the evening session, a man who had been insistent on speaking rose and faced the audience. Don Stephan braced himself for the worst. But what he heard couldn't have sounded sweeter if it had been drafted by the PR man himself. "I hope to God you're doing the right thing. But I think that all of us in this room support you and appreciate the courage it took for this family to come forward." The meeting ended in applause.

The McCardles' decision to come forward, to share their secret with the town, moved many parents. But that weekend brought new fears, spread by supporters of political extremist Lyndon LaRouche. LaRouche was known all too well in the Chicago area. The previous spring, in a stunning bit of political guerrilla theater, two of his handpicked candidates had walked off with the Democratic Party's nominations for two statewide offices. The ensuing attempt by honest-to-God Democrats to disassociate themselves from the LaRouche Democrats probably cost the party the Illinois statehouse.

LaRouche had made AIDS a cornerstone of his political agenda with the slogan "Spread panic, not AIDS." His National Democratic Policy Committee platform called for mass AIDS testing and quarantining of all —by now numbering a million and a half—who carried the virus. In California the previous fall, LaRouche followers had gotten an AIDS quarantine proposition on the ballot. It took a two-million dollar campaign to defeat the proposition, and LaRouche had vowed to go to the voters again.

Schools were an obvious place for LaRouche's forces to fo-
ment panic. As early as the fall of 1985, they had tried to stir
things up in the Brighton neighborhood of Boston. More recently in Granby, Connecticut, a small town just outside Hartford, Paul Cameron, a LaRouche ally who calls homosexuals
"highly mobile infectious disease factories," a psychologist who
had been read out of the American Psychological Association
for his bizarre views, had been crusading, also unsuccessfully,
against allowing a child with AIDS in school.

The LaRouchites know how to fight dirty—to shut up an op-
ponent they are trained to shout "He has AIDS! He has
AIDS!"—but in sedate Wilmette they prudently couched their
message in the quieter language of pseudo-science. LaRouche
supporters handed out leaflets to parents attending the informational meetings and stuck fliers on the windshields of parked
cars. Several hundred families received a fat packet of articles
from *The New American,* the LaRouche party's house organ,
warning what happens "When Perversion Prospers" and issuing an "AIDS Warning: The Surgeon General's Report May Be
Hazardous to Your Health." The weekend after Wilmette's announcement, a sound truck cruised the streets broadcasting the
LaRouche message of fear.

Wilmette police quickly put a stop to this campaign. They escorted the sound truck to the edge of town and shooed off the
leafleters. Such tactics were constitutionally questionable, for
even speech that offends the sensibilities of the right-minded
enjoys the protections of the First Amendment, but the police
could cite local ordinances banning sound trucks and requiring
permits before leafleting.

Wilmette was not yet home free. At the third forum, held on
Monday, January 26, 1987, three visibly anguished women made
their way to the front of the auditorium. They turned toward
the massed and waiting cameras as they entered the assembly
hall. Throughout the meeting, the women seethed. "That's not
so," they muttered while Phair and Gussner were answering
questions from the audience. "Tell the truth."

A 3 x 5 card turned in to Stephan, who was chairing the
meeting, greatly worried the school board president. "The

AIDS patient is in my son's special education class," the card read. "Not only will the school district not remove the student from the class, they will not allow us to remove our children to save them. The AIDS patient constantly puts toys and pencils in his mouth." Stephan ignored the raised hands of the women until the end of the meeting, when the TV crews had left to file their stories. Then the mother who had written down her accusation turned to the assembled parents and said her piece. "At that moment," Stephan recalls, "I thought it had come undone."

Yet what the audience apparently heard in the voice of this mother was the unraveling edge of hysteria, not a factually rooted demonstration of danger. Over the course of three meetings, seemingly all the parents' hardest questions had been answered, all the contingencies explored. It was time, almost, for business as usual.

Still, it was clear that some of the parents whose children were in Jamie's class had unanswered questions. Jamie had been sensitive to all the talk about AIDS and had innocently told one of his classmates that he was the one who had the disease. His classmate's mother turned out to be the woman who had submitted the 3 x 5 card, and that night she and her son telephoned everyone else in the class with the news. This alarmed both the other youngsters and their parents.

Among all the parents, these were the ones most likely to be alarmed. They were also the fathers and mothers whose understanding and support mattered most if Jamie was to continue leading a normal life in class. At this point, Fran and Bill McCardle took a brave step. They decided that a meeting was needed for all these parents at their house. Ellen Chadwick, Jamie's doctor, would be there, as would teacher Jane Gold and Principal Paul Nilsen. And everything, including the story of how Jamie had contracted AIDS, would be told.

It was a tense group that gathered up all the seats in the house, the big rocker and the plaid couch and the oak dining chairs, to listen to the McCardles tell how Jamie came into their lives. Shortly after Jamie had been diagnosed, they were told, both Fran and Bill McCardle had been tested for AIDS, as had two of their children who wanted reassurance that they were not infected—wanted it badly enough to brave the taking of blood. At the meeting, the McCardles could tell the parents of Jamie's classmates that "for years, we didn't know that he had AIDS and we took no precautions. None of us has AIDS."

All the parents in that living room talked about how sorry they were for what the McCardles were going though. And they praised their bravery in coming forward—trusting their neighbors enough to place the family's fate in their hands. "We feel good that you told us," they said. One couple, both doctors, who described themselves as hypochondriacs about their own child's health, added reassuring words. "If we thought that there was one chance in a million that our child could catch this virus, we wouldn't be here tonight."

The mother who had worried so about Jamie's biting on pencils and toys was too overwrought to hear what was being said. But it was Ellen Chadwick who made the biggest impression on the parents. It wasn't just that the doctor had the facts to back up her reassurances: she was very visibly pregnant. "Do you think that I would be caring for children with AIDS if I believed that I was endangering my child?" she asked.

By then, the controversy really was over—at least the public part. A bomb scare a few days later was treated matter-of-factly. And when the *Wilmette News/Voice*, a local shopper, tried to make an issue out of the famous 3 x 5 card, townspeople lit into the paper for being irresponsible. Support for the family came from all sides. The Central School PTA passed a resolution offering whatever help might be needed to a family whose identity they still did not know and, in the spring, the Junior Auxiliary of the Wilmette Women's Club asked Superintendent Gussner to find out if the family had a favorite charity to which they could contribute. The answer came back: please make the donation to the Howard Brown Memorial Clinic, which had seen the McCardles through the roughest times.

It fell to Jamie's teacher, Jane Gold, to talk with his classmates about AIDS, explaining in simple terms how the disease spread, and about Jamie's condition. "What you have heard is true," she

said. "And I wish I had had the chance to tell you first. Jamie
has AIDS. Eventually he is going to die."

Some children needed reassurance that they would not catch
AIDS; others were simply caught up in personal grief. "He's my
friend, I don't want him to die!" one boy in the class said, while
another asked whether "AIDS is going to hurt Jamie."

It was fine to talk about Jamie and AIDS in class, Gold said,
but "this is a family matter, we're not going to talk about it in
gym or music or art," and the class kept the confidence. They
discussed how to keep his identity secret from the reporters
who, it was feared, would snoop around. "If a reporter asks, we
can all say we're the kid who has it," one child suggested, a sentiment that recalls the historic moment when Adolf Hitler demanded that Danish Jews wear yellow armbands and everyone
in Denmark wore them.

In class, Jamie's behavior was unobtrusively monitored—
to make sure, for instance, that he wasn't sharing his food.
Hugging time, a daily ritual, was abandoned because it made
Gold uncomfortable, but the children continued to hug one
another and went out of their way to hug Jamie. For several
weeks, Gold scrubbed Jamie's desk with bleach solution every
time he sneezed, but eventually she decided that she was being
hypercautious.

"We suffered together, and we all learned to be kind and to
love one another," says Gold, who recalls when she was almost
too sad to teach, when only her sense of obligation to the children kept her going. The lesson was heeded. A parent of one
of Jamie's classmates told Ms. Gold that her boy had been walking around the house dressed up in a doctor's costume. "I'm
going to find a cure for AIDS," he told his mother, "Jamie isn't
going to die."

As the teachers at Central listened to the children ask why
one among them had to die of this bad disease, they realized
that Wilmette needed instructional materials not only about
AIDS but also about death, pitched at a level young children
could understand.

The school district responded with its customary efficiency, hiring a specialist to produce the needed curriculum. The McCardles, meanwhile, tried to absorb the implications of what was happening. Their son had been welcomed into the Wilmette schools. Their neighbors had rallied around them. And, within a few years, their son was going to die.

In Wilmette and elsewhere, the public school is a place where adults congregate to decide questions of value. It is also the single public institution that teaches something about values to the nation's young.

Despite the fond hopes of the 1960s radical educators, the Paul Goodmans and John Holts who in their warmhearted innocence imagined every schoolhouse as a miniature democracy, teachers are firmly in command except under rare and unappealing circumstances of anarchy. This is true whether the school's aim is to turn out obedient good citizens or inhabitants of some new Atlantis of loving-kindness. Nor should this be surprising. The social meaning of being young is that inevitably *some* hovering adult presence will guide, if not dominate, one's life. "You cannot be a ruler unless you have first been ruled," as Aristotle counsels in the *Politics*, and since so much of a child's life is spent in schools, the teacher naturally assumes that authority.

Schools involuntarily conscript not just the presence of children but their most intimate participation. All too often, though, they mostly use their authority to keep order. In an institution where, by one count, as many as a thousand interchanges between students and teachers take place each day, order keeping is assuredly needed; the problem is one of emphasis. One study reports that, in the primary grades, teachers rank following the rules above any other lesson, including reading and arithmetic. And if rules are emphasized somewhat less in the upper grades, it is only because, by and large, students have made the rules their own.[2]

"They got politics in their dreams," said one black mother, speaking about the lessons her eleven-year-old son and her twelve-year-old daughter were taking away from school. "That's

the way it is with all God's children. They take in everything and
no one can say for sure when they'll jump down from where
they were setting."³ Students quickly learn that, although life
in school can bring out their entire repertoire of feelings—
docility, competitiveness, confession, and a sense of vulnerability—the classroom is not an away-from-home family.⁴

In the drama of unfolding childhood, school plays an ex-
quisitely delicate part. It deals in intimacy, particularly in the
first years when the teacher is the nine-to-three "mom" and
sometimes more than that. But even as one mom is routinely
replaced by another at year's end—an intolerable custom if the
teacher really were a parent—the school does not—cannot—
always respond sensitively to the special needs of individual
children. Instead, it relies basically, though as humanely as
possible, on the application of general yardsticks. The mix of
personalism and universality—the incident that catches the
teacher's eye, and the checked-off categories on the report
card—is intended to prepare children for adult life. What occurred in Jane Gold's class was extraordinary: almost never
does the life-and-death fate of a young classmate become explicitly the object of attention.

Educators have made a somewhat oversimplified distinction
between two basic kinds of primary schools: traditional schools
in which obedience is the sum of the message—what matters
most are the rules themselves and the awful consequences of
breaking them, not the forging of principles that transcend
classroom commandments—and modern schools in which, under the tutelage of the teacher, children learn to reason about
moral rules for themselves. "When a school ties a child sternly
to a disciplinary structure," one study of a half-dozen schools
over a period of years concludes, "when it presents the child
with the task of keeping constant track of the rules of acceptable behavior, it may defeat its own goal of shaping a morally
mature individual."⁵

Other aspects of schooling, including the institution's commitment to the idea that learning means thinking, not rote
learning, can powerfully affect children's capacity for moral
maturity. So too does life at home and on the streets, as well as

the core of individual identity that is beyond manipulation. But the point remains: more than fear or respect for one's elders is needed to build a free and powerful character, one able to cope intelligently and humanely with the kind of moral crisis signaled by the presence of AIDS.

At Case Junior High School in Swansea, Massachusetts, where Principal Harold Devine urged students to "practice taking responsibility" for their lives, Mark Hoyle's classmates responded with sophisticated moral reasoning to his wish to be in school, thoughtfully considering his rights and imagining themselves in his place.

Although the students in Jane Gold's Wilmette classroom were younger than those in Swansea, they could understand something one of their mothers failed to grasp: the importance of treating Jamie's illness as a "family matter." And one of these wise children could propose that they would all protect their classmate by each pretending, if asked, to be the child with AIDS.

PILSEN

Paul Nilsen, the Wilmette Central School principal, drove down to Chicago's Pilsen Community Academy the morning of February 27, 1987. Three days earlier, Bill Levin, Pilsen's principal, had been summoned to the office of Deputy Superintendent Joseph Lee and told that a preschool child who had been exposed to the AIDS virus would soon be enrolling in his school. Levin had called Nilsen seeking help, and Nilsen had offered to spell out Wilmette's strategy at a meeting of Pilsen community leaders.

This was not like dealing with the Wilmette town manager or the principal at St. Xavier; that much Nilsen quickly figured out. All the other building principals in Pilsen Academy's district (one of twenty elementary school districts in Chicago) were in attendance that morning, together with officials from the Chicago Health Department and Board of Education and priests from the six Catholic churches in Pilsen.

The community organizers were there, too. They ran the neighborhood action programs that handled job training and day care, renovated rundown homes, and mediated among rival gangs—programs that made Pilsen a true community.

Chicago would be picking a mayor and a new city council in just six weeks, and both candidates for alderman were also present. A Democratic mayoral candidate, Thomas Hynes, had asked if he could come, but Levin diplomatically demurred. To invite Hynes meant inviting Harold Washington, the Democratic incumbent; if Washington and Hynes both showed up, Pilsen's AIDS problem might become a citywide political issue.

Bill Levin knew there was no way to keep the Pilsen Academy situation wholly out of politics, in a city where even the most trivial event of daily life can become a matter of clout. The principal's hope was to keep the politics localized, which meant persuading all the constituencies in the neighborhood, the parents and politicians and priests, that they could live with the AIDS decision. Levin knew that if he failed, if the community split, there would be serious trouble.

The meeting of Pilsen community leaders came off without a serious hitch, as did Bill Levin's other attempts that week to touch base with everyone who had a stake in the AIDS issue. It was only some days later, when Lyndon LaRouche's followers made a determined effort to broaden the issue by evoking a panic that knew no geography, that the attempt to emulate Wilmette began to unravel.

"Hog Butcher for the World/Tool Maker, Stacker of Wheat": Carl Sandburg's description of his "broad-shouldered" hometown remains famous, three-quarters of a century after it was written, but the image doesn't reflect contemporary Chicago. The slaughterhouses are long gone, the appliance factories and steel mills, too; manufacturing now provides jobs for fewer than one worker in five. The city of three million, gradually losing population to the surrounding suburbs, is fast becoming a center for the new service economy. The idea of trading in options was invented in Chicago in 1973 and has brought prosperity to the money men. Downtown—the Loop, as Chicagoans call it— has been made over by a building boom, second only to New York City's, that gave Chicago some of the most distinguished, and more of the most monumental, architecture in America.

The old Chicagoans—middle European, proletarian, living in modest frame bungalows in industrial villages—are also slowly disappearing. Along Lake Michigan and in the neighborhoods just north of downtown, gentrification is in full swing. Condominium prices keep going up, and Michigan Avenue may become Chicago's answer to Fifth Avenue and Rodeo Drive. "A decent, potbellied working man's city is now wearing a turtle-neck sweater . . . and a suave look on its face," laments Mike Royko, columnist and conscience of Chicago. "And its nose is stuck in a brandy snifter."

Elsewhere in the city, though, in old ruined neighborhoods from which the Irish and the Poles have fled, stretch acre after acre of endless blight, territory largely abandoned to new immigrants, poor and nonwhite. Between them, blacks and Hispanics make up 57 percent of Chicago's population, double the proportion of 1970, and cluster, apart from the rest, in the nation's most racially segregated city.[6] It was to Chicago that Martin Luther King came in 1965 to open up housing to blacks, for Chicago symbolized all that was evil about race relations in the North. "The people of Mississippi ought to come to Chicago to learn how to hate," King said during his failed campaign.

To such accusations, and to the lingering memories of police brutality at the 1968 Democratic national convention, Chicagoans have responded with instinctive defensiveness. "Locals used to call Chicago the city that works, and contrasted New York's financial tumult (during the 1970s)," political scientists Kathleen Kemp and Robert Lineberry observe. "But if it works, it works because, some suspect, it runs on grease."[7] A decade ago, the *Sun-Times* opened its own bar, "The Mirage," and used its experiences to report on how everyone from the policeman on the beat to the plumbing inspector was looking for a payoff; the account caught Chicago in the act of being itself. "Chicago isn't so much a city," Nelson Algren had written some years earlier, "as a vast way station where three and a half million bipeds swarm with a single cry, 'One side or a leg off, I'm getting mine.' It's every man for himself in this hired air."

Chicago is the place where Mayor Richard Daley—Boss Daley for twenty years, until his death in 1976—took out the patent on machine politics. If you wanted a city job, a zoning variance, a sewer connection, you went to the ward leader where you lived, and paid back the favor come election time. It was, one of Daley's critics said, "a kind of municipal totalitarianism."

Although the ward system worked well enough for whites, blacks and Hispanics were largely shut out. Things began to change after a series of court orders in the late 1970s reduced the number of patronage jobs in Chicago from 40,000 to 900. And when Harold Washington was elected mayor in 1983, the pace of change picked up noticeably. Washington billed himself as the reform candidate and the candidate of the minorities. When he pledged that the city would become "ours," everyone knew whom he was talking about.

Another and very different kind of politics had grown up in Chicago in the Daley years—the politics of community organizing. Saul Alinsky, a native Chicagoan, was the acknowledged master of organizing, and during the 1960s neighborhood after neighborhood learned from the tactics Alinsky put into practice in Chicago's Woodlawn area. If City Hall wasn't going to create new housing and libraries and decent schools on its own initiative, if the politicians weren't going to take care of potholes and dope dealers unless pushed, organizers would mobilize their communities to do the pushing. Boycotts and demonstrations were added to the arsenal of Chicago's political tactics. These new community groups, largely frozen out of the patronage dispensed by the bosses in the city's fifty wards, found new dollars— and new clout— in the War on Poverty programs that President Lyndon Johnson launched.

"Native leadership was crucial for community organizations," Alinsky wrote,[8] and few Chicago neighborhoods have generated more forceful leaders than has Pilsen, home to three-quarters of the Mexican community in Chicago. Though Pilsen is just a mile south of the Loop, the two places literally do not speak the same language. Pilsen was developed a century back by Czechs, Poles, and Germans; its architecture has the solid feel of a middle-European city, all gables and steep pointy roofs. But the shops that once sold bratwurst and schnappes have long since been replaced by *bodegas* and *fruterías*, whose Day-Glo colors contrast with wooden beams and somber stained glass.

Since Mexicans first began settling in Pilsen in the aftermath of the 1917 revolution, it has been a cohesive neighborhood, with its own traditions and its own organizations. It is not Mexico in *Yanqui*-land, though, for the Anglo culture inevitably intrudes. Stores in Pilsen have names like "Descuento Center," and the children speak their own made-up language of Spanish and English.

The poverty of the families has meant that, even three-quarters of a century ago, residents of Pilsen had to look outside, to places like Jane Addams' Hull House, for help. Nearly four families in ten continue to live in overcrowded housing, more than double the citywide average, and one resident in four lives in poverty. Mexicans emigrating to Chicago still come first to Pilsen, while second- and third-generation Chicanos move away, if they can.

The six Catholic churches that line the neighborhood's main street are the backbone of the community; all draw huge crowds for Sunday mass. It stood to reason that the planners of Pope John Paul II's trip to Chicago in 1979 included a stop in Pilsen. The priests, a number of them Hispanic, see their mission in social terms, taking up issues like immigration as their cause, finding common ground with a host of community groups.

In Pilsen, as in other black and Latino neighborhoods, a new generation of leaders emerged from the events of the 1960s. These were people who fought for their own neighborhood high school and bilingual education, for decent jobs and health care, who were not afraid to conduct a sit-in at City Hall or stage a walkout at the local school. Under Mayor Washington, some of these leaders moved on to city jobs. With federal dollars scarce on the ground, the local organizations—Casa Aztlán, the Latino American Association, the Pilsen Youth Organization—

are no longer as strong as a decade earlier and are given to bickering with each other. Some people complain that Pilsen Neighbors, which over the years became the most powerful of these groups, has lost its commitment to local concerns. Nonetheless, it was to the local leaders that Pilsen Academy Principal Bill Levin turned, out of instinct and necessity, when the AIDS issue arose.

"One night, a few weeks before I got the call from the central office," Levin remembers, "I had a nightmare that a child with AIDS was being sent to Pilsen. I couldn't go back to sleep, couldn't stop worrying." Worrying is habitual with Levin, a Chicago native who pushes himself ten and twelve hours a day, six and a half days a week, teaching drivers' ed and adult courses, jogging three miles and doing fifty push-ups daily, as well as running Pilsen Academy. He is a perfectionist by nature, constantly wondering whether he could be doing a better job. "My family," he says, "calls me Calamity Jane."

Levin has headed Pilsen Academy since 1973. The venerable building, once called the Jurika School, is hooked to a faceless contemporary wing and now enrolls 1,040 students, ninety-eight percent nonwhite and almost entirely Hispanic. From the outset, Levin was the foreigner, the Jewish Anglo who speaks no Spanish assigned by downtown bureaucrats to a Latino world. A boycott organized by neighborhood groups had forced out his predecessor, a woman with a reputation as a disciplinarian, who displayed too little love for her charges and, it was said, looked down on the Pilsen community. Some years later, the neighborhood organization cut a deal with the Board of Education to secure a Hispanic superintendent for the district. This history has led Levin to cultivate the leaders of the neighborhood groups as if they were hothouse orchids. "I'm always walking a thin line," he says.

Over the years, Bill Levin has remade his school. He has been able to do what any successful principal must do in the city of clout; use his contacts in the bureaucracy to wheedle extra books and state-of-the-art computers out of a central office that chronically pleads poverty. When Pilsen became a magnet school in 1982, able to offer special programs and attract students from a wider geographical area, Levin secured not only additional teachers but, equally important, the authority to pick and choose his staff. "What matters most is the quality of the teachers in the classroom," he says. "If you don't have good teachers, you don't have anything." Perhaps the best testimony to Levin's perfectionism is his file of fifty staff members whom he has eased out or banished over the years, a startlingly high number in a strongly unionized school system where every dispute about teaching is a potential incitement.

Though Levin is not without ambition—he imagines himself in the future as a high school principal or superintendent in a suburban town—it is not personal power but institutional performance that drives him. In several grade levels, his new teachers have brought the reading and mathematics scores of Pilsen Academy students up to nationwide averages. School attendance figures are among the highest in Chicago, partly because Levin cares so much about students' coming to class that he hands out awards—Pilsen Academy pencils and extra field trips—for good attendance. A sophisticated testing program developed at the school, which identifies the learning problems of kindergartners, has won national attention. All this has earned Bill Levin the Citizens School Committee's annual award as Chicago's outstanding principal.

While Levin has sometimes gotten into hot water with the union for his handling of teachers, the parents have rallied to his defense. So has Pilsen Neighbors, which received help from the principal in raising money. "I cut a political deal," he recalls, describing the nastiest of the teachers' battles. "They appealed for one teacher . . . . I wrestled with the question for twenty-four hours. If I didn't make that accommodation, I'd lose the war." The principal knows that he can never become district superintendent in this part of the city. "We need one of our own," he was told by one of his closest allies in the community. But he figures he is in solid with the parents and the teachers. "I get maybe sixty Christmas presents a year from the teachers and 'superior' evaluations from almost all of them. . . . Right after the AIDS thing settled down they chipped in $400 for an escape weekend."

Principal Levin wasn't the picture of confidence, though, as he headed for Deputy Superintendent Joseph Lee's office on February 24, 1987, in response to a cryptic summons. "What have I done wrong?" he was asking himself. Joe Lee had been Levin's district superintendent before moving up to the number two job, the man who ran day-to-day operations for the system, and he was Levin's godfather in the bureaucracy. But in the web of fragile alliances that forms the 430,000 student Chicago school system, things could fall apart at any time.

In his office at what is derisively known as Pershing Gardens, a fortress-like colossus of a building that had previously been an Army headquarters, Lee explained the reason for the secrecy: a child who had the AIDS virus had been reviewed by the systemwide medical screening panel and was being assigned to Pilsen. "Does the youngster live in the neighborhood?" Levin wanted to know, thinking that the answer would affect how parents in Pilsen reacted. No, Lee answered, but added that the child—who is Mexican—"belongs in Pilsen Academy because the school is the appropriate educational placement."

"Like a good second lieutenant," says Levin, "I took my marching orders." A teachers' meeting would be held the next day, with school officials and a nurse—but no doctor—present to answer questions, followed a few days later, by a meeting of community representatives; a letter explaining what was happening would be sent out, under Lee's signature, to all the parents. It was "chancy" to inform so many people, Lee acknowledged, since information invites problems, but not telling the community could create far greater problems if the news ever leaked out. Bob Saigh, the head of public information for the Chicago schools, volunteered to assist Levin. Otherwise, the principal was on his own.

The procedure the deputy superintendent followed for Pilsen had been generally laid down in the AIDS policy hammered out by the Chicago Board of Education the previous year—a policy that itself had been controversial. For months on end, AIDS had been deliberated by the eleven-member Board of Education, a racial and ethnic microcosm of the Chicago schools picked by the mayor for five-year terms. The school

administrators were anxious to adopt guidelines that tracked
the recommendations of the Centers for Disease Control—
keep children with AIDS in school unless some special reason
justified fear of contagion—but some board members had disagreed. Draft after draft was sent up for review, first to the
board's management committee and then to the full board.

Dissenters got their ammunition from Dr. Robert Mendelsohn, a local pediatrician, whom one of the unhappy board
members, Betty Bonow, invited to consult. Early in the history
of the AIDS epidemic, Mendelsohn had urged that people with
the disease be quarantined and that researchers announce their
sexual orientation, supposedly to reveal bias. In his testimony
before the board, Mendelsohn dismissed the "so-called prestigious experts," attacked studies showing that AIDS had not
been spread in the households of AIDS patients, and derided
the CDC as "hysterical." Experts on "both sides of the question"
should decide whether a child infected with the AIDS virus
could attend school, Mendelsohn argued.

The school administrators feared that they had lost their
fight. Eventually, they persuaded the board members with
masses of reassuring information on how AIDS is transmitted.
Or almost persuaded them: When the Board of Education finally adopted its AIDS guidelines, in June 1986, Mendelsohn
was selected for the medical screening panel.

In January 1987, when the youngster eventually assigned to
Pilsen came before the medical panel, Mendelsohn's was the
only vote against admission to school. What the public knew
was only that, although the child had tested positive for the
AIDS virus, no symptoms of the disease itself were present.
The public was never informed that the child's mother and two
siblings had full-blown AIDS.

The school administration treated the decision of the medical
panel, and the subsequent placement recommendation by a
committee of educators, as part of the bureaucratic routine laid
down in the guidelines. What they hoped for, recalls Deputy
Superintendent Joe Lee, "was a quiet, purposeful approach—
a low-key approach. No one thought the LaRouchies were
working that neighborhood." George Muñoz, then president of

the board, learned about the decision through channels, in a matter-of-fact memo from Superintendent Manford Byrd, Jr., and when Muñoz inquired further he was told that things were in capable hands.

The Chicago school administrators saw little reason to take special measures in Pilsen. After all, the act of adopting a policy had put them in the forefront on AIDS in Chicago. Although the city has some 2,000 AIDS cases, the seventh largest number in the country, it has not really awakened to the epidemic. The public health bureaucracy has been chronically embattled: its director, Dr. Lonnie Edwards, drew criticism from all sides for not moving quickly on AIDS. The city's six medical schools were too busy fighting over AIDS research money to cooperate. And while the staff at the Howard Brown Memorial Clinic has dispensed endless amounts of care and counsel to AIDS patients, the harried volunteers are seriously overworked.

With AIDS a largely unnoticed issue, it made bureaucratic sense to play Pilsen by the book: that was what the thousands of school bureaucrats who worked out of Pershing Gardens habitually did. They were leaving matters in the hands of the locals, a strategy assiduously promoted by Superintendent Byrd, who believed that principals had credibility that the central office sometimes lacked.

Manford Byrd had been a Chicago schoolman for a third of a century, passed over four times for the top job before finally being appointed superintendent in 1985. His immediate predecessor, a dynamo named Ruth Love, was regarded as charismatic by her allies, dictatorial by her enemies in the school system. Byrd is seen as easygoing, soft-spoken, a gentleman and a survivor in a harsh and calculating world. On AIDS, as on many other things, he believes in delegating. And if some members of the school board would have preferred to be more involved in putting the new AIDS policy into effect, they were lulled into inattention by the numbing language of the superintendent's memorandum.

With such a laissez-faire attitude, it was indeed "providential that the first AIDS case should be in a school headed by someone with Bill Levin's capabilities," as Deputy Superintendent

Joe Lee observed—the same sentiment Bill Gussner expressed about Paul Nilsen in Wilmette. And Levin recalls thinking, "We'll be compared to Wilmette. It's important to leave no stone unturned."

On the morning of February 25, the teachers at Pilsen Academy heard the news. It was an awkward session. "The top brass just said, 'There is no choice,'" recalls one of the teachers, Nydia Gonzalez. "There were lots of unanswered questions when we walked out of that room." But once the Pilsen teachers recovered from their initial shock, once they had had a chance to ask all their questions about risk and health insurance, about bringing the disease home to their families, and about the district's legal liability, they came around. None took up Levin's offer to arrange a transfer to another school, and Mary Jane Andrade, a teacher's aide, volunteered to work with the youngster. "I had tuberculosis as a child," she said, "and I know how it feels to be pushed aside."

Levin helped restore the teachers' confidence by making himself available every day that week, before and after school, to talk through their concerns. He was collecting articles on AIDS, informing himself and passing along the materials. "If this had to happen anyplace in Chicago, it is a godsend that it happened at Pilsen," became the teachers' mantra.

That same day, February 25, Levin contacted his allies in the neighborhood. Among the key people was Lucy Gutierrez who, as a member of the local alderman's staff, had been helping out the residents of Pilsen for years. Gutierrez had collected 10,000 signatures for a new health center in the early 1970s; now her daughter was a teacher's aide at the school. There were also Lourdes Ortega and Sylvia Domingues from the school's parents council, and Mary Jane Andrade, who had been so helpful at the staff meeting and whose daughter was enrolled at Pilsen Academy. And there was Raquel Guerrero, an organizer with a migrant workers' group, who had moved to Pilsen with her family in 1957, fixing up a falling-down house and shepherding her children through the public schools.

Guerrero had achieved a measure of fame in Pilsen for haranguing Mayor Daley, calling him a liar for failing to deliver the bilingual education he had promised. And Guerrero wasn't afraid to take the unpopular side in a fight, if that seemed the right thing to do. She had stood up for Levin's predecessor, arguing that the woman was a good educator. "She wasn't a warm person," Guerrero recalls, "but she knew her job. Who needs hugs all the time?"

Early in the 1980s, Guerrero had come to the rescue of Pilsen Neighbors, mortgaging her own home to bail out the community organization when it was in danger of folding. That gesture put her in a financial bind, yet Guerrero never took a cent from any neighborhood group. Nor would she accept a job as a school aide; the money would keep her from speaking her mind, she felt.

"We're number one in everything," said Guerrero. "But why are we number one in this?" Yet she agreed to help Levin. "I had a son who died of hepatitis," Guerrero says. "My neighbors weren't sympathetic. They said, 'What did he die of? I need to take my child for a shot.' I knew how the mother of that child was feeling."

The support from these women gave Levin some credibility at the February 27 meeting of the school officials and the Pilsen community leaders, the session that Paul Nilsen attended. But the principal had a hard selling job. The community organizers expressed their support for the school, but not for the Chicago school system or its AIDS policy. All they would promise was to stay away and keep mum, not risking turmoil by making their worries about AIDS generally known.

When Levin asked Ortega of the parents' council how families would react to the news, her response was graphic: she mimed slitting her throat. Juan Soliz, the soon-to-be-elected alderman from Pilsen, posed the questions that would be repeated regularly during the next several weeks: "Why Pilsen? Why now?" Carlos Valencia, president of Casa Aztlán, angrily accused the school district of plotting against Pilsen, and Bob Saigh, spokesman for the school system, replied: "Do you think we would pick a school in the most politically active neighborhood in Chicago to place a child with AIDS if we had any choice?"

As Bill Levin walked out of that meeting, he believed he was over the worst. The letters to parents had gone out, and the school had set up a hot line to answer questions. The priests would speak out from their pulpits in support of the schools, and in devoutly Catholic Pilsen their voices would be heard. The principal, working with Bob Saigh, had lined up a raft of speakers for the public forum scheduled for the following Thursday, March 5. Politicians, school officials, and doctors would reiterate that the enrollment of the child was a compassionate act that posed no medical risk. Chicago's auxiliary archbishop, who happened to be the brother-in-law of one of the city's top school officials, would offer a homily in Spanish. Following the procedure that had worked well in Wilmette, questions would be submitted in advance; since many of the parents spoke only Spanish, several teachers had been lined up to translate. But before the Q-and-A period could begin, Lyndon LaRouche's legions had turned the public meeting into a wide-open brawl.

This was not the LaRouchites' first adventure in Pilsen, nor were they all outsiders. "I was born in Pilsen," says Herman Garza, a staunch LaRouche supporter. "We work here, we organize." In 1979, the LaRouche organization had held its first public meeting in Pilsen; a year later, when Lyndon LaRouche ran for president, he campaigned in the streets of Pilsen.

Driving home from his meeting with Joe Lee earlier in the week, Bill Levin had spotted a van belonging to the National Democratic Policy Committee, LaRouche's party, which was fielding candidates in the upcoming Chicago elections. "Quarantine All AIDS Cases," read the banner hanging from the van, and Levin shuddered. During the first days of March, while the principal readied himself for the forthcoming community meeting, things were quiet in Pilsen. The hot line had almost no calls, and Levin caught himself thinking that "this could be a piece of cake." But the LaRouche activists were busy taking their message of fear door to door in Pilsen.

It wasn't clear until the March 5 meeting just how effective the LaRouche forces had been, and by then it was too late. "When I came home at three o'clock that morning," Levin recalls, "I crawled into bed and told my wife that I wanted to cry. . . . We had tried so hard to keep the LaRouchies out by using lists of all the parents, but they slipped past us by posing as spouses of single parents."

Nearly five hundred people crowded into the school's auditorium that Thursday night. Every seat was filled, and people stood in the aisles to hear what was being said. For the first half hour, things went smoothly enough. But when Levin began to speak about the "misconceptions" that surrounded the youngster who would be enrolled at Pilsen, the LaRouche supporters, who had positioned themselves in the front rows of the auditorium, made their move. "Liar, liar," they started shouting, as Levin pleaded vainly for a chance to communicate the facts. "Where are the guarantees?" they yelled, and then demanded that the matter be put to a vote.

Levin tried switching to the Q-and-A, but when the shouting kept up he returned to the planned format. A brief calm greeted Dr. Lonnie Edwards, Commissioner of the city's Health Department, when he beseeched the audience to "open up your ears, and hear the truth we have to tell you. Use your minds, use your hearts." Then the tumult began all over again.

Levin turned to Herman Garza, who had loudly been demanding the floor, and invited him to speak. Levin thought he had a deal—Garza would talk and the session would continue—but Garza rushed the stage, bent on taking over. At that moment, a furious Raquel Guerrero gave Garza a shove, and pandemonium broke out. It was *mano a mano* in the auditorium, as LaRouche backers mixed it up with angry parents. "Is this Russia?" the LaRouche minions cried when members of the Chicago police force, who had let the school administrators know that they would intervene only if things got rough, began carting off the antagonists. The meeting collapsed.

As Levin and Saigh spent the succeeding days planning a series of twenty-four simultaneous AIDS information sessions, to be held a week later in Pilsen Academy's classrooms and carefully limited to parents, the LaRouche forces stepped up their noisemaking. They spent the weekend cruising the neighborhood, exhorting parents to keep their children home. On

Monday, March 9, 190 children stayed away from the 1,040-student school, four times the usual number of absences. Many parents had brought their children to school but were scared off by talk of a bomb inside.

Children who did come to class that day were learning about AIDS. When Bill Levin visited a sixth-grade classroom, the youngsters recited the ways AIDS could be transmitted. One child asked the principal a question that had become all too familiar: "Why don't our parents vote on whether to admit a child exposed to AIDS to school?" Levin explained that this wasn't the kind of thing people voted on—"Would you want people voting on whether you were in school?"—and then took an informal poll. Almost unanimously, the youngsters said that the child should be allowed in school. "You've got more compassion than the people out there," the principal told them.

Outside the school, the LaRouche activists were picketing, blasting their message in Spanish. "This school is being used as an AIDS experiment because it is a minority school," they claimed. Raquel Guerrero stood down her antagonists. "Go home! Go home!" she demanded, waving her finger in the face of the leaders, while other parents encircled the LaRouche contingent with signs saying "LaRouche Must Go" and "LaRouchies Are AIDS." Bill Levin, who had anticipated the LaRouche protest, called the police; when officers tried to move the demonstrators along, the LaRouche forces became "very combative," in the words of the police. Six protesters were arrested, including the party's candidate for Chicago city clerk and two parents of Pilsen children.

By now, the Chicago news media were all over the Pilsen story. The Spanish TV stations, which had never previously paid much attention to AIDS, now offered lengthy coverage. Levin became a TV fixture, talking about "hand-to-hand combat with the LaRouchies." Raquel Guerrero and Lucy Gutierrez, the veteran Pilsen organizers, and José Cerda, one of the principal's familiar adversaries, were also regulars on the nightly news.

"They don't ask the parents," Cerda complained. "We have no rights." But other parents, quizzed by the newsmen, contended that the LaRouche activists were "here to twist our

minds, they said the whole school is contaminated with AIDS."
When Walter Jacobson, a TV commentator with a large audience and a reputation for being rough on his subjects, questioned Levin closely about the risks involved, the principal
came off looking like a man who knew his stuff.

Levin looked like a leader too. "We will listen to parents and
respond to their concerns," Levin told the TV reporters. "We've
got ninety percent of the parents now," he said on March 10,
the second day of the LaRouche-organized boycott, when absences had been cut in half. "Our job is to convince the other
ten percent." By week's end, as even the most skeptical parents
began bringing their children back to school in the aftermath of
the AIDS informational meetings, both the *Tribune* and the
Sun-Times offered editorial pats on the back to the "responsible" citizens of Pilsen.

Bill Levin was putting up a brave front—"We'll be like Wilmette in a couple of weeks," he declared—but behind the scenes
things weren't going entirely smoothly. The mother of the child
with AIDS had suddenly vanished, unnerved by the outcry,
taking her child with her, and for several days the principal
could not locate them. In the face of the school's troubles,
the administrators at Pershing Gardens were remaining mute.
"They were behind me," Levin recollects. "Way behind." Other
principals were calling Levin, telling him he was crazy to let a
child with AIDS in his school. "I'd be fighting this," they said.
Rumors began circulating that a teacher at Pilsen Academy had
AIDS. And several of the principal's allies in the community,
people he had gone to when he first sought support, were being
manhandled by their neighbors. Lourdes Ortega, from the parents' advisory group, had it particularly rough: her car tires
were slashed, and rocks were heaved through the windows of
her home.

These women had been led to believe that the AIDS dispute
could be readily contained, that there really were no serious
medical concerns. And the appearance of LaRouche backers
gave them another reason to side with the schools, for it was
important to them that Lyndon LaRouche not gain a toehold in
Pilsen. Several years earlier, in a fight over the placement of a

drug treatment center in Pilsen, Lucy Gutierrez and Raquel Guerrero had been wooed by LaRouchites who had concealed their identities. "They wound us all up," remembers Gutierrez. Guerrero had even been sent to a convention of the National Democratic Policy Committee in Detroit. "A bunch of walking mummies," Guerrero called the conventioneers who cheered every word of their leader. "I didn't want to listen to their philosophy of hatred." Pilsen had to be preserved as the *doñas'* turf, not Lyndon LaRouche's.

Yet in the days before and after the disrupted meeting, as Pilsen parents kept hearing stories about AIDS in mosquitoes, saliva, and sweat while the Health Department and the Board of Education were nowhere in sight, the women started wondering whether they had been set up. Their credibility, their only resource, was suddenly on the line.

The small in-school meetings organized by Levin and Saigh, from which the LaRouchites were effectively barred, answered some of the parents' questions. But Gutierrez, Guerrero, and the others had already decided it was time to enlist some new allies. On Wednesday, March 11, a Pilsen contingent marched into a Board of Education meeting to demand that the board— particularly George Muñoz and Linda Coronado, the two Chicano board members—make an appearance in the community.

Coronado, the board's newest member, was a familiar and trusted face in Pilsen, for she had been an organizer in the neighborhood and had run the women's center there. Muñoz, the board chairman, was less well known. Though Muñoz had grown up poor, one of twelve children in a home where only Spanish was spoken, his brains and industriousness had been his ticket out—to Harvard Law School and a partnership in one of the most prestigious downtown law firms.

It was Muñoz's status as an outsider that had made him an attractive board candidate to Mayor Harold Washington, who had promised to take the schools out of politics. And as a board member, Muñoz had seen his role in citywide terms; he had been instrumental in forcing out Superintendent Ruth Love two years earlier, when she persisted in running a one-woman show. But Muñoz knew that his Hispanic heritage was a principal reason for his being on the board. Now, in Pilsen, he was being called upon to test his credibility for the sake of his constituency.

About 200 people were in the auditorium the evening of Friday, March 13, to hear Muñoz and Coronado—to hear, also, three Hispanic doctors, including Jorge Prieto, the avuncular president of the Board of Health who, over a third of a century, delivered a thousand babies in Pilsen. Muñoz regarded Prieto as the ideal medical spokesman for Pilsen; Prieto, chafing under what he regarded as Health Commissioner Lonnie Edwards' ineptitude, was only too happy to oblige.

Three checkpoints to the school were heavily guarded to keep LaRouche agitators away. When Bill Levin made his appearance, Raquel Guerrero politely but firmly ushered him out. "You are part of the system," Levin was told. "And the parents want to hold this discussion without any influence from the school system." Though the principal understood, he couldn't help feeling hurt; he went back to his office and listened to the proceedings on the PA system. He had done his part. Now it was time for the community leaders to take charge.

The doctors were closely questioned by parents who, by now, knew all the questions to ask. And the *doñas* kept things calm. "Don't get too emotional, doctor," Lucy Gutierrez said, when one of the medics started slipping into a passionate peroration about the risks of everyday life. Prieto, when asked about guaranteeing the safety of the children at Pilsen, won over some of the parents by saying: "I'll sign a guarantee that your child won't get AIDS in school—if you, as a parent, will guarantee that your child won't have sexual intercourse, in school or out."

The Chicano board members, Coronado and Muñoz, got a thorough going-over too. "Why did you abandon us?" one parent asked. And another raised the possibility of putting the matter to a vote. A community organizer framed the matter of accountability squarely, "We trust you. If you tell us it's OK to let this child in our school, we'll do it."

That Sunday, March 15, AIDS was what the parish priests spoke about. The priests had joined to send a pastoral letter to their parishioners about the youngster who had been exposed to AIDS—a politically delicate gesture, for in Chicago the Catholic Church's antipathy toward homosexuality had kept it from addressing AIDS. At Providence of God Church, where the Pope had briefly stopped in 1979, Father Tim McCormick preached about AIDS in Spanish to 800 parishioners. "It is the outsiders who are the problem," McCormick said. "We have to remember who we are. We know more than anyone what oppression is. We can't become the oppressors."

George Muñoz had politics on his mind that weekend. He had told the people of Pilsen that he would talk through the AIDS issue as long as they wanted to, but the board president felt that something more was needed to mollify the Gutierrezes and the Guerreros, the people who had stuck their necks out for their school; otherwise, they would come out of this as losers. Muñoz got Superintendent Byrd to commit a full-time nurse to Pilsen and confirmed that the medical advisory panel would closely monitor the situation at the school. At a session at Pilsen the following Monday, the board president tossed out these ideas as possibilities; they quickly became community demands, which Muñoz could then satisfy.

That strategy proved almost too clever. "You keep telling us there is nothing to worry about," one parent said to Muñoz. "Why are you taking all these extra precautions?" Yet by this time, nearly three weeks after Bill Levin had first learned that a child exposed to AIDS would be assigned to Pilsen, things were back to normal. The LaRouche contingent had vanished; community skeptics were quiet; and José Cerda, who had demanded that his children be allowed to transfer, sent his wife to apply for a job on the school bus that took the infected youngster to and from school.

Inside the school, too, things had returned to normal—in one case, far too normal. When Levin went to observe how the AIDS-infected pupil was being treated, he was horrified to learn that teachers who saw the child daily were being very casual in cleaning up the youngster's nosebleeds; the principal promptly bought disposable gloves from a medical supply house.

By the end of the school year, it was hard to locate a parent in Pilsen who would admit to harboring serious misgivings about what the school had done, harder still to find anyone who would acknowledge any LaRouche sympathies. Bill Levin was still working his six-and-a-half-day weeks, still handling ques-

tions about AIDS in the schools—and still hadn't had a chance
to take his wife on the holiday weekend the teachers had
chipped in to pay for.

NETTELHORST

"I can't keep him in a bubble," the foster father of a young boy
suffering from AIDS-related complex (ARC) complained to a
reporter on the *Chicago Sun-Times*. It was early in February
1987, and the school district hadn't decided how to handle the
case of the child who, a few weeks later, would be assigned to
Pilsen Academy. This second case was potentially even more
problematic.

While the youngster being sent to Pilsen carried the AIDS
virus, this second child already displayed the signs of a weak-
ened immune system. Medically, that made little difference, but
it was a comfort to those at Pilsen that the youngster who would
be coming to their school was, and indeed might remain, perfectly healthy.

Another element complicated the case of the second Chicago
schoolchild, one that was never on the table but was clearly in
the minds of the decision makers: the foster father was forty-
three years old, single, and lived in Newtown, the Chicago
neighborhood that much of the city's gay community calls
home. What would the LaRouche zealots, who in Pilsen were
fulminating against the threat posed by gays, make of this
opportunity?

Chicago school officials maintained a scrupulous silence
about the particulars of the case. But the boy's father, who did
not identify himself by name, talked to the *Sun-Times* reporter
about his anger at the school system for having delayed its
decision.

In June 1986, nine months earlier, Paul Swenson* had finally
succeeded in beating the bureaucracy. For two years, Swenson
had been trying to become a foster father in the Parent to

---

*The name is changed, as is the youngster's first name, to preserve confidentiality.

Parent program, run by a Catholic service agency, which placed troubled teenagers with foster parents with the hope of eventually reuniting the youngsters and their natural families. Swenson was an obvious choice: since 1981 he had been a volunteer at Chicago's Children's Hospital and before that had worked with retarded youngsters.

Working with children, says Swenson, was "a mission." That's why the Vietnam veteran had saved up enough of a nest egg to quit his high-powered management job; he wanted nothing to do with "the Yuppie bag." Yet for some never-explained reason—Swenson thinks the social service officials believed, mistakenly, that he was homosexual—he never got the required foster-parent license from the Illinois Department of Children and Family Services. Just as he was contemplating going to court, he was contacted by a social worker from the state agency. A boy named David with AIDS-related complex had just been handed over to them for placement. If Swenson took this child, he would get his license.

The call made Paul Swenson mad. "They want to put the two hot potatoes together," he speculated. But Swenson was "frustrated with all the Mickey Mouse," and his savings were almost gone. He went to Children's Hospital and talked with the pediatric AIDS specialists, including Ellen Chadwick, David's doctor, who six months later would be involved in the Wilmette story. Then he met the youngster, a curly-haired moppet with pie-sized brown eyes. "The boy needs a guardian angel," Swenson figured, and he was it.

Paul Swenson brought David home from what he calls a war zone. David's mother, who divided her life between Chicago and San Juan, was a drug addict, diagnosed as having AIDS, and barely able to care for her son; she died a month after giving him up. Feces littered the floor of the apartment where David was living; he had no blanket, no food, no clothes. "It's a miracle that he didn't die there," says Swenson. From the outset, though, David was an irresistible urchin unafraid of strangers, filled with enough energy for two kids, finding affection wherever he could. The foster father and his son spent all their time together and quickly became inseparable. "I haven't done a conventional parent trip," says Swenson. "I didn't know how long he would live and I didn't want to deprive him of anything. The only thing I make him do is to eat healthy foods."

When the issue of enrolling David in a school program first came up, Swenson worried about the risks of infection that contact with other youngsters might entail for his foster son. "The risk is all on his side," he thought. During the spring of 1986, when he was diagnosed as having ARC, David had been through a bout of pneumonia. He had been healthy since then, hadn't picked up the flu his foster father contracted during the winter, or developed any of the opportunistic diseases that mark full-blown AIDS. So appealing, so full of life, were the child and his father that they were asked to talk at a meeting of the Children's Home and Aid Society, which was just beginning to work with AIDS children, and at Lenten mass in posh Lake Forest. "We're like show horses," Swenson proudly declares. "While I speak, David works the crowd."

The boy's doctors and nurses agreed that "he's doing so well. He needs the chance" of being in school, and in January 1987 Swenson tried to register David for Nettelhorst Elementary School, just a few blocks from his condo. Things didn't go as planned. "I thought the agency would have warned the schools but they didn't. When we came to the place on the application where it asks about AIDS, their jaws dropped."

Swenson filed all the necessary forms. Ellen Chadwick wrote to the schools, urging that David be admitted, for he was a healthy and happy boy. From the Chicago public school system came only silence. The next month, Swenson sought out the *Sun-Times* reporter. "I had no other influence," he says. In early May, he contacted the Chicago Public Guardian, Patrick Murphy, a civil rights lawyer whose courtroom victories over the Chicago Establishment have given him considerable influence. Murphy made a threatening phone call to the school board, then drafted a "see you in court" letter. "Let's wait until after Memorial Day, then if we have to, we'll file a lawsuit."

Nettelhorst Elementary School, a solid brick building dating to the early days of the century, stands in the middle of Chicago's predominantly gay neighborhood, north of downtown.

It is a mixed community, with young professional couples moving in and black and migrants from Appalachia hanging onto places they've lived in for years; it is also where many of Chicago's most popular gay bars and restaurants are located. This is Chicago's decidedly Midwestern answer to Christopher Street in New York and the Castro in San Francisco.

The preschool-through-grade-eight school is not a central part of this community. Many of the parents in the neighborhood who are most ambitious for their youngsters send them to better-equipped and more generously staffed magnet schools elsewhere in the district, or to private schools. And many of the children at Nettelhorst come from outside the neighborhood, referrals from nearby overcrowded Hispanic schools and youngsters with behavioral, emotional, and learning problems. A quarter of the school's five hundred pupils are in its thirteen special classes.

Since 1978, Peggy Lubin has presided over this racially balanced confederacy of instructional offerings. While Lubin doesn't have the power to select teachers, enjoyed by a magnet school principal like Bill Levin at Pilsen, the able and energetic black Chicago native has put her stamp on Nettelhorst. "We take whoever shows up at the door," says Lubin. "That's great, it works."

Lubin was intensely screened for her job by a parent committee—"Twenty-three people sat in a circle around me; for an hour they asked questions"—and a parents advisory council meets monthly. But a school that draws on such a dispersed population has difficulty keeping more than just a few parents involved in broad issues. Most parents who do spend time at the school are concerned with one of the special programs; they join the special education support group or the bilingual parents' council.

Peggy Lubin made AIDS the topic of the advisory council meeting held early in May 1987. A dozen parents and teachers showed up to hear Dr. Roberta Luskin, a pediatrician at nearby St. Joseph's Hospital, explain the medical facts. The earlier AIDS case at the Pilsen school had drawn the attention of school administrators throughout Chicago; immediately after the troubles in Pilsen began, Lubin's district superintendent, James Maloney, had asked all the principals to speed up the AIDS education effort.

A pamphlet on AIDS was attached to spring report cards at Nettelhorst, which parents had to pick up at the school. "That," says Lubin, "is where you put the information you want to make sure isn't lost." She had wanted to set up an AIDS session with the advisory council earlier, but local budget hearings and scheduling conflicts got in the way. Lubin didn't know yet that a child infected by the AIDS virus would be sent to her school. But she had read the *Sun-Times* article mentioning a second youngster exposed to AIDS and had a hunch that "because Nettelhorst is in the gay community, we're going to get that child."

Soon after the advisory council session on AIDS, Lubin began receiving a series of strange phone calls from Deputy Superintendent Joe Lee. "I'm going to ask you questions about your enrollment," Lee told Lubin. "Your answers have to be absolutely accurate, and I can't explain anything." Lubin called the district office and asked for Maloney, only to learn that he was in conference with Lee. On May 22, Lubin was told to come to a meeting at Lee's office. "You've figured out what's going on, haven't you?" Lee asked. "Yes," Lubin replied.

The Chicago schools had learned something from the Pilsen experience, and Bill Levin had collected extensive materials on AIDS, which he now turned over to Lubin, offering to give her whatever help she needed. Again, as in Pilsen, parents and teachers would be informed. This time, though, the principal was asked whether she wanted any of the top officials to attend the parents' meeting. Lubin declined the offer. Her intention, she told Lee, was to keep things as normal as possible, and it wasn't normal for the deputy superintendent to appear at the Nettelhorst Elementary School.

"When should the child be enrolled?" Lubin was asked. "As soon as possible," she replied.

Near the end of the school year, children begin counting down the days and hours until vacation. For teachers and parents, too, attention is focused elsewhere than on school. That was why Lubin wanted to admit the child then, rather than wait until fall when school would again become the center of so many people's lives.

"For two weeks, AIDS was all that I did," Peggy Lubin recalls. Immediately after the session in Deputy Superintendent Lee's office, she and District Superintendent Maloney met with all the Nettelhorst staff. That day and the next, Lubin visited each of the teachers, enlisting them in the effort to inform parents. "What should we be doing?" she asked. Two hours after a request for disposable gloves and other AIDS precautions, the supplies were on the scene, breaking all school district speed records and helping to allay teachers' concerns. Students in the upper grades got a plain-talk lecture on AIDS. "When you think of AIDS," they were told, "think of blood and sex."

Letters pinned to the shirts of all the students, noting that a youngster with AIDS-related complex would be enrolling at the school, were sent home to all the Nettelhorst parents. On May 28, the parents met to talk about AIDS—this time not in the abstract.

Lubin didn't know whether to expect a repeat of Pilsen, but nothing of the sort happened. Only parents came to the meeting—thirty-eight of them, mostly mothers—at which they talked about the basics on AIDS transmission with Roberta Luskin. The young doctor was knowledgeable without being intimidating. She easily fielded questions, using language the parents could understand.

The one potentially explosive moment came when a parent declared: "I won't send my child to this school, no matter what. You don't know the answers." A mother who had been to the earlier advisory council session replied: "You don't know if the waiter in a restaurant where you're eating has the virus. What are you going to do, stop living?"

A second meeting, conducted in Spanish, was held a few days later for Spanish-speaking parents, who had more questions. But the discussion stayed within the four walls of the Nettelhorst Elementary School. There were no LaRouche activists on the scene, no calls for a boycott.

Paul Swenson, biding his time before taking legal action to get his foster son into school, knew nothing about these gatherings. "That's because he wasn't a school parent at the time," says Lubin, "and the meetings were only for parents." The first word Swenson had from Nettelhorst came the Tuesday after Memorial Day. "You can bring David in to class tomorrow," he was told.

The event drew no publicity, not a single news article or TV piece about what was happening at Nettelhorst. Peggy Lubin thought it was a miracle: "All those announcements of the meeting were floating around the community, and nobody picked up the story." Bob Saigh, the spokesman for the Chicago schools, had heard from reporters that, in the aftermath of Pilsen, they were "all AIDS-ed out." "Don't tell us about your next AIDS case," the journalists had told Saigh, only half-jokingly.

During the last days of the school year, life at Nettelhorst proceeded without incident. Only one parent, the woman who had expressed her upset at the meeting, kept her child out of school. At kindergarten graduation, a cap-and-gown affair, several parents told Peggy Lubin they would be sending their children to parochial school in the fall, but that happens every year. And actually fewer parents than usual were seeking to transfer their children from Nettelhorst to a magnet school for first grade.

Peggy Lubin thought that the previous events in Wilmette and Pilsen, as well as the AIDS education materials the Nettelhorst parents had been given in the spring, made her job easier. "If you get that word—AIDS—in front of parents," she says, "they have a chance to think through the issue before being confronted with a case of AIDS in their own school."

One morning at the very end of May, Peggy Lubin happened to be present when a young boy—a "gorgeous little boy," the principal describes him—came into the classroom holding his father's hand. "He was thrilled to be there," says Lubin. "He wasn't shy at all. 'I'm going to play,' he said, and then he dived right in."

Over a period of five months during 1987, in three separate episodes, children with AIDS had the support of the authorities when they enrolled in Chicago-area public schools. That is noteworthy in itself, for school officials have not been uniformly on the side of these youngsters, and the particular circumstances make this show of support even more remarkable.

These were no easy cases, no Ryan Whites or Mark Hoyles. They were young—as young as nursery school age. And in two of the three instances, they were assigned to classes for children who, for one reason or another, cannot easily manage their feelings—children who, in the jargon of the trade, have behavioral or emotional disorders. This is the category of children for whom the CDC has recommended the closest case-by-case evaluation.

When the unknowns linger, when the experts differ on a matter of life and death, the possibility for trouble arises. Trouble, in the form of withdrawal of children to private schools, could have broken out in the well-to-do town of Wilmette. On the Wilmette scene were three Central School mothers who claimed to know that the child in question was a menace in the classroom, and a doctor, mother of a child in the school, who used her professional credentials to demand the kind of guarantees only God can give.

Trouble, in the form of a split among the parents, did indeed erupt in the Pilsen community of Chicago, a Chicano neighborhood suspicious of the dictates of the Board of Education and susceptible to the divisive manipulations of Lyndon LaRouche's radical camp followers. In Pilsen, for a time, the testimony by doctors and educators that the unidentified child posed no risk was shouted down by a band of zealots who sought to turn the episode to their political advantage by driving away a child with AIDS.

And it is all too easy to imagine what Lyndon LaRouche's gang could have made of the Nettelhorst circumstances: a preschool foster child living with a never-married man, whose names were not made public, was enrolled in a school in the Chicago neighborhood most heavily populated by homosexuals.

Yet in each of the Chicago stories a child who had been exposed to AIDS remained in school while tensions dissipated—or, in Nettelhorst, failed to materialize. These successes can be attributed partly to the people who happened to be in charge, three principals and a suburban superintendent who came out strongly for what was right and had the backing of parents who had known them for years. They stood down their antagonists. They managed their encounters with fame as if they had been in the limelight all their lives.

Perhaps the most important thing these leaders did was to trust the communities whose children they educated, resisting the temptation to slip the decision by unknowing parents. The conversations they launched were taxing, even treacherous. But all that talk—sometimes impassioned, sometimes reasoned, seemingly endless, and always pointed—was eventually the convincer. It gave parents a chance to have their say about something that intimately touched their lives.

In Wilmette the parents who brought their sharp questions to the January 1987 meetings went away convinced that the medical experts and school officials they knew well were right, not the mothers intoning their lamentations. Besides, as the parents kept telling the newsmen, who wanted to be another Kokomo? In Pilsen, two months later, the day was carried by the Chicano doctors and the Chicano educators—and a Jewish school principal—whom parents knew and trusted from other fights. The lesson of Wilmette helped the *doñas* of Pilsen to banish the outsiders and their scare tactics. Without the commitment of those remarkable women and the leadership of that conscientious and politically savvy principal, Pilsen could easily have degenerated into another Queens—only this time, with LaRouchites on the scene, the boycott might have been more protracted, the festival of panic more frenzied.

Nettelhorst proved to be a happy anticlimax for the Chicago school authorities, in part because a great deal had been learned in Pilsen. And a great deal had been said about AIDS at Nettelhorst during the weeks immediately preceding the critical time. "It was as if the word AIDS had lost some of its terrifying power," says Peggy Lubin. "The parents could understand that AIDS was—well, just a disease."

Chicago does not enjoy a particularly savory reputation when it comes to politics: it is, after all, where bossism, not the town meeting, was perfected. The reputation is earned, for Chicago remains the city where clout talks loudest and where, as is evident in the handling of AIDS by the public health bureaucrats, competence is often in short supply.

Yet there are other, less visible strands of Chicago politics: widespread citizen involvement in more liberal suburbs like Wilmette, and the politics of community organization in neighborhoods like Pilsen that know how to defend themselves against City Hall. In the triptych of Chicagoland tales, it is this kind of politics, together with a breed of leaders remarkable for their bravery, that enabled three small children touched by the AIDS virus to go to school.

This story has no tidy ending. The coming years will see other towns facing similar circumstances, other reenactments of community pride and prejudice. During August and September of 1987—two years after Kokomo, Indiana; two years, too, after the very different story of Swansea, Massachusetts— towns in Pennsylvania and Tennessee were doing whatever they could to keep children with AIDS out of their schools. And the Ray family's burning house in Arcadia, Florida, came to symbolize the madness that fear of AIDS can bring to the surface.

Much closer to Chicago, in the suburb of Dolton, the school board voted, 6–1, in September 1987 to keep a child with ARC out of school. "The concept of the greatest good for the greatest number" was the reason for the decision, said Board President Joyce Forbes, even as school officials acknowledged that the child being barred posed no danger to anyone. Within days of the board's vote, the family of the unnamed child filed a lawsuit. Eventually, the family would win its case, but meanwhile the child in Dolton, described in the legal complaint as "extremely depressed and disappointed," had to sit at home and wait.

In Wilmette at the same time, things were very different. Until the end of the school year, Jamie McCardle remained one of his gang—the three musketeers, Fran called them—but during the early days of summer, she talked to the other two mothers.

"Don't feel that your boy has to see so much of Jamie during the vacation. Maybe they all could use a break from the sadness."

Jamie himself was beginning to understand the meaning of his own inevitable death. When his ten-year-old sister Sally told him, "I don't want you to die!" he answered stoically: "I just have to."

One day, as Jamie and his mother drove past a cemetery on their way to an appointment with Dr. Chadwick, Jamie asked: "That's where I'll go when I die, isn't it?" "That's where your body goes," Fran answered. "The inner you goes to heaven—a great big bakery, with lots of cookies and cakes."

Jamie could live for years, the doctors told the McCardles, or he could die suddenly, and that uncertainty weighed on the family. Meanwhile, Bill and Fran McCardle and the Wilmette parents whose children attended school with Jamie would be sharing more cups of coffee, more revelations about the plague that had entered all their houses.

Our Towns

An epidemic was never just an epidemic. It was a reflection on the health of government.

Ian Watson, *The Martian Inca*

In A.D. 808, a plague ravaged the Japanese city of Kyoto. When all other expedients failed, the emperor summoned a priest, in hope that he could stop the people's suffering. The priest climbed to a hilltop where, some years earlier, a miracle had supposedly occurred. There he gathered up mounds of brush, formed it into the shape of the Chinese character *dai* (meaning great), and ignited a bonfire that could be seen from one end of Kyoto to the other. The supplication succeeded, or so legend has it, and the plague miraculously vanished. Ever since, whenever Kyoto has suffered from disease the *dai* has been set afire.

To moderns, the igniting of the *dai* sounds like nothing more than a tribal ritual; what we want is science—proof—not magical coincidence.[1] But even in our times, as Antonin Artaud has written, plagues "take images that are dormant . . . and suddenly extend them into the most extreme gestures"; they touch on feelings imbedded deeper than reason.[2]

The burning *dai* did not save the people of Kyoto—that much science can teach. But, visible to all and so reaching all, it can be seen as a timeless emblem of solidarity, symbolizing the common impress of disaster and the inescapable need to face disaster together. AIDS has delivered another incendiary symbol, the burning house in Arcadia. It speaks, very differently, to a separation from one another, a sense that protection in these times of dread resides in keeping up barriers between *us* and *them*.

It is in communion with one another, not acts of segregation, that we can best do battle with the AIDS epidemic: this is the pragmatic lesson of science on the one side, experience on the other. Segregation is not only morally offensive, it would also be logistically impossible. In 1988, the Centers for Disease Control conservatively estimated that one and a half million Americans carry the AIDS virus. Rounding them up and forcing them into camps would create problems of transport and housing, care and education (there would be thousands of children) far worse than did the internment of the Japanese during World War II. And since AIDS carriers, unlike the Japanese, are in no way readily identifiable, who is to be rounded up by the AIDS Police, forced to wear yellow armbands (or tattoos, as columnist William Buckley offhandedly proposed)? Who will search for the AIDS resisters—and who, like the Good Gentiles of Europe during Hitler's reign of terror, will shelter the resisters? The idea of quarantine was bruited in the Reagan White House. But the whole unspeakable scheme sounds as batty, and as horrific, as the indelibly memorable internments of this century.

If the spread of AIDS is to be slowed, cooperation is necessary between the infected and those still untouched. This means, at the least, self-restraint on the part of people who carry the virus and an end to discrimination by those who don't. An everyperson-for-himself individualism, a devotion to self-interest narrowly construed, a denial of responsibility for the impact of one's conduct on one's neighbors: that attitude, if it came to dominate, could all too literally spell the death of many of us. The need for cooperation to ensure survival is why communities of compassion, places as different from one another as Swansea and Pilsen, are not just Sunday school pieties but powerful weapons in the war on AIDS. It is why communities of isolation, the Kokomos and Ocillas, will ultimately fail to protect their members—and, in the process, be corroded by fearfulness and distrust.

Empathy for the AIDS sufferer is not just the surest path to that day when the course of the disease is checked. It also allows us to express an emotion akin to love of our neighbor, and this is a feeling that rarely surfaces in the hyperrational, bureaucratized world of the modern welfare state. That is why these gifts of communion from the parents and schoolchildren in Swansea and Wilmette, Chicago and Lorraine, are so special. They reveal something about our natures, our selves, that we can point to with pride, as "a good in common that we cannot know alone."[3]

The outstretched hand of community is as powerful a force for us as it was for the citizens of ninth-century Kyoto—so the stories about AIDS in our towns make plain. Yet it is a force rarely acknowledged.

As Americans, we are "don't tread on me" individualists by history and instinct, suspicious of the very idea of community as amounting to no more than Jeremy Bentham's description at the time of the Revolution—"a fictitious body composed of the individual persons who are . . . its members" and whose "interest" is only "the sum of the interests of the several members who compose it."[4]

Contemporary America honors students of politics who find in the adroit management of contending factions our government's highest calling. We attend seriously to the speculations of sociobiologists, who insist that concern for others is no more than a genetic trait that helps the tribe survive. We deliver our highest praise, including a Nobel Prize, to economists who identify a selfish reason for everything that we do, both as leaders and led, and who deny any logical underpinning for acting together other than self-aggrandizement.[5]

The American public language is rich in references to the spirit of individualism, and the patriotic texts of our civil religion are shot through with paeans to liberty and freedom and rights. We are much more wary about any claim for loyalty that reaches beyond the atomistic individual and the circle of intimates linked by blood or friendship—understandably enough for, once unmasked, these claims have too often proved only appeals to a universal, and potentially imprisoning, Truth. It was the too-binding ties of imposed obligation that the American colonists left behind, and each succeeding generation of immigrants—whether fleeing madmen like Hitler or Pol Pot, or the deadening yoke of authority—has pursued in America a vision of greater individual freedom.

Yet from the beginning America has also seen itself as a new kind of community—a "city on a hill," as John Winthrop called it, whose goodness would stand as a rebuke to corrupted Europe—and the idea of a good held in common remains a part of our tradition. No one better understood the tension between Americans' individualism and our remarkable capacity for popular sovereignty than Alexis de Tocqueville. A century and a half after his *Democracy in America* first appeared, it remains, astonishingly, the most clear-eyed account of who we are. Tocqueville does not slight the difficulties of "draw[ing] a man out of his own circle." In other countries, he reports, appeals aimed at getting people interested in public affairs go unheard. But the genius of American politics is that the "administration of minor affairs" is entrusted to the citizenry. It takes a homely event (the example Tocqueville uses is building a road that borders a man's property) to engage someone's attention in the affairs of his neighbors—to demonstrate "that there is a connection between this small public affair and his greatest private affairs." But once this connection is understood, the consequences reach well beyond the building of a road. "Men attend to the interests of the public, first by necessity, afterwards by choice; what was intentional becomes an instinct, and by dint of working for the good of one's fellow citizens, the habit and the taste for serving them are at length acquired. . . . The free institutions which the inhabitants of the United States possess, and the political rights of which they make so much use, remind every citizen, and in a thousand ways, that he lives in society."[6]

We pay less attention to "the interests of the public" these days, habitually letting the bureaucrats and the politicians, the pros at this game, run the show. Yet some issues touch our lives with an immediacy and power that can turn even couch potatoes into amateur politicians: the prospect of a hazardous waste dump nearby, for instance, or a post office closing or a freeway slicing through town. It was just such a concrete issue, how to respond to a schoolchild with AIDS, that in town after town renewed old associations or turned strangers into momentary intimates. The need to respond meant that people had to decide where the boundaries of their community lay, to recognize "that 'we' have a different set of obligations and rights when acting toward those who are seen as part of 'our' community than toward those who are seen as outside that community."[7]

"Community" in this sense is a measure not of place but of a shared state of mind, a common consciousness that AIDS brought out. In towns where people couldn't reason beyond the fact of irreducible risk, where they didn't know or couldn't accept what the scientists were saying, they sought protection against contamination by walling out the stricken child. Such reactions were defended, not as acts of selfishness, but in terms of the paramount public good—survival.

"What would you do in our place?" these parents asked, when outsiders challenged their motivation; in Kokomo in the summer of 1985, when the specter of AIDS among the young was entirely new, that was a potent rhetorical question. But over time, as the scientific evidence—that the presence of a youngster with AIDS in school did not threaten the survival of one's own children—became unshakably solid and more widely known, these enclaves came to seem, not places of caring, but mean-spirited communities defined by self-imposed isolation. By the fall of 1987, the burning of the Rays' home in Arcadia could be widely understood as a deed driven not by love but by unreasoning fear.

Communities of isolation have traditionally defined themselves as apart from and against the outside world, as represented by the dramatized menace of Manhattan or Los Angeles or Atlanta. The leaders in such communities constructed boundaries to keep a child with AIDS out because, by contracting the dread disease, the child had somehow become part of the dangerous outside. Such attempts to preserve the purity of place, to maintain a sense of distance and its promise of safety, are a familiar aspect of communal life. Traditional depictions of demons and witches are one way to make these formless threats real; banishing the noticeably different person, the deviant, is another. The outcast becomes a model showing those inside what evil looks like and marking the difference between *us* and *them*—between being inside and being outside.[8]

These acts of segregation, and the "us-them psychologies of discrimination and exclusion" that they generate, are a commonplace of American community life.[9] Historically, when we have come together it has often been not as congregations of the tolerant but as aggregations of the like-minded eager to impose our orthodoxies on others. For all its commitment to virtue, John Winthrop's "city on a hill" had no use for dissenters.

Minorities have perpetually been victimized by such insularity and have absorbed its hard lessons. This is where we live, the have-nots realize, but we cannot count on the other-side-of-the-tracks townspeople for understanding or support. In the 1950s, it was not to the leaders of towns like Ocilla or Fletchers Crossing that civil rights activists turned in their efforts to integrate schools or secure the right to vote. And it was not to the local elite in towns like Atascadero or Kokomo that advocates for the poor went for help during the 1960s. In these places, a particular family in need, especially one regarded as a "good" family, might count on a handout from neighbors. Yet calls to assist not only people with familiar faces but all who require help have often gone ignored, and so too have urgings that communities defend their weakest citizens against the harshness of second-class treatment. To the vulnerable but newly mobilized minorities, such towns became understood as the enemy, and respect came only from far-off Washington.

There is no reason why AIDS should have been handled differently, and sometimes it wasn't. What is remarkable, though, is how often things *were* different—how the authority of communities over AIDS, an authority subject to criticism for being

hierarchical, parochial, and even irrational, was used to em-
brace rather than reject.

This kind of compassion doesn't come naturally, the social
scientists say, but develops through practice and social learning.[10] This is what transpired in the open forums on AIDS, as
people changed their minds after talking things through, in
sessions shaped and informed by exemplary leaders. National
opinion surveys often showed sizeable segments of the populace opposed to allowing children with AIDS in school.[11] But
those responses do not mean much, since they are generally the
offhand and fear-inspired reactions of people who likely have
never given a second's thought to the question. Such sentiments
are often transformed by the kinds of conversations, with neighbors and school chiefs and experts, that occur when a child with
AIDS actually enters their lives.

What is striking is the number of cities and towns that carried
on public discussions about schoolchildren with AIDS. It is
rare, after all, for Americans to approach issues this way. Most
decisions are not made by us but by our proxies—elected representatives or the mandarins who run the agencies of state.
When we are called upon as citizens to decide something, usually it is only a yes-or-no response to a referendum. In hierarchical communities, AIDS was handled in this business-as-usual
way, and the public was not invited in.

The officials who took matters into their own hands said they
were motivated by a benign desire not to create trouble. But the
consequence was either reinforced paternalism and depen-
dence, as in Ocilla, or rebelliousness, as in Queens, which drew
its strength from popular resentment at having been misled by
officialdom. Once made public, the hidden enrollment of a
schoolchild with AIDS, however just, could be expected to
arouse the kind of resentment any imposed tax invites.

In these situations, parents were treated as objects, not subjects. They had no opportunity to come to terms with their
fears, or to situate themselves as givers on the moral landscape.

Even more troubling, from a communitarian perspective, is a

judge's ruling requiring a school district to enroll a child with AIDS. Everywhere, the court is a voice from outside; while bureaucrats may be argued with, the word of the court is final—it is, after all, the law. As such, the court becomes the enemy of public conversation whose aspiration is consensus. The impact can be softened by treating the trial as a kind of community classroom, as happened in Queens. But however open-ended the process, the final judgment is still an order which, when it grants the child formal community membership, does so as a matter of right.

The role of law has not been entirely unhappy. Sometimes, fear of an adverse court ruling helped prod school districts into accepting children with AIDS. And the kind of community imposed by a legal judgment is sometimes the best that can be hoped for. Better the rule of reason, even without a clear sense of place, than the rule of unreason. In Kokomo and Atascadero, the exchange of voices had degenerated into a conspiracy of insiders, and resort to persuasion was hopeless; in Queens, the reservoirs of distrust may have made real talk unattainable from the start. But whatever the circumstance, the legal ruling—like the fulminations of that other familiar outside voice, the national media—can command only a begrudging and resentful response. A judgment does not secure acceptance, let alone love; for children with AIDS, and for their families, love is what is most wanted.

Community meetings proceeded very differently from decision making by school chiefs or judges. They were nothing less than transforming experiences.

In negotiating the terrain of AIDS, some towns adhered to procedures resembling *Robert's Rules of Order* and others were more freewheeling. But the reality of public conversation is that, whatever the formal rules, certain kinds of statements are effectively forced out of bounds. During the hundreds of public conversations not many overt appeals to prejudice were made, and only infrequently did speakers resort to superstition or lapse into hysteria. People harbored such feelings, of course, but sensed that to express them would not persuade anyone. Such sentiments would discredit the speaker—not only on the immediate occasion but in the future as well—for they are the building blocks of an unwelcome reputation in communities that have memories. Neighbors who know that they will be living together long after the AIDS debate is history often temper their rhetoric. It is mostly the outsiders, the followers of Lyndon LaRouche and their kind, who toss the verbal grenades.

The most open of the public conversations about AIDS prompted people to speak in terms of public values—caring and risk—and to test their sentiments against the realities others introduced. When they talked self-consciously about their own community, when they used words like compassion and decency, they moved beyond artifice or script—for when individuals express themselves this way, they can have a powerful effect on how their neighbors, and how they themselves, think.

Public conversations are hardly immune to the closed mind or the appeal to unreason. But when, amidst all the posturing and venting and emoting, people rediscover the meaning of concern for others in these "new contexts of association and moral cohesion," then remarkable things happen.[12] It exaggerates, but not by much, to describe a neighbor as "a stranger transformed by empathy and shared interests into a friend."[13] The newly minted neighborly affection and the skills of citizenship developed in these forums transcend the particular and seem likely to last much longer than the inflated civic pride that, say, a World Series championship momentarily brings. This kind of conversation builds trust among those who participate by acknowledging the gift of their own goodness, even as it builds solidarity and communal competence. And those lessons get passed on to the children, in the classroom and around the dinner table.

Conversation has this potential to take the straight path to hearts and minds. But conversation may also wander in circles or detour into cul de sacs. What transforms idle talk into a discussion that reaches consensus is a unique sort of leadership—a leadership that creates the conditions for arriving at a decision, rather than imposing that decision on the participants. The discussions that tamed initially fearful opinions about AIDS were directed, not spontaneously instigated. School and medical officials took the lead, motivated not by the thrill of command but by the aim of talking to reach agreement.[14]

The AIDS issue called upon the talents of different kinds of experts—to help unravel its scientific complexities, to sift out the questions of risk, and to parse the meanings of empathy. If communities were going to learn about AIDS, they required rational leadership, doctors who knew their science and could make it comprehensible, experts with the patience to ease people away from their dread. They needed organizer-leaders to keep the talk going, to appeal for forbearance—to stay calm in tense times. And they depended on moral leadership, trusted authorities who, as Ralph Waldo Emerson wrote a century ago, "teach us the qualities of primary nature, admit us to the constitution of things."[15] The men and women who rose to the occasion—school principals and politicians, journalists and doctors and priests, superintendents and citizen-advocates—put themselves on the line, articulating both the pragmatics and the rightness of fellow feeling.[16]

If expertise mattered, so too did the old-fashioned virtues of experience and character. The doctors who were most persuasive were those who moved beyond science to personal connection: Peter Smith in Swansea, for instance, whose earnest sincerity helped to carry the day, or Ellen Chadwick in Wilmette, whose own pregnancy was a visible reminder of her certainty that AIDS was not easily passed on. The principals and superintendents who knitted their towns into communities of compassion, in Swansea and Wilmette, Chicago and Lorraine, had histories of personal trustworthiness to bank on.

There were parents who became moral leaders, and their own experiences mattered too. They could invite empathy with an AIDS-stricken child by relating the youngster's plight to the cruelties visited on children with hepatitis or polio or physical handicap—or even, in the case of one school board member, to the horrors visited on the Jews in Nazi Germany. They could look to their own life histories—as when the woman who founded Friends of Mark in Swansea recalled how, terrified of

AIDS, she had kept her gay brother away from her home—and vow to protect a child with AIDS from such destructive passions. They could comprehend the simple human truth, and the relevance, of the testimony of a Polish Catholic woman who at considerable personal risk had rescued Jews during World War II: "What would you have done in my place, if someone comes at night and asks for help? What would you have done in my place: One has to be an animal without a conscience not to help."[17]

Even in our private lives, we are seldom asked to make decisions with moral significance, and almost never do we reason publicly about the meaning of fairness. Such talk is risky, because of its unfamiliarity and because communities have so often found their identity in driving out the unwanted among them. But when this kind of democracy succeeds, the transforming power of discussion—not votes, not representation, but talk that leads to agreement—is revealed.

A nation of democrats, Berthold Brecht says in *Galileo*, needs no heroes; it finds its heroes in its ordinary citizens. When the subject was AIDS, the citizens, decidely low-key heroes in the American tradition, could offer full membership in the community to their neighbor in need, something that not even the ablest politicians or bureaucrats could deliver.[18] What grows out of this process, a sense of the moral meaning in everyday living, has reverberations that reach far beyond AIDS.

On July 30, 1985, when Kokomo School Superintendent J. O. Smith told Ryan White that he could not attend school because he had AIDS, 12,000 AIDS cases had been recorded in the United States. By 1991, the Centers for Disease Control estimates, the number will be 270,000—a twenty-fivefold increase—and nearly 180,000 Americans will be dead from AIDS. More Americans will die from AIDS during that year alone than during the entire Vietnam War. And by 1993, just two years later, the casualty count will have more than doubled again.

Little groups of neighbors can care for one another. They can offer an open hand, and the respect and dignity—the love and affection—that come with that welcome. They can minister to those who need their help. But they cannot manage a pandemic. Neighbors are intimates, and that is their source of strength. But our communities do not have the authority to pull together the disparate parts of the country into a community of the whole. They cannot accomplish the mission of leadership that the apostle of democratic localism, John Dewey, reserved for the nation—to "order the relations" and "enrich the experiences" of all its communities.[19]

Leadership on AIDS poses tasks of surpassing difficulty. No obvious language of belonging—a language that includes and does not segregate—cuts across all the familiar lines of fragmentation, race and class and sexual preference.[20] No readily discernible set of ideals held in common embraces isolated villages like Ocilla, crossroads towns like Fletchers Crossing, freeway outposts like Atascadero, and megacities like New York. Yet at moments in our history, we have put aside our differences to address economic depression and technological progress and civil rights in terms that AIDS also demands: as a transforming issue, a national cause that requires national leadership.

It is an ancient and vexing question: What, as the Apostle Paul asked, can fairly be required of individuals as "members one of another"? What is the relation between self-interest and public interest, between personal impulses and rights held in common? The typical American answer is as pragmatic, and in ordinary times as sensible, as the nation itself. There is no abstract idea of the general welfare—nothing except counting the votes to set selfishnesses against one another, weighing the competing claims of separate interests. But plagues, like wars, cannot be fought this way. Or fought effectively—Vietnam has this much to teach us about AIDS.

When the history of the American 1980s is written, AIDS will occupy a position of prominence. The historians will wonder how it was that the nation's president through much of the decade—a man whose oratorical gifts won him the White House and who largely occupied himself by turning his office into a bully pulpit for causes as varied as the Nicaraguan *contras* and drug wars—could have been mute on AIDS for so long; and how, when he finally spoke out, could have been so inarticulate. The right words from the President, at the right moment, could have made all the difference. In the aftermath of the tragedy in Arcadia (when townspeople burned the house of a family that dared to send its three children, carriers of the AIDS virus, to school) imagine the impact of a televised speech from the White House, with those children sitting alongside the President as he explained the facts about AIDS. But such words went unspoken. To be sure, exponentially increasing amounts of federal dollars were spent on AIDS research. But the money came late, in amounts that lagged far behind what the scientists needed; it came, always, from Congress, which found itself forcing dollars on an unwilling administration; and it came without anything approximating a vision of the nation's responsibility.

Spokesmen for the Reagan administration publicly described AIDS as the nation's "number one public health priority." Yet to listen in on the backstairs whispers recorded in the Reagan White House, from beginning to end AIDS was little more than a gay joke gone awry.[21] In the summer of 1986, the Justice Department interpreted the federal Rehabilitation Act as permitting employers to fire workers with AIDS if the employers feared that the disease might be contagious. Even an irrational fear would suffice, said the government lawyers, and thus—until the courts set the record straight—did panic and prejudice become national policy. The conspicuous exception within the administration was the septuagenarian surgeon general, C. Everett Koop, a distinguished doctor with impeccably conservative credentials, who delivered no-nonsense advice on the need for AIDS education beginning in primary school. For his realism, Koop was derided by White House staffers as an amoralist.

The White House misrule directly relates to the stories told in earlier chapters, for it is the reason those cities and towns found themselves generally adrift, forced to come to terms with AIDS largely on their own. For years, the administration in Washington vacillated between dithering and derisiveness, and offered no national policy. It also denied Americans the moral tutelage to help us respond to AIDS out of our own virtues—to locate a language of belonging broad enough for all of us and to discern ways of mobilizing our altruism. Because gay and lesbian organizations were among the most visible altruists, collecting blood for depleted blood banks and ministering to the sick, the Reagan adminstration pointedly stayed away lest it be charged by its right-wing allies with "legitimization of a lifestyle repugnant to the vast majority of Americans."[22] In place of a collective ethic of responsibility, the social equivalent of "I and Thou," the administration resorted to a finger-pointing moralism that placed the blame for the disease on its victims—those who hadn't "just said no" to sex and drugs and were suffering the consequences of their alleged moral failings.

Harsh judgments of the administration's handling of AIDS had been voiced, both by outside critics and knowledgeable insiders, almost from the onset of the epidemic, but the appraisals drew little attention.[23] In 1987, however, Randy Shilts's powerful critique, *And the Band Played On*, became a national bestseller, and in 1988 Establishment figures joined the attack.

During a single week in June 1988, the National Academy of Sciences issued a blistering report assailing the White House for its lack of leadership on AIDS, and a commission appointed by President Reagan echoed many of the same charges.[24] The commission's findings were especially devastating because they came as such a surprise: when the panelists had been named a year earlier, many were derided as administration catspaws, inexpert ideologues, and in the intervening months several independent-minded members had quit in disgust. Yet the commission was able to overcome its own origins and resurrect itself—to transform itself "from ignorance to brilliance," in the words of its chairman, retired Admiral James Watkins—by witnessing firsthand the ravages of the epidemic.

Predictably, the recommendations of both reports went largely ignored during Ronald Reagan's final days in the White House, and this leaves the shaping of a national AIDS policy to the new administration. It also leaves unsettled a basic choice of policy direction: between a *contain-and-control* strategy, of the sort generally favored by the Reagan administration, which aims at identifying and isolating those with the disease in order to halt its spread, and a *cooperation-and-compassion* strategy, which enlists those most vulnerable to the disease by calling upon them to act responsibly, inviting their participation, and offering the protection of nondiscrimination and assured treatment. The fundamental choice of direction decides all else—the nature and explicitness of AIDS education; the emphasis placed on testing for AIDS, either for the general population or groups seen as particularly at risk; the relationship between drug addiction and AIDS prevention, specifically the government's willingness to provide clean needles for addicts; and the treatment of those whose lives are directly controlled by government, including schoolchildren, prison inmates, the military, and aliens.

Here too the experience of the communities that confronted the issue of AIDS among schoolchildren is relevant, for it shows that the contain-and-control approach cannot work. And not only for schools: neither punishment nor testing is rational AIDS policy.

The criminal penalties some have urged are aimed at the person with AIDS who deliberately spreads the disease. Such willful irresponsibility is as rare as it is contemptible; it hardly amounts to a ripple in the tidal wave of the epidemic. It is more common within marriages, as AIDS-infected spouses have often kept their condition a secret, but this behavior is unlikely to be affected by the threat of a jail sentence.

The ostensible reason for expanding the regime of AIDS testing is to protect us from contagion—so its proponents have argued, in locales as different as Washington, D.C., and Ocilla, Georgia. Such protection is the least we ask of government; even the minimalist night-watchman state is on guard against pestilence. But the experts are agreed that the promise of protection made by proponents of AIDS testing is false. The proposed measures, including the screening of aliens and prisoners, and especially of people applying for marriage licenses, would cost a great deal of money and have little effect on the spread of the disease. The major impact of such testing would actually be to unravel the lives of thousands of individuals, whom, predictably, the tests would falsely label as carriers of the virus.

Mandating massive AIDS testing as our national policy makes about as much scientific sense as a tribal purification ritual. But the alternative approach urged by the National Academy of Sciences and the presidential commission—expanding AIDS education, research, and medical care, as well as policing against discrimination—points to new national commitments. And not just for AIDS: since many of the dilemmas faced by AIDS patients are familiar to anyone who is sick and impoverished, AIDS highlights the broader problem of inadequate care and the pain of imposed helplessness. In that sense, AIDS also stands as a judgment on the Social Darwinism of the Reagan administration, which reserved membership in the national community to those strong enough to insist upon weak government while giving the back of the hand to the most vulnerable among us.

The policy of containment and control promises to keep dollar costs down and minimize Washington's involvement. But for the national community the real cost is too high. As social scientists have warned, "the ways in which society organizes and structures its social institutions—and particularly its health and welfare systems—can encourage or discourage the altruistic in man; such systems can foster integration or alienation; they can allow the 'theme of the gift' . . . to spread among and between social groups."[25] Instead of providing a pathway to mutual caring, the maxim of containment and control had—and still has— the potential to ignite the war of all against all.

Nearing the end of the first decade of AIDS, America has not yet chosen between compassion and cooperation on the one hand, containment and control on the other. The tales of AIDS and schoolchildren, of Swansea and Chicago set against Ocilla and Kokomo, and all the variations in between, particularize that choice and suggest its human consequences. They show us what we are capable of becoming, at our most frightened and at our most enlightened. Within ourselves and in our politics, on state ballots that urge quarantine and in ordinary conversations, the engagement continues: the power of dread against the power of love, the illusion of safety in separateness against the necessity of pulling together as neighbors and citizens. The choice must be made again and again, in the cities and in the remotest corners of the republic—for soon, the Centers for Disease Control reports, scarcely a county will not have recorded at least one AIDS case.

Most of the new AIDS patients of the 1990s will be poor and nonwhite, heroin users, convicts, and hustlers, communities of outcasts with their own life and logic. They will strain our capacities for empathy, for they inhabit worlds that seem psychologically remote from the communities most of us know and understand. Why didn't these people—*them*, not *us*—remake their own lives, some will ask. Others, less polite, will insist that these sufferers are better off, if not dead (that remains the great unspeakable), then at least out of our sight. And these spokesmen will have followers, for as the number of AIDS cases continues to mount, the burdens of compassion will only seem greater, and the idea of safety in cordoning off risk will sound more appealing.

Nor will the plight of children with AIDS, an estimated 20,000 by 1991, capture our attention with the startling impact of a Ryan White. These youngsters are not likely candidates for *People* magazine cover stories. A majority are nonwhite, many of them the abandoned offspring of intravenous-drug users— children who will fill one in ten of the nation's pediatric hospital beds, and who will die in those hospitals without ever knowing a home. Will the response of the parents in places like Wilmette and Swansea and Lorraine—acceptance of an infinitesimally small risk of harm to their own children in order to keep a youngster with AIDS among them—come to seem naively sentimental?

In remote Hindu villages of India, where famine is endemic, anthropologists report that a morality has evolved to cope with this predictable contingency. As the supply of food dwindles, the sacrifice is not borne equally. Instead, those who in ordinary times are socially marginal and politically vulnerable get short rations, while the elite are protected according to the usual principles of security and privilege in those societies. The worst-off may be almost decimated by the famine, but they do not rise up in resentment. Instead, they accept the idea of selective starvation as their fate. This is how the social arrangements in these

Hindu villages remain intact from one famine—one generation—to the next.[26]

We imagine ourselves to occupy a different moral universe
from these famine-haunted people. We would call them primitive, intending the insult—even as we regard as primitive the
ninth-century citizens of Kyoto who put their faith in the *dai*.
Our civic religion decrees that to be an American is, at the least,
to undo such differences of status, "to be a member of the
'covenanting community' in which the commitment to freedom
under law . . . takes on transcendental importance." And not
just freedom in the sense of being left alone: students of our
national character say that to be an American means aspiring to
membership in a "public household" that is akin to our own
households, "a social cement for the society."[27]

AIDS puts these ideals of contemporary citizenship to a hard
test. How we, as neighbors and as a nation, respond to those
touched by this disease who seek entrance to the public household—that is our credo in action. Our words and deeds can tell
us, past all self-delusion, who we really are.

N O T E S

CHAPTER 1: TELLING TALES

1 This history is recounted in Randy Shilts, *And the Band Played On: Politics, People and the AIDS Epidemic* (New York: St. Martins Press, 1987), pp. 103–104.

2 See, for example, Colin Turnbull, *The Mountain People* (New York: Simon and Schuster, 1972); Albert Camus, *The Plague* (New York: Knopf, 1948).

3 William McNeill, *Plagues and Peoples* (Garden City, NY: Anchor Press/ Doubleday, 1976).

4 See Joan Trauner, "The Chinese as Medical Scapegoats in San Francisco, 1870–1905," *California History*, vol. 57 (Spring 1978), pp. 70–87.

5 Paul Starr, *The Social Transformation of American Medicine* (New York: Basic Books, 1982). See generally McNeill, *Plagues and Peoples*.

6 The attribution of meanings to diseases is elegantly discussed in Susan Sontag, *AIDS and Its Metaphors* (New York: Farrar Straus & Giroux, 1989), and, less elegantly, in Talcott Parsons, *The Social System* (Glencoe, IL: Free Press, 1951). On social understandings of sexuality, see generally Michel Foucault, *History of Sexuality* (New York: Vintage, 1980); Jeffrey Weeks, *Sexuality and Its Discontents* (London: Routledge and Kegan Paul, 1985). On the history of approaches to venereal diseases in America, see Allan Brandt, *No Magic Bullet: A Social History of Venereal Diseases in the United States* (New York: Oxford University Press, 1987).

7 See generally Mary Douglas, *Purity and Danger* (London: Routledge and Kegan Paul, 1979).

8 On blacks and syphilis, see James Jones, *Bad Blood: The Tuskegee Experiment* (New York: Free Press, 1981); on prostitutes, see Judith Walkowitz,

Prostitution and Victorian Society: Women, Class, and the State (Cambridge: Cambridge University Press, 1980).

9 See generally Dennis Altman, *The Homosexualization of America* (Boston: Beacon Press, 1982) and *AIDS In the Mind of America* (Garden City, NY: Anchor Press, 1986); Cindy Patton, *Sex and Germs: The Politics of AIDS* (Boston: South End Press, 1985).

10 Quoted in Robert Sunley, "Early Nineteenth-Century American Literature on Child-Rearing," in Margaret Mead and Martha Wolfenstein, eds., *Childhood in Contemporary Cultures* (Chicago: University of Chicago Press, 1955).

11 Viviana Zelizer, *Pricing the Priceless Child: The Changing Social Value of Children* (New York: Basic Books, 1985). See also Carl Degler, *At Odds: Women and the Family in America from the Revolution to the Present* (New York: Oxford University Press, 1980).

12 See Christopher Lasch, *Haven in a Heartless World* (New York: Basic Books, 1977); Kenneth Kenniston and the Carnegie Council on Children, *All Our Children* (New York: Harcourt Brace Jovanovich, 1977). For a skeptical view of the demise of families see Mary Jo Bane, *Here to Stay: American Families in the Twentieth Century* (New York: Basic Books, 1976). W. Norton Grubb and Marvin Lazerson, *Broken Promises* (New York: Basic Books, 1982), contrast public stinginess with private beneficence toward children.

13 James Coleman and Thomas Hoffer, *Public and Private High Schools: The Impact of Community* (New York: Basic Books, 1987). See generally Sarah Lawrence Lightfoot, *Worlds Apart: Relationships between Families and Schools* (New York, Basic Books, 1978).

14 William Boyd, "The Public, The Professionals, and Educational Policy Making: Who Governs?" *Teachers College Record*, vol. 77, no. 4 (May 1976), p. 539. The issue of who *should* govern is taken up in Amy Guttman, *Democratic Education* (Princeton, NJ: Princeton University Press, 1987).

15 David Tyack and Elizabeth Hansot, *Managers of Virtue* (New York: Basic Books, 1982); Larry Cuban, *School Chiefs Under Fire* (Chicago: University of Chicago Press, 1976); Raymond Callahan, *Education and the Cult of Efficiency* (Chicago: University of Chicago Press, 1962).

16 The national survey we carried out in selecting seven communities to write about suggests that one hundred secret-keeping towns would be a modest estimate. In Indiana alone, just during the several-month period before the start of school in September 1987, state Health Commissioner Woodrow Myers, Jr., reports that a dozen school districts with AIDS cases were in contact with his office; not one of the cases was made public.

Doctors sometimes urge parents of children with AIDS to keep that fact from school officials. This was the advice that St. Petersburg, Florida, pediatrician Jerry Barbossa gave the Ray family, and Barbossa reports that at least one other patient has followed this advice.

17 Thomas Timar and David Kirp, *Managing Educational Excellence* (New York: Falmer Press, 1988).

18 See Garry Wills, *Reagan's America: Innocents at Home* (Garden City, NY: Doubleday, 1987).

19 See Dennis Altman, *AIDS in the Mind of America;* Randy Shilts, *And the Band Played On.*

20 Burton Clark, "The Organizational Saga in Higher Education," *Administrative Science Quarterly*, vol. 17 (June 1972), p. 184. Very different are the "fictions" that some leaders invent to justify their actions where things have gone badly.

21 John Dewey, *The Child and the Curriculum* and *The School and Society* (Chicago: University of Chicago Press, 1956 edition).

CHAPTER 2: "NO PLACE TO DIE": KOKOMO, INDIANA

1 Theodore Caplow et al., *Middletown Families: Fifty Years of Change and Continuity* (Minneapolis: University of Minnesota Press, 1981), pp. 4–5. See also Robert Lynd and Helen Lynd, *Middletown* (New York: Harcourt Brace, 1929) and *Middletown in Transition* (New York: Harcourt Brace, 1937).

2 Although Jeanne White was interviewed briefly, the discussion of the Whites is primarily drawn from published materials—newspaper and magazine articles—and the recollections of the other central figures, with whom we spoke at length.

3 J. Oleske, A. Minnefor, R. Cooper, Jr., et al., "Immune Deficiency Syndrome in Children," *Journal of the American Medical Association*, vol. 249 (May 6,1983), p. 2345. In a related editorial, Anthony Fauci of the National Institutes of Health warned that "if routine close contact can spread the disease, AIDS takes on an entirely new dimension."

4 "Education and Foster Care of Children Infected with Human T-Lymphotropic Virus Type III/Lymphadenopathy-Associated Virus," *Morbidity and Mortality Weekly Report*, vol. 34 (August 1985), p. 517. The American Academy of Pediatrics released a similar report. Charles Marwick, "AIDS-Associated Virus Yields Data to Intensifying Scientific Study," *Journal of the American Medical Association*, vol. 254, no. 20 (1985), p. 2865.

5 When Myers quit that post in October 1987 his action was treated as confirming the perception that the federal panel would not play a useful role in shaping AIDS policy.

CHAPTER 3: ORDINARY HEROES: SWANSEA, MASSACHUSETTS

1 James Bryce, *The American Commonwealth* (London: Macmillan, 1891), p. 591.

2 Jay Hoyle, *Mark* (South Bend, IN: Langford Books, 1988).

CHAPTER 4: PASSION PLAY: NEW YORK CITY

1 Mario Cuomo, *Forest Hills Diary* (New York: Random House, 1974).

2 See David Rogers and Norman Chung, *110 Livingston Street Revisited: Decentralization in Action* (New York: New York University Press: 1983); David Rogers, *110 Livingston Street: Politics and Bureaucracy in the New York City Schools* (New York: Random House, 1968).

3 In 1987, he was eased out of his job.

4 See Dorothy Nelkin and Stephen Hilgartner, "Disputed Dimensions of Risk: A Public School Controversy over AIDS," *Milbank Quarterly*, vol. 64, suppl. 1 (1986).

5 S. H. Weiss, C. Saxinger, D. Rechtman, M. H. Grieco, J. Nadler, et al., "HTLV-III Infection among Health Care Workers: Association with Needle-Stick Injuries," *Journal of the American Medical Association*, vol. 254 (1985), p. 2089; R. Melbye et al., "Anal Intercourse as a Possible Factor in Heterosexual Transmission of HTLV-III to Spouses of Hemophiliacs," *New England Journal of Medicine*, vol. 312 (March 1985), p. 857. No members of AIDS-infected hemophiliacs' households except sex partners were found to have acquired the virus. The "toothbrush" study discussed at the CDC meeting was published several months later. While the findings were known to AIDS specialists at the time of the Queens trial, they were not discussed in the popular press until that later publication. G. H. Friedland, B. R. Saltzman, M. F. Rogers, et al., "Lack of Transmission of HTLV-III/LAV Infection to Household Contacts of Patients With AIDS and AIDS-related Complex with Oral Candidiasis," *New England Journal of Medicine*, vol. 314 (January 1986), p. 344.

6 See Barbara Ehrenreich and John Ehrenreich, *The American Health Empire: Power, Profits, and Politics* (New York: Random House, 1970); Ivan Illich, *Medical Nemesis: The Expropriation of Health* (New York: Pantheon, 1982); I. K. Zola, ed., *Ordinary Lives: Voices of Disability and Disease* (Cambridge, MA: Applewood Books, 1982).

7 William McNeill, *Plagues and Peoples*, p. 257. On science and magic, see Keith Thomas, *Religion and the Decline of Magic* (New York: Charles Scribner's Sons, 1971).

Medical researchers' oft-repeated statements that studying AIDS will reap benefits to science by increasing understanding of the immune system and cancer offered no real reassurance to a worried public.

8 See Frederick A. O. Schwarz, Jr., and Frederick P. Schaffer, "AIDS in the Classroom," *Hofstra Law Review*, vol. 14, no. 1 (Fall 1985); Deborah Jones Merritt, "Communicable Disease and Constitutional Law: Controlling AIDS," *New York University Law Review*, vol. 61, no. 6 (November 1986).

9 See generally David L. Kirp, *Just Schools: The Idea of Racial Equality in American Education* (Berkeley and Los Angeles: University of California Press, 1982). For New York City, see David Rogers, *110 Livingston Street.*

10 Ken Auletta, *The Streets Were Paved With Gold* (New York: Random House, 1980).

11 The estimate of abandoned children born with AIDS is drawn from a survey of twenty-five states conducted in June 1987 by the Massachusetts Adoption Resource Exchange.

CHAPTER 5: BURIED FEELINGS: OCILLA, GEORGIA

1 Marshall Frady, *Wallace* (New York: New American Library, 1968), p. 11.
2 Robert Dubin, "Organizational Fictions," in Robert Dubin, ed., *Human Relations in Administration with Readings* (Englewood Cliffs, NJ: Prentice-Hall, 1966), p. 493.

CHAPTER 6: "CLEAR AND PRESENT DANGER": FLETCHERS CROSSING

1 See Erving Goffman, *Stigma: Notes on the Management of Spoiled Identity* (Englewood Cliffs, NJ: Prentice-Hall, 1963).

CHAPTER 7: THE BITE: ATASCADERO, CALIFORNIA

1 M. Sande, "The Case Against Casual Contagion," *New England Journal of Medicine,* vol. 314 (February 1986), p. 380.
2 Virus-positive saliva is a quite infrequent occurrence among people with the AIDS virus. The leading study was able to isolate the virus in the saliva of just one of seventy-one seropositive men. See D. D. Ho, R. E. Byington, R. E. Schooley, et al., "Infrequency of Isolation of HTLV-III Virus from Saliva in AIDS," *New England Journal of Medicine,* vol. 31, no. 3 (1985), p. 1606.
3 See XII International Congress, World Federation of Hemophilia (January-March 1986); M. Berthus et al., "Transmissibility of Human Immunodeficiency Virus in Hemophiliac and Non-Hemophiliac Children Living in a Private School in France," *Lancet,* vol. 11, no. 8507 (September 13, 1986), p. 598.
4 C. Tsoukas et al., "Risk of Transmission of HTLV-III/LAV from Human Bites," *Proceedings of the 2d International Conference on AIDS,* Paris (June 1986), p. 125.

CHAPTER 8: TRIPTYCH: CHICAGO

1 Carleton Washburne and Sidney Marland Jr., *Winnetka: The History and Significance of an Educational Experience* (Englewood Cliffs, NJ: Prentice Hall, 1963), describes the ethnic and neighborhood politics behind the drawing of boundaries for a new high school in the Winnetka area.
2 See Robert Hess and Judith Torney, *The Development of Political Attitudes in Children* (Chicago: Aldine, 1967); David Nyberg and Kieran Egan, *The Erosion of Education: Socialization and the Schools* (New York: Teachers College Press, 1981).
3 Quoted in Thomas Cottle, *Black Children, White Dreams* (Boston: Houghton Mifflin, 1974).
4 See Jules Henry, *Culture Against Man* (New York: Vintage, 1963); Edgar Friedenberg, *Coming of Age in America* (New York: Vintage, 1965).

5 Barbara Biber and Patricia Minuchin, "The Impact of School Philosophy and Practice on Child Development," in Melvin Silberman, ed., *The Experience of Schooling* (New York: Holt, Rinehart and Winston, 1971), pp. 39–54.

6 Reynolds Farley and Walter Allen, *The Color Line and the Quality of Life in America* (New York: Russell Sage Foundation, 1987).

7 Kathleen Kemp and Robert Lineberry, "The Last of the Great Urban Machines and the Last of the Great Urban Mayors? Chicago Politics, 1955–1977," in Samuel Gove and Louis Masotti, eds., *After Daley: Chicago Politics in Transition* (Urbana: University of Illinois Press, 1982), p. 14.

8 Saul Alinsky, *Rules for Radicals* (New York: Random House, 1972), p. 72.

CHAPTER 9: OUR TOWNS

1 See Lucien Levy-Bruhl, *Primitives and the Supernatural* (London: G. Allen, 1936, translation by Lilian A. Clare).

2 Antonin Artaud, *The Theatre and Its Double* (New York: Grove Press, 1958).

3 Michael Sandel, *Liberalism and The Limits of Justice* (New York: Cambridge University Press, 1982). See also Herve Varenne, *Americans Together* (New York: Teachers College Press, 1977).

4 Jeremy Bentham, *An Introduction to the Principles of Morals and Legislation*, J. H. Burns and H. L. A. Hart, eds. (London, University of London, Athlone Press, 1970), p. 12.

5 See, e.g., Anthony Downs, *An Economic Theory of Democracy* (New York: Harper, 1957); James Buchanan and Gordon Tullock, *The Calculus of Consent* (Ann Arbor: University of Michigan Press, 1965); Mancur Olson, *The Logic of Collective Action* (Cambridge: Harvard University Press, 1965). Edmund O. Wilson, *Sociobiology: The New Synthesis* (Cambridge: Harvard University Press, 1975); Christopher Lasch, *The Culture of Narcissism* (New York: Norton, 1978); Russell Jacoby, *Social Amnesia* (Boston: Beacon Press, 1975). But see Robert Bellah et al., *Habits of the Heart: Individualism and Commitment in American Life* (Berkeley: University of California Press, 1985).

6 Alexis de Tocqueville, *Democracy in America,* J. P. Mayer and Max Lerner, eds. (New York: Harper and Row, 1966), vol. 2, pp. 109–112.

7 Joseph Gusfield, *Community* (New York: Harper and Row, 1975), p. 30.

8 Kai Erikson, "Notes on the Sociology of Deviance," in Earl Rubington and Martin Weinberg, eds., *Text and Readings in the Sociology of Deviance* (New York: Macmillan, 3d edition, 1968), p. 25. See also Howard Becker, *Outsiders* (New York: Free Press, 1973).

9 Benjamin Barber, *Strong Democracy* (Berkeley: University of California Press, 1984), p. 152. See Herbert McCloskey and Alida Brill, *Dimensions of Tolerance: What Americans Believe about Civil Liberties* (New York: Russell Sage, 1983). Compare Wilson Carey McWilliams, *The Idea of Fraternity in America* (Berkeley: University of California Press, 1973).

10 McCloskey and Brill, *Dimensions of Tolerance.*

11 An August 1988 Gallup Poll, for example, finds 24 percent of Americans

opposed to children with AIDS attending public school, and an additional 19 percent undecided.

12 Robert Nisbet, *Community and Power* (New York: Oxford University Press, 1962), p. 278.

13 Benjamin Barber, *Strong Democracy*, p. 189.

14 On the role of leadership in dealing with the 1950s controversies over fluoridation, which are interestingly parallel, see Robert Crain, Elihu Katz, and Donald B. Rosenthal, *The Politics of Community Conflict* (Indianapolis, IN: Bobbs-Merrill, 1969). Crain and his colleagues find leadership—the support of the mayor—to be the crucial factor in understanding a community's position on fluoridation; the relationship between leaders and led goes unexplored, however.

15 Ralph Waldo Emerson, *The Collected Works*, Wallace Williams and Douglas Emory Wilson, eds., vol. 4 (Cambridge, MA: Harvard University Press, 1971).

16 See Reinhold Neibuhr, *The Nature and Destiny of Man* (New York: Charles Scribner's Sons, 1949).

17 Nehama Tec, *When Light Pierced the Darkness* (New York: Oxford University Press, 1986). See also Philip Hallie, *Lest Innocent Blood Be Shed* (New York: Harper and Row, 1979).

18 See Michael Walzer, *Spheres of Justice* (New York: Basic Books, 1983).

19 John Dewey, *The Public and Its Problems* (New York: Henry Holt, 1927), p. 211.

20 See Michael Ignatieff, *The Needs of Strangers* (New York: Viking Press, 1985).

21 See, e.g., David Talbot and Larry Bush, "At Risk," *Mother Jones* (April 1985), pp. 29–37.

22 Randy Shilts, *And the Band Played On*, p. 456. See Ronald Bayer, *Private Acts, Public Consequences: AIDS and Politics of Public Health* (New York: Free Press, 1989).

23 See, e.g., Office of Technology Assessment, *The Public Health Service's Response to AIDS* (Washington, D.C.: Government Printing Office, 1985).

24 The National Academy of Science, *Confronting AIDS: Update 1988* (Washington, D.C.: National Academy of Sciences, 1988); *Report of the Presidential Commission on the Human Immunodeficiency Virus Epidemic* (Washington, D.C.: Government Printing Office, 1988).

25 Richard Titmuss, *The Gift Relationship: From Human Blood to Social Policy* (New York: Vintage, 1972), pp. 12–13.

26 The research is described in Mary Douglas, *How Institutions Think* (Syracuse, NY: Syracuse University Press, 1987).

27 Irving Kristol, "The Spirit of '87," *Public Interest*, no. 83 (1987), p. 3; Daniel Bell, *The Cultural Contradictions of Capitalism* (New York: Basic Books, 1976), p. 278.

ACKNOWLEDGMENTS

"Think of it like if you were in his position—how would you feel?" These words from a thirteen-year-old girl in the small Massachusetts town of Swansea, explaining to a reporter in September 1985 why she so wanted her AIDS-striken classmate Mark Hoyle to return to school, became the inspiration for this book.

Just weeks earlier, in the outwardly not-so-different town of Kokomo, Indiana, the prospect of a student with AIDS attending school had provoked hysteria and rage. What accounted for the difference between these two places? And, more generally, why did America respond in such varied ways to AIDS among its schoolchildren?

Our search for answers—in the collective lives of communities and the private lives of families throughout America—has been, at once, an anguishing and illumining experience. How could it be otherwise, in a book about people confronting firsthand their deepest concerns, dread and deviance, disease and death.

The first-person voice is not part of these accounts. But there is nonetheless an implicated "I" (or "we"), molded by powerful telling moments, defining moments of intimacy, in the gathering of these tales. There is, for instance, the memory of Mark Hoyle in Swansea—everyone's kid brother, everyone's son—capering around his house with a just-bought video camera, chased after by his puppy Chipper as he records the writer recording the circumstance. And there is Marcella Jackson sitting in a darkening room in Ocilla, Georgia, whispering that she can never allow herself to cry for the death of her daughter, for "if I ever got started . . . I could never stop." There is young Jamie McCardle in Wilmette, Illinois, too shy to say anything, even in response to his parents' promptings, but sweetly giving hugs to his inquisitive visitors. And there is Marcus Robinson, visibly pleased with his new

home and his new life, proudly talking about how he's going to make it—
going to "be someone."

In each of the communities we visited, dozens of people—school officials,
parents, teachers, students, politicians, reporters, doctors, ministers, and all
manner of interested citizens—gave hours of their time talking over recollections. They dug into their personal archives to turn up the news clips, memos,
letters, minutes of meetings, and mimeographed fliers we rely on. The families most directly affected, and the AIDS-striken children themselves, walked
us through the stories of their lives with remarkable candor and patient thoroughness. They answered with grace and courage our deepest questions:
took us to the central questions we were too reticent to ask, about the impact
of AIDS on their lives and their personal sense of mortality.

These families were not selected as subjects to write about because of their
extraordinariness. Quite the contrary: they are ordinary people, school-
teachers and housewives, ad men and welfare recipients, who were touched
by AIDS as if by lightning; and that fact makes the strength of character they
reveal so powerful.

It is on behalf of those familes that we are donating half the royalties of this
book to organizations that help families and children deal with AIDS.

Without the financial support of the Spencer Foundation, the research and
writing could never have been undertaken. And Spencer's backing has meant
much more than dollars. From our first mention of the project, Spencer's
President, Lawrence Cremin, and its Vice President and Secretary, Marion
Faldet, were persuaded of its importance; and throughout, their enthusiasm
was contagious.

Colleagues and old friends—David Cohen, Nathan Glazer, Judith Gruber,
James Kinsella, Kristin Luker, Robert Post, Philip Selznick, Ann Swidler, and
David Tyack—paid us the compliment of giving a scrupulously close reading
(sometimes more than one reading) to a draft of the book. Audiences at
Berkeley, Harvard, and the University of New South Wales turned presentations into lively seminars. If the critiques of our readers and listeners kept us
busily rewriting for months, they encouraged us to write a more interestingly
complicated account. An earlier version of the Atascadero story appeared as a
cover story in *Image*, the *San Francisco Examiner*'s Sunday magazine; and an
earlier rendering of the Chicago stories was published as a cover piece in the
Chicago Tribune Sunday Magazine. In both instances, we learned from our
editors.

Talented editors at Rutgers University Press—Kenneth Arnold, Karen
Reeds, Marilyn Campbell; and Norman Rudnick, who gently massaged the
prose to bring its nuances to light—saw to it that the book was published with
considerable speed without cutting corners.

The authors' friends, spouses, and lovers lived through the intensity of the
research and writing. They helped keep us whole, even as we, a kind of community, kept each other whole during these many months that an understanding of AIDS and schoolchildren—AIDS and America, really—was
taking form.